Leavenworth Papers

No. 9 🛢️

Defending the Driniumor: Covering Force Operations in New Guinea, 1944

by Dr. Edward J. Drea

Combat Studies Institute
U.S. Army Command and General Staff College
Fort Leavenworth, Kansas 66027

February 1984

Drea, Edward J., 1944-
    Defending the Driniumor: covering force operations
in New Guinea, 1944 / by Edward J. Drea. — Fort
Leavenworth, Kan. : Combat Studies Institute, U.S.
Army Command and General Staff College; Washington, D.C., : For sale by Supt. of Docs., U.S. G.P.O.,
1984.

    xi, 182 p. : ill., maps ; 25 cm. — (Leavenworth
papers ; no. 9)

    "February 1984."
    Includes bibliographical references.
    S/N 008-020-01000-6
    Item 359-C
    Supt. of Docs. no.: D 110.9:9

    1. World War, 1939-1945—Campaigns—Papua New
Guinea. 2. Papua New Guinea—History. I. United
States Army Command and General Staff College.
Combat Studies Institute. II. Title. III. Series.

D767.95.D73   1984 940.54'26—dc19   84-603862
                                    AACR 2   MARC

Library of Congress

Contents

Conclusions

Illustrations

Maps

Figures

Acknowledgments

During the course of researching and writing this *Leavenworth Paper*, many persons and agencies contributed their time and resources to assist the project. In particular, Mr. John Taylor, National Archives and Records Center, Modern Military Branch, was especially helpful in sorting through the mass of declassified Ultra documents. The National Security Agency also provided valuable assistance in this study. At the U.S. Army Military History Institute, Dr. Richard Sommers and Messrs. John Slonaker and Dennis Vetock were very considerate and helped me to investigate many documents in a short period.

As for the records of military units, the Washington National Records Center's Record Group 407 contains the 32d Infantry Division's (Persecution Task Force) G-3 Journal and File; the division's "Report After Action, Aitape, New Guinea"; "Persecution Covering Force After Action Report"; "Headquarters 112th Cavalry Regimental Combat Team Journal and Log"; "Diary, 2d Squadron"; and "112th Cavalry Historical Report, 112th Cavalry Regiment, Aitape, New Guinea." In addition, Mr. Claude Rigsby, then president of the 112th Cavalry Association, gave me a partial copy of the historical report. These documents, particularly the historical report, are the basis for this narrative, although I also compared their contents with the official Japanese military history of the campaign in order to present a balanced account of the battle.

The members of the 112th Cavalry Association kindly allowed me to attend their 1981 and 1982 reunions in Dallas, Texas, and I also attended the 1982 reunion of the 32d Infantry Division in Milwaukee, Wisconsin. On all three occasions I had the opportunity to talk to veterans of the New Guinea fighting, and this essay has profited from their insights. Time limitations, unfortunately, meant that I could talk to only a handful of veterans, although ideally all of the members should have been able to contribute to the human dimension of this battle. I extend my deepest appreciation to the members of both organizations, particularly Mr. Rigsby and Col. (Ret.) Thomas Makal, past president of the 32d Infantry Division Veterans Association, for their help in arranging my interviews at their respective reunions.

The Aitape campaign is little remembered, and consequently few reliable secondary accounts of the fighting exist. General Walter Krueger's memoirs provided details as did Jay Luvaas's editing of General Robert Eichelberger's letters in *Dear Miss Em*. Lt. Col. Millard Gray's *Military Review* article was illuminating because Gray had been G-3, 32d Division, during the operation. D. Clayton James's work on MacArthur was helpful in understanding the strategic background. The standard work on the Aitape campaign remains Robert Ross Smith's *The Approach to the Philippines*. This *Leavenworth Paper* adds tactical detail to a single phase of the complex operations that Smith describes so well.

1982   Edward J. Drea
                                  Combat Studies Institute
                                  U.S. Army Command and General Staff College

Preface

The Allied invasion of Aitape, New Guinea, on 22 April 1944 was one of three simultaneous invasions far to the rear of what conventional military wisdom considered the front line of Japanese resistance. It recently has been revealed that the U.S. ability to read the Imperial Japanese Army's (IJA) most secret codes, the information from which was disseminated as the so-called Ultra intelligence, contributed significantly to these bold operations. Armed with special intelligence, General Douglas MacArthur, commander in chief, Southwest Pacific Area (SWPA), conducted a series of amphibious flanking maneuvers that forced the Japanese to fight at places of MacArthur's choosing. Aitape was one of those places.

In the lexicon of historians of World War II, "forgotten" has become a popular modifier. One reads of the forgotten front, forgotten soldiers, the forgotten army, and so on. The operations in New Guinea also qualify for the forgotten label. As James Jones wrote about those campaigns, "A year it had taken from Guadalcanal to Sansapor. And how many invasions? Fifteen? Almost all of them names people in the United States never heard of, and still haven't."[1] The landings at Aitape and the subsequent Driniumor River campaign were two such names.

If military readers related the historical lessons of the Driniumor River fighting to today's doctrine, they would discover striking similarities. Although today's FM 90—5 has incorporated many lessons from the past, it is intended to serve as a how-to-fight manual for the individual soldier. Guidance for the intricacies of larger unit operations—battalion and above— is lacking. Current U.S. Army jungle warfare doctrine, for instance, uses the same terminology as its 1941 predecessor to describe the general conduct of operations in jungle terrain through the use of covering force, main battle, and rear areas. It does not, however, spell out the exact role of a covering force or how to establish the respective battle areas in such a situation. Instead, the interested reader is referred to FM 100—5, which describes the covering force in terms of a European style battlefield. In 1929, B. H. Liddell-Hart wrote, "The practical value of history is to throw the film of the past through the material projector of the present onto the screen of the future." He naturally assumed that the audience paid attention to the film. If the "film of the past" is forgotten, so too are the U.S. Army's tactical and doctrinal legacies from World War II.

As John F. Morrison Professor of Military History at the U.S. Army Command and General Staff College, D. Clayton James, MacArthur's foremost biographer, often expressed his puzzlement about the U.S. Army's historical neglect of its extensive campaigns in the Pacific theater. An exclusive focus on northwest Europe, he suggested, misrepresented not only the global role of the U.S. Army and its adaptability to the diverse conditions of World War II but also the very nature of that war. If we did not understand the Pacific War, we could not comprehend the nature of global conflict. Professor James spoke of the highest strategic levels, but he also suggested to the Combat Studies Institute that the battles along the Driniumor River would be a suitable topic for tactical analysis as a *Leavenworth Paper*. The immediate question was how to translate his strategic perspective into a tactical framework. In one sense, the paradox of New Guinea as a theater of war solved the problem.

New Guinea was so large that it absorbed vast numbers of troops, more than nine U.S. infantry divisions by July 1944, but the jungle terrain fragmented the deployment of large formations attempting to operate en masse. At the tactical level, company- and platoon-size actions were the norm. The actual number of U.S. combat troops was small, their combat service support large.[2] The Japanese situation was the reverse, mainly because MacArthur's leapfrogging strategy had isolated the Japanese from their logistic support. From MacArthur's strategic viewpoint, Aitape was hailed as a classic victory, but to the few men who actually fought the battle, it was a swirling, confused melee.

Chronologically, the Aitape campaign fell into distinct phases, the strategic-operational and the tactical. The strategic and operational phases began in January 1944 when Southwest Pacific Area commander and staff first conceived the leap to Hollandia-Aitape. It culminated in early July when 6th Army completed the operational deployment of Persecution Task Force, the code name for the American forces at Aitape. Although occasional skirmishes punctuated this period, the full tactical fury of protracted battle did not commence until the night of 10—11 July 1944, when the entire Japanese 18th Army attacked Persecution Task Force defenders along the Driniumor River. By extending this dichotomy, the first phase was preparatory as both sides deployed for combat. At this time, Ultra intelligence revelations about Japanese capabilities and attack plans were instrumental in American operational deployment.

The planning and maneuvering that brought Japanese and American forces to the Driniumor River serve as the focus for the first part of this study. As the battle raged, however, the respective commanders had to depend on the collective skills of their individual soldiers and hope that their operational deployments, training, and tactical doctrine would bring them victory. The tactical struggle, or second phase, then, was as removed from the strategic and operational phase as the experience of the officers and men on the front line was from the abstract map symbols that represented their units at higher headquarters.

The purpose of this *Leavenworth Paper* is to integrate American and Japanese strategic, operational, tactical, and human dimensions into a narrative form. The focus is on the 112th Cavalry Regiment because that unit played a significant role in defeating a numerically superior Japanese force that tried to outflank an American covering force. Official histories in both English and Japanese languages illuminate the decision-making processes of the combatants at the strategic and operational levels that resulted in the deployment of men and their war-making equipment to the Driniumor. Ultra adds the intelligence dimension to American decision making. At the tactical level, however, events are less clear. For the purposes of organization, three major engagements occurred along the Driniumor River in July and August 1944. On the night of 10—11 July 1944, Japanese troops of the 18th Army broke through and overran American covering force defenders on the Driniumor. An American counter-attack characterized by bitter fighting eventually sealed this penetration. The third major battle—more correctly a series of company and platoon level engagements lasting three weeks—raged around the south flank of the American positions as the Japanese tried to turn the U.S. line. This more specific level is difficult to reconstruct with exactitude because of the confused nature of jungle fighting when men only a few yards distant were out of sight and earshot. Small parties of Japanese and Americans fought and died in anonymity. Nevertheless, reference to contemporary military reports and war diaries makes it possible to impose a degree of order, necessarily arbitrary, on the operations and then to describe the fighting.

The motivations of the troops who fought in such a hideous environment are central to an understanding of the battle from the small unit perspective. I relied on the personal accounts of American and Japanese veterans for an understanding of these complex and highly significant questions. Oral history, if obtainable, becomes invaluable because it personalizes the official accounts and fills in the gaps in the historical record.

The U.S. Army's 32d Infantry Division and 112th Cavalry Regiment fought for forty-five days along the Driniumor. Those who survived the hardship, terror, or rare exhilaration of the firing line can provide an insight into the emotions and impressions of their struggle. It was a savage battle in primitive conditions where no quarter was asked or given.

Part I

Strategic
and
Operational
Perspectives

Ultra and Pacific Strategy

1

Background

In the early spring of 1944 the prospects for a quick Allied victory in the war against Japan seemed remote. It is true that the Allied counter-offensive in the Southwest and Central Pacific had forced the Japanese to assume the strategic defensive, but despite these blood-soaked Allied gains, the Japanese home islands remained secure behind a vast defensive perimeter. The Japanese primary defense line in March 1944 stretched from the Burma-India border through the Netherlands East Indies, most of New Guinea, the northern part of the New Britain and the Solomon Island chain, and then northward to the Kamchatka Peninsula. A glance at maps 1 and 2 shows that in two years of hard fighting the Allies had taken the Gilbert and Marshall islands, Guadalcanal in the Solomon chain, and the south tip of New Britain and had pushed the Japanese back along the north coast of New Guinea. Nevertheless, Japan seemed a long way off to the common soldier as well as to the strategic planners.

The Joint War Plans Committee in October 1943 estimated that in the spring of 1945 Formosa could be captured. This would be followed as soon as possible thereafter by an invasion of Hokkaido, the northernmost of the main Japanese home islands. These same planners envisioned an invasion of Honshu in the summer of 1946.[1] If, in retrospect, these men appear to have been unduly pessimistic, one should recall that on 1 January 1944 the closest American infantryman to Tokyo was more than 4,800 kilometers away, at Tarawa in the Gilbert Islands or at Lae, New Guinea. The distances staggered the imagination. The area from Milne Bay on the southeast tip of Papua, New Guinea, where the Australians had first repulsed Japanese invaders in August 1942, to the most forward Allied base at Dumpu, Northeast New Guinea,* was approximately 800 kilometers and had taken the Allies sixteen months to recapture.

*In 1828 the Dutch annexed the western half of New Guinea, but in 1885 the British established a protectorate over the southeastern coast and its nearby islands. Twenty years later, Australia gained control of British New Guinea and renamed it Papua. During World War I, Australian forces occupied the German controlled region of Northeast New Guinea and, after the war, received that area as a mandated territory.

4

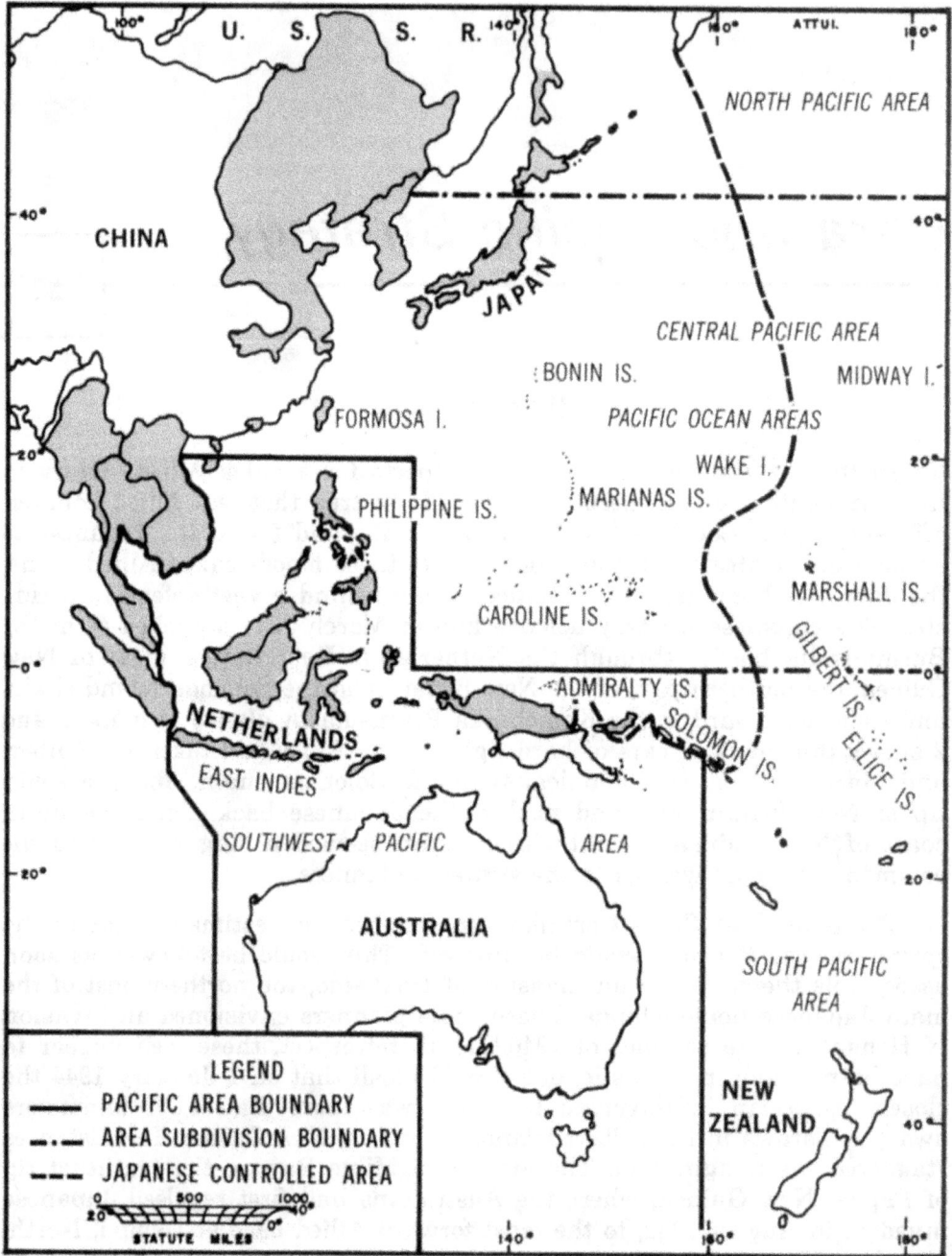

Map 1. Japanese controlled area, March 1944

5

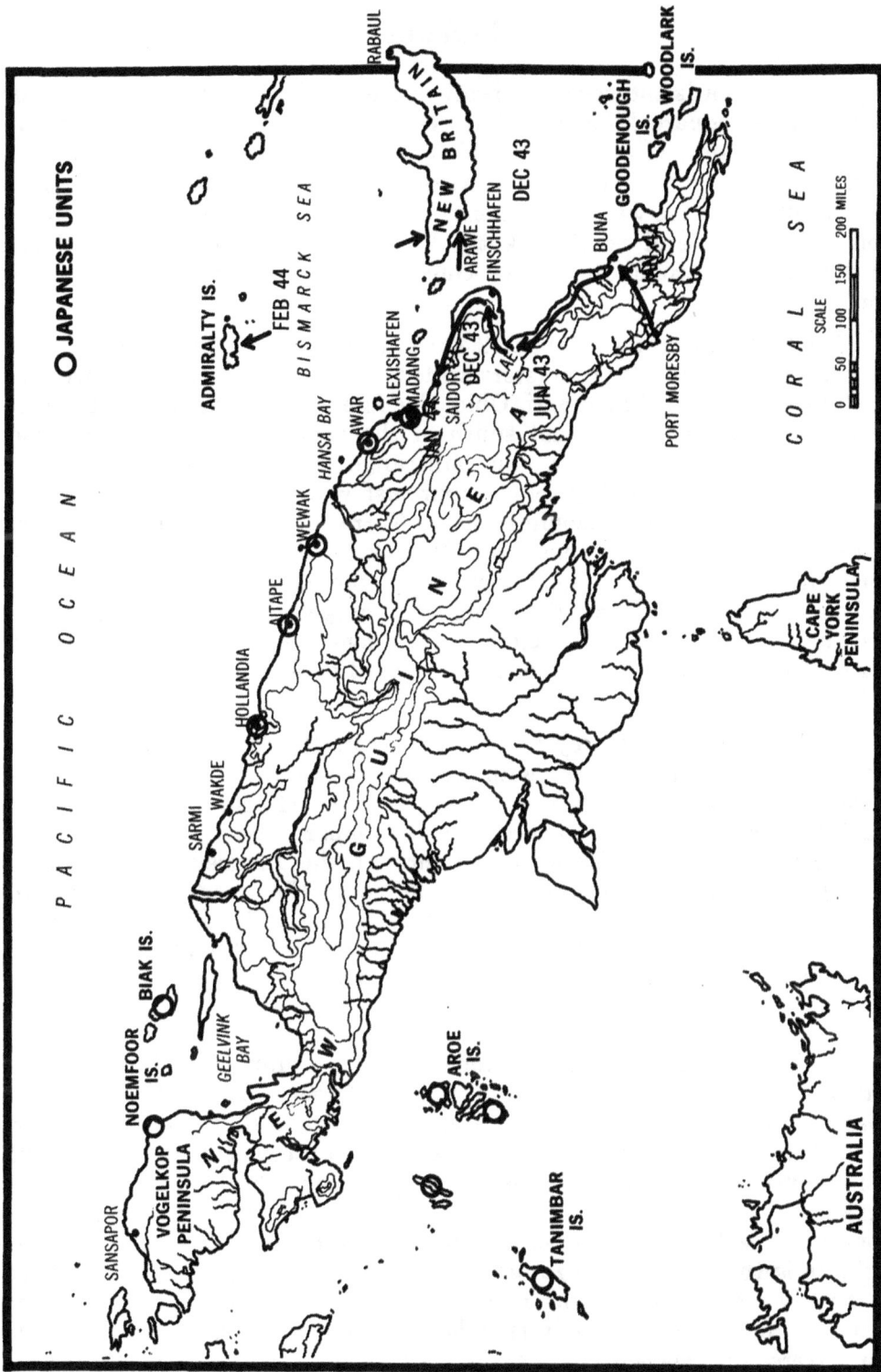

Map 2. Allied advance in New Guinea, January 1943—February 1944

Terrain

New Guinea is the second largest island in the world and covers more than 885,000 square kilometers.[2] If New Guinea were superimposed over the United States, Milne Bay would be south of Norfolk, Virginia, Lae at Pittsburgh, the major Japanese base of Wewak at Detroit, Biak Island at Minneapolis, and the westward extension of Dutch New Guinea would extend well into the state of South Dakota. A rifleman could hardly be faulted if he thought the reconquest of New Guinea alone would be an endless task. For many it was.

The north coastline is about 2,400 kilometers long, and the island, at its widest point, is 645 kilometers wide, approximately the distance from Washington, D.C., to Cincinnati, Ohio. The island extends from about twelve degrees south latitude to just south of the equator and has a monsoon climate (see map 3). A major mountain range runs from the eastern end of the island to Geelvink Bay, but a spur just west of the Sepik River leads to a smaller complex of mountains, the Torricelli Range, which runs near and parallel to the north coast from Wewak to the Mamberamo River. The Torricellis rise as high as 1,420 meters, but the mountains are considerably broken with many rough ridges and deep gorges that bar the passage of large military formations. The crest of the range, about twenty-five kilometers south of Aitape, canalized Japanese westward deployment between the foothills and the coast.

Bordered on the north by the Pacific Ocean, the Aitape area is a coastal plain covered by rain forest with numerous swampy places (see map 4). Streams and rivers running north from the Torricelli Range cut the narrow coastal plain at numerous places. The Driniumor is one of six main rivers in New Guinea, and it flows rapidly through the Torricelli foothills before it enters the plain at Afua, a native village on the river's west bank and the scene of heavy fighting in August 1944. Normally the Driniumor can be waded. It is 1 meter deep with a course of 145 meters and a bed 37 meters wide, but both width and depth vary greatly depending on the amount of rainfall.

Aitape receives nearly 250 centimeters of rain annually. The wet season during the northwest monsoon lasts from December to April. Although there is an appreciable difference in the amount of rainfall from May through November, monthly averages are more than 17.5 centimeters. During July and August (the period of the major fighting along the Driniumor in 1944), torrential tropical downpours are the rule, and quick runoff from the mountains results in rapid stream risings on the plain. Humidity is naturally high, as is the temperature range of 38° to 20.5° C. Clouds are least likely at the lower elevations in the morning after sunrise. Fog is not a problem near the coast, but inland it is quite common, especially in valleys and near rivers. In 1944 sunrise was at 0635 on 5 July, sunset at 1833. Comparable figures for 5 August were 0636 and 1835. There was a full moon on 6 July and 4 August, and moonrise varied from 1713 on 5 July to 1924

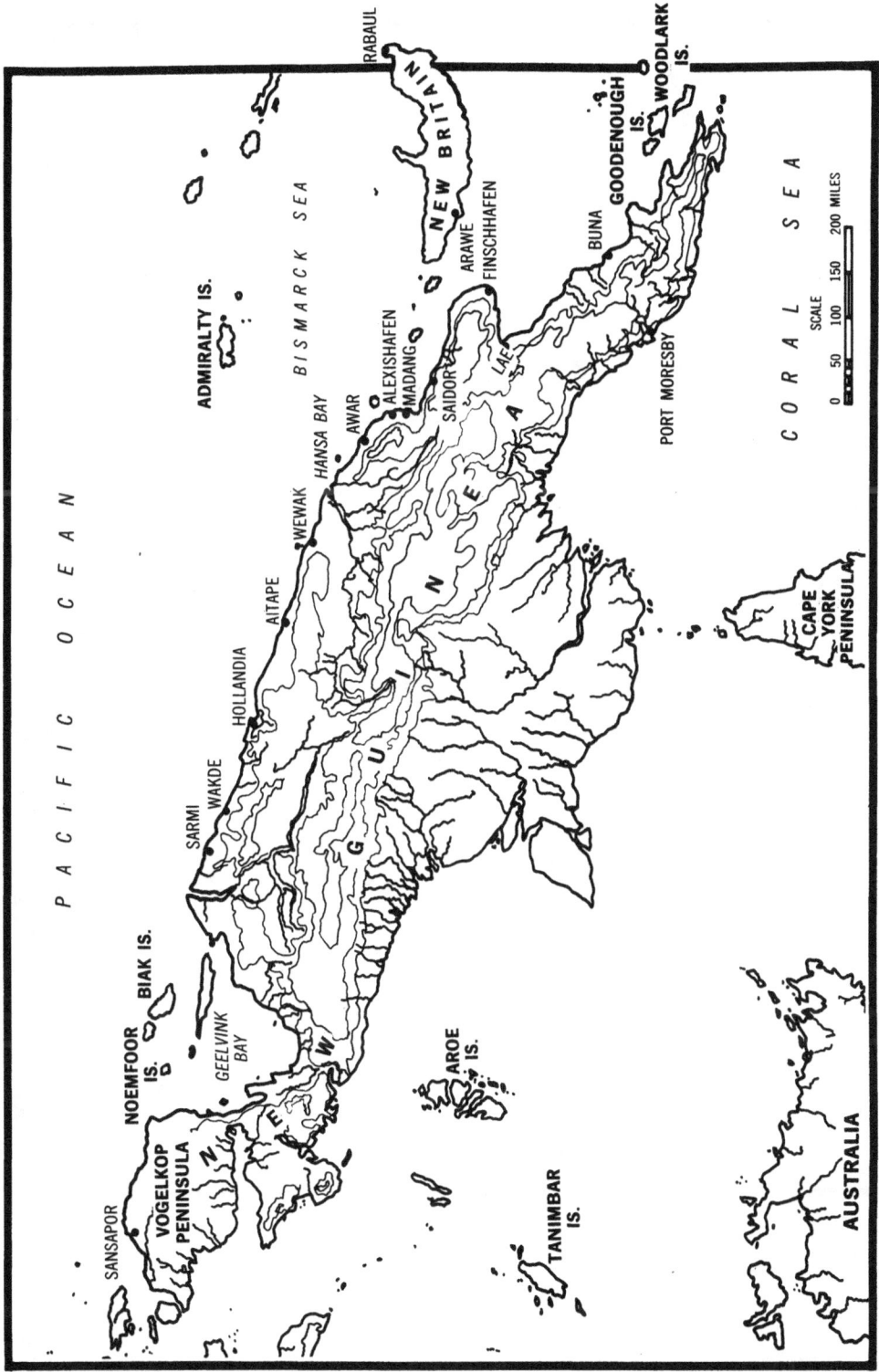

Map 3. Terrain relief map, New Guinea

8

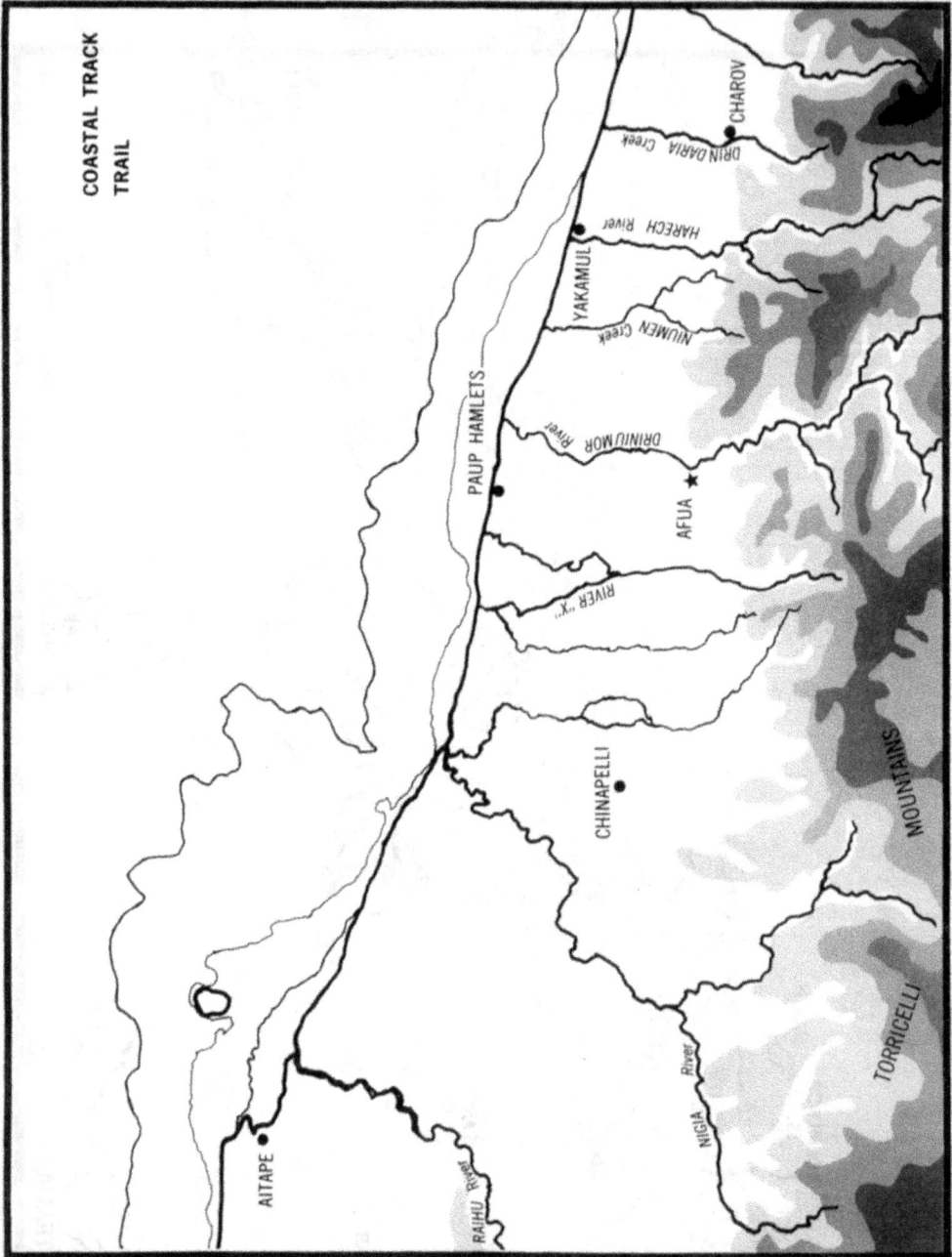

Map 4. Terrain relief map, Aitape region

on 5 August. Aitape is not a particularly pleasant place to live. Deteriorating into a slithery morass capable of engulfing the unwary soldier, it is a worse place to conduct large-scale military operations.

Invasion Planning

By early 1944 General MacArthur's planners had begun the process that would bring Americans and Japanese to battle in this heretofore remote spot. Aitape was about 200 kilometers east of the major Japanese base at Hollandia, but nearly 650 kilometers west of the nearest Allied ground forces. It was thus beyond the approximately 500-kilometer operational radius of land-based Allied fighter aircraft and accordingly was lightly defended by the Japanese. Based on their previous experience fighting MacArthur, Japanese planners believed that the next Allied landing would be made between Madang and Hansa Bay. These Japanese estimates were remarkably similar to those of the Combined Chiefs of Staff in Washington.

After the deliberations of Allied statesmen at the Quadrant Conference in Quebec, 14—24 August 1943, the Combined Chiefs approved bypassing rather than capturing the major Japanese naval base at Rabaul, New Britain, and neutralizing the Japanese forces in eastern New Guinea to Wewak, about 160 kilometers east of Aitape.[3] The decision to bypass Rabaul and to give top priority to Admiral Chester A. Nimitz's drive across the Central Pacific seemed to leave MacArthur in a backwater, far removed from the main action. As D. Clayton James has observed, the disappointing Quebec decisions set MacArthur to thinking of ways to adopt this bypassing or leapfrog strategy to his own operations.[4] The shaping of MacArthur's strategy was enhanced by the availability of Ultra-derived intelligence about Japanese defensive preparations. While it remains difficult to demonstrate a direct causal relationship between Ultra-derived intelligence and MacArthur's leapfrog strategy, it does seem apparent that Ultra was instrumental in MacArthur's decision to scrap his notions for an invasion of Rabaul in favor of a series of seaborne flanking maneuvers along New Guinea's northern coast.

MacArthur's Southwest Pacific Area (SWPA) Command had its own signals intercept organization called Central Bureau. Central Bureau, which operated out of Brisbane, Australia, in early 1944, had been activated on 15 April 1942 as a combined Australian-American intercept and decryption service.* Maj. Gen. S. B. Akin, SWPA's chief signal officer, was the guiding force in Central Bureau's evolution and technical development. By 1943 the bureau had more than 1,000 members and had become a high quality intercept network.[5] Its Washington counterpart was the Military Intelligence

*Headquarters, Central Bureau, followed MacArthur from Melbourne to Brisbane (September 1942), to Hollandia (late summer 1944), to Leyte (October 1944), to San Miguel (May 1945), and to Tokyo (September 1945) and was deactivated in November 1945.

10

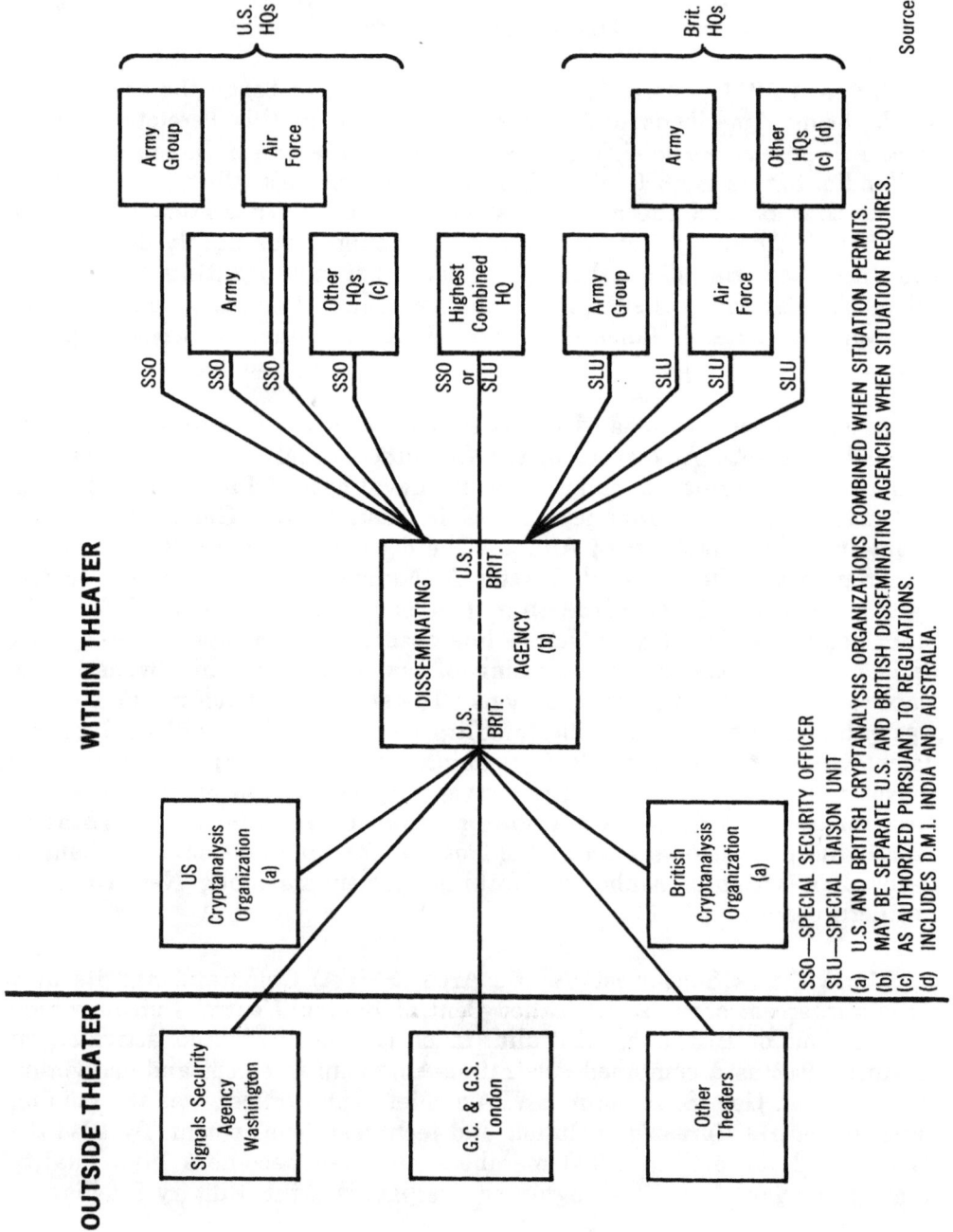

Fig. 1. Flow of Ultra information

Service (MIS) headquartered at Arlington Hall Station, Virginia. Friction characterized the relations of these two intelligence organizations, but by early 1944 they were regularly exchanging information, although MIS was never pleased with Central Bureau's and SWPA's seemingly casual treatment and dissemination to field units of Ultra-derived intelligence information (see fig. 1).[6]

Despite Herculean efforts and technical breakthroughs, the complete recovery of Japanese Army codes still defied the Central Bureau's skilled decryptanalysts, and consequently much of the Japanese Army order of battle information depended on the less reliable system of traffic analysis.[7] Then in late January 1944 the capture of the main Japanese Army codes and ciphers "brought a sudden embarrassment of riches to Arlington Hall, and early in February the Japanese section began to be deluged with a daily flow of thousands of readable Japanese Army messages."[8] With the veil shrouding the Japanese 18th Army's dispositions in New Guinea pulled away, MacArthur and his staff were privy not only to enemy order of battle information, but also to the very intentions of Lt. Gen. Adachi Hatazo, commander of that army.

Japanese messages transmitted and intercepted in late January revealed to SWPA by early February the precise location of each Japanese unit assigned to the defense of Madang, Hansa, and Alexishafen. Beyond that, Ultra provided the Allies specific figures on Japanese casualties, personnel shortfalls, and supply shortages, especially of small arms ammunition. MacArthur's decision to seize the Admiralty Islands on 29 February 1944, one month ahead of the originally scheduled invasion date, was based on his knowledge that Japanese air and sea arms were withdrawing from that area and that there was little to fear from them.[9] The Admiralty operation, in turn, allowed him to accelerate his drive up the New Guinea coast and provided him air bases in the Admiralties that could support operations along that coast.[10] The acquisition of those bases and Ultra revelations probably led MacArthur to cancel his proposed Hansa Bay operations in favor of a direct jump to Hollandia.[11] A decrypted Japanese message, transmitted 28—29 February and available shortly thereafter, offered SWPA planners another opportunity to peer over the shoulders of their Japanese adversaries.

The message formed the core of a staff appreciation of Japanese defensive planning for New Guinea and subsequently appeared in a SWPA G-2 (Intelligence), "Memorandum to the Assistant Chief of Staff, G-3, (Operations) SWPA." According to the intercepted communications, the Japanese foresaw the next major Allied amphibious operation occurring on the north New Guinea coast between Madang and Awar. Lt. Gen. Adachi Hatazo, commander, Japanese 18th Army, planned to counter such a landing by attacking from the south with his 41st Infantry Division and from the north with his 20th Infantry Division, thereby "ambushing" any Allied invaders (see map 5). In fact MacArthur originally had planned to invade the Hansa Bay area.[12] Then on 5 March 1944, through his chief of staff, Lt. Gen.

12

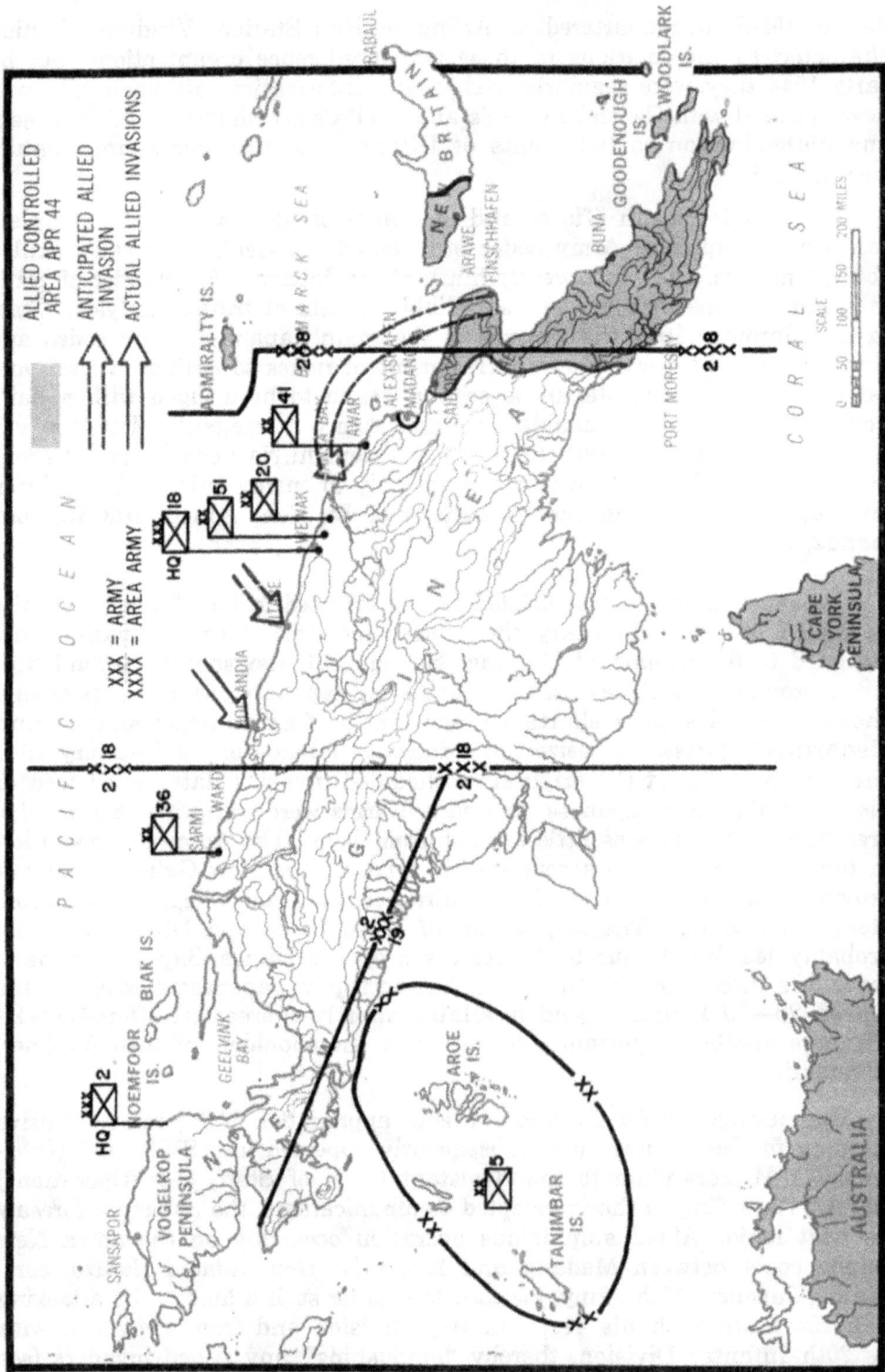

Map 5. Anticipated and actual Allied landings, April 1944

Richard K. Sutherland, he instead proposed to the Joint Chiefs of Staff that two SWPA divisions, supported by the U.S. Pacific Fleet, attack Hollandia on 15 April as a step toward MacArthur's goal of returning to the Philippines. One week later, the JCS approved MacArthur's plan with the understanding that Hollandia could be developed into a heavy bomber base for subsequent air operations against the Palaus and Japanese air bases in western New Guinea and Halmahera.[13]

Hollandia was attractive for SWPA forces because its combination of potential harbor and airfield facilities offered the possibility of a major supply and staging base to launch MacArthur's much heralded return to the Philippines. A leap to Hollandia would bring him 800 kilometers closer to that goal and allow him to bypass the Japanese stronghold at Wewak. The major drawback to the Hollandia operation was its distance from Allied fighter air bases. Hollandia lay beyond the fighters' effective range, yet SWPA required continuous fighter support for its amphibious landing operation. To carry off the operation, MacArthur needed the carrier-based aircraft, but the Navy was in the midst of preparations for the invasion of the Marianas. Cognizant of the upcoming Saipan operation, and despite his earlier promise of air support for MacArthur, Admiral Chester A. Nimitz, commander in chief, Pacific, refused to allow his carriers to remain in the Hollandia area for the eight-day period MacArthur wanted. Instead, Nimitz offered his naval air arm for the first three days after the initial Army landings. Thus denied sustained naval air support, MacArthur's staff then opted to obtain the vital land-based air support for the Hollandia operation by seizing Aitape, 200 kilometers to the east, where the Japanese had three airfields in various stages of construction and one strip operational. These fields could serve as the forward bases for Army Air Force fighter aircraft. Furthermore, U.S. planners reasoned, American troops at Aitape could protect the eastern flank of Hollandia against any westward counteroffensive by the Japanese 18th Army.

As SWPA intelligence officers well knew, 18th Army was moving west. On 13 March a major redisposition of 18th Army appeared in signal traffic. Throughout March, via Ultra, SWPA followed the painful progress of 18th Army's withdrawal from eastern New Guinea. As the Japanese pushed westward, MacArthur responded by organizing Persecution Task Force for the purpose of establishing an airbase at Aitape to support the Hollandia landings and to serve as a blocking force against the approaching Japanese forces. In order to confuse the Japanese about MacArthur's objective, SWPA G-2 developed and executed a classic deception operation designed to convince the Japanese that the main targets of the Allied invasion forces were indeed Hansa Bay and Wewak.

As part of the deception effort, 5th Air Force intensified its attacks against Madang and Wewak, and dummy parachutes were dropped in the Hansa Bay area. Increased and conspicuous reconnaissance flights were sent on mapping and photographic missions over Hansa Bay, and the Navy was directed to make suitable demonstrations along the coast. SWPA ordered PT boats to stage isolated operations in Hansa Bay, and empty rubber landing boats, indicative of disembarked scouting parties, were spotted along the Hansa Bay shoreline. Ultra intercepts confirmed that the Japanese had swallowed the bait. So successful was this deception effort that on 21 April, just one day before the actual Allied landings, the Japanese still expected the Allied invasion behind their lines to occur between Madang and Hansa.[14]

Ultra also confirmed to SWPA intelligence analysts that the Japanese accepted the fact that the Allies intended to occupy Madang and Hansa. The Japanese, however, had no serious expectation of the Hollandia invasion and anticipated no major Allied operations before June. In the meantime, signals intelligence, confirmed by aerial reconnaissance, detected a major Japanese Army Air Force buildup near Hollandia. The mission of this Japanese 4th Air Army, according to Ultra, was "to break up enemy operations and landings in the Madang area." Forewarned, MacArthur's 5th Air Force and U.S. Navy carrier-based aircraft struck first and often. In a series of heavy raids lasting four days, U.S. airmen crippled 4th Air Army, reducing its effective strength to almost zero.[15]

In addition, Ultra allowed Allied intelligence analysts to monitor the dispositions of Japanese ground forces near the invasion areas. An Ultra-derived signal revealed that among the 16,000 Japanese near Hollandia, more than 7,600 were Army Air Force personnel and that an "overwhelming number" of the remainder were service troops. Ultra also divulged the weakness of Japanese defenses at Aitape. On 14 April, for instance, the Magic Summary—Japanese Army Supplement (MSJAS) Summary reported that "at Aitape only two guns were available for AAA defense" and that "malaria was rampant" in the area. There is little doubt that Ultra's contribution at the operational level of the Hollandia-Aitape campaign was significant, but without SWPA's skillful and imaginative planning and use of the intelligence information, it might have died aborning. Moreover, the employment of Ultra intelligence before and during the Aitape campaign was regarded by SWPA G-2 and MIS—in a rare moment of agreement—as a classic application of special intelligence to combat operations. Such an assessment on the strategic and operational levels was justified; on the tactical level, it proved an oversimplification.

Japanese 18th Army

On 9 November 1942 Imperial General Headquarters (IGHQ) in Tokyo had established the Eighth Area Army Headquarters at Rabaul to coordinate Japanese Army operations in the Solomons and eastern New Guinea. The 18th Army, organized that same day, was subordinated to the Eighth Area Army. Lt. Gen. Adachi Hatazo commanded 18th Army and was responsible for Japanese Army operations in eastern New Guinea. Adachi was sixty-one years old. His father had been an army officer, and two older brothers were major generals. Adachi graduated from the Japan Military Academy in 1910 and from the War College in 1922. He had commanded the 12th Infantry Regiment, 26th Infantry Brigade, and the 37th Infantry Division in combat. His operational experience was mainly in Manchuria and North China. In early 1943, IGHQ assigned the 20th, 41st, and 51st Infantry divisions to Adachi's command.

The 20th Infantry Division arrived in New Guinea from China in January 1943. Organized in 1917, this division had extensive combat experience in China dating from 1937. Its 78th and 80th Infantry regiments had distinguished combat records in North China, and the 79th Infantry Regiment had also gained extensive combat experience there. The 41st Infantry Division was organized in 1939. Its three infantry regiments, the 237th, 238th, and 239th, had widespread operational experience in North China and Inner Mongolia. The 51st Infantry Division, organized in 1940, had garrisoned the Canton region in South China from the summer of 1941 to November 1942, when IGHQ transferred the division to Rabaul.

All three divisions had fought against the Americans and Australians on New Guinea and had suffered serious losses. In January 1943, the 51st Infantry Division, for example, had spearheaded General Adachi's counterattack against Wau, where it had been repulsed by the Australian defenders. A convoy carrying reinforcements for the division's 115th Infantry Regiment met disaster when Allied aircraft attacked the ships. Most of the reinforcements perished when, after jumping from the sinking transports, they were strafed in the water by Allied fighters. The 51st and 20th Infantry divisions subsequently engaged combined American and Australian forces at Lae and Salamaua from June into September 1943 and at Finschhafen in late September and early October. The 238th Infantry Regiment, 41st Division, had participated belatedly in the Salamaua fighting, and its sister regiment, the 239th, had counterattacked and driven back elements of the Australian 7th Division from Kesawai in December 1943. The grueling jungle fighting had exacted a severe toll on the Japanese, in terms of both battle casualties and illness. Thus, in early 1944 Adachi was trying to rebuild the fighting strength of his units in anticipation of resisting future Allied attempts to retake eastern New Guinea. These preparations and Adachi's urgent signals for resupply and reinforcement were what Ultra revealed to the Allies.

As General Adachi reorganized his troops, Eighth Area Army Headquarters transmitted ambiguous orders that led to conflicting interpretations of Adachi's mission. On 27 February 1944 they sent two orders to Adachi. The first directed 18th Army to defeat the enemy troops advancing towards western New Guinea in a holding action at Madang. According to IJA doctrine, a holding action was designed to gain time in order to readjust to the changing operational situation, to deceive the enemy, or to delay the enemy's advance so that a stronger main defensive position might be established. Simultaneously, Adachi received a second signal directing him, together with the Japanese 4th Air Army, to defeat the enemy advance in eastern New Guinea. Was Adachi's defense to be passive, simply holding a line, or active, counterattacking vigorously to disrupt the enemy's offensive preparations? Apparently higher headquarters left this decision to Adachi.

Moreover, the Japanese expected the next Allied attack to fall on Madang, particularly after MacArthur's seizure of the Admiralty Islands put Madang within range of Allied fighters. The Japanese used the rule of thumb that the effective fighter range for the continuous type of support required in Allied amphibious invasions was about 480 kilometers. Madang fell within that range, but Hollandia and Aitape were beyond it. General MacArthur had heretofore not used carrier-based fighters for tactical air support, so Japanese planners downgraded the immediate threat against Hollandia and Aitape because of their distance from Allied airfields. They concentrated 4th Air Army near Hollandia, presuming that it was beyond effective Allied fighter range and that the Allies would not attack the base with unescorted bombers. They overlooked the possibility that MacArthur might employ carrier-based aircraft not only against the major concentration of Japanese aircraft at Hollandia, but also in a close air support role at Hollandia and Aitape. Consequently, defenses at both bases languished as the Japanese strengthened those areas where they believed MacArthur's next blow would fall. Based on these assumptions, Japanese staff officers concluded that MacArthur's next landing would occur between Madang and Hansa Bay.[16] Accordingly, IGHQ ordered 18th Army to abandon Madang and to withdraw rapidly west of Wewak, but only after striking a "heavy blow" against the invaders.[17] General Adachi deployed his 51st Division at Madang, his 20th at Bogia, and his 41st at Wewak. From this disposition he hoped to trap Allied invaders between Hansa Bay and Wewak in a pincer movement, a stratagem Ultra revealed to Allied planners.[18]

MacArthur's capture of the Admiralties also isolated Rabaul. As Eighth Area Army at Rabaul could no longer effectively control 18th Army, IGHQ assigned 18th Army and 4th Air Army to General Anami Korechika's Second Area Army, headquartered at Davao, Netherlands New Guinea. Anami's command was responsible for the defense of western New Guinea, a strategic area controlling the southern approach to the Philippines and the Caroline Islands. The Japanese primary defense line, decided at an imperial conference on 30 September 1943, ran south of Timor and Tanimbar islands, through the western side of Geelvink Bay, thence to Truk, the major Japanese naval base in the Caroline Islands. Second Area Army's front line included Tanimbar and Aroe islands, extended to Sarmi, and then swung back through Sorong to Halmahera (see map 6).

General Anami ordered Lieutenant General Adachi to move 18th Army westward to Wewak, thence to deploy his forces to defend Wewak, Aitape, and Hollandia. The 18th Army's main strength, however, still remained east of Hansa Bay. In order to implement Second Area Army's orders, Adachi had to move his battle-depleted, poorly supplied, and scattered units 500 kilometers west, from Wewak to Aitape, and nearly 850 kilometers from

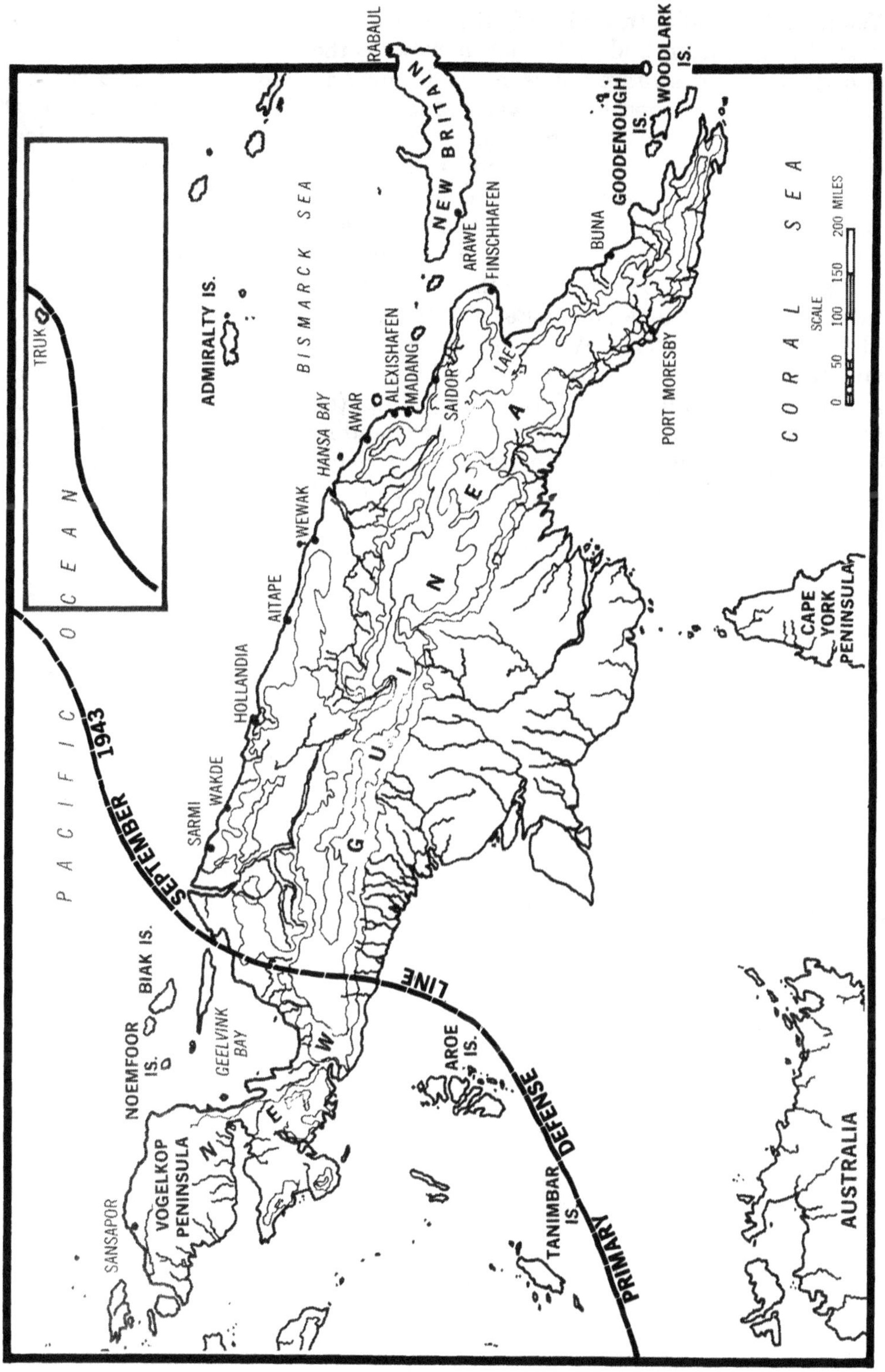

RABAUL

NEW BRITAIN

BISMARCK SEA

ADMIRALTY IS.

WOODLARK IS.

GOODENOUGH IS.

CORAL SEA

BUNA

ARAWE

FINSCHHAFEN

ALEXISHAFEN

MADANG

SAIDOR

LAE

PORT MORESBY

SCALE
200 MILES
150
100
50
0

AWAR

HANSA BAY

WEWAK

TRUK

PACIFIC OCEAN

AITAPE

HOLLANDIA

SARMI

WAKDE

N E W   G U I N E A

CAPE YORK PENINSULA

BIAK IS.

NOEMFOOR IS.

GEELVINK BAY

AROE IS.

SANSAPOR

VOGELKOP PENINSULA

TANIMBAR IS.

PRIMARY DEFENSE LINE

SEPTEMBER 1943

AUSTRALIA

Map 6.   Japanese primary defense line, 30 September 1943

Wewak to Hollandia. In mid-April 1944, during the redeployment, the elements of the 51st Division had just reached Wewak, the 20th Division was passing through the vast swamp between the Ramu and Sepik rivers, and the 41st Division was stretched out between Madang and Hansa. More than 30,000 Japanese troops were scattered east of Hansa, and 18th Army staff officers estimated that they would need another fifty days to get through the rugged terrain.[19] The main reason for the slow pace was a lack of gasoline-powered transport. The 18th Army lacked both trucks for overland movement and barges for sea transport. A forced march was their last resort. Beyond the sheer physical demands of such a move, they made their trek under increasingly dangerous circumstances. Intensified Allied aerial activity made all movement hazardous. While sudden tropical downpours would temporarily curtail the air threat, the rain would wash out jungle tracks and turn swamps into small lakes, further impeding the westward progress of the Japanese. Thus, at the time of the Allied landings at Hollandia and Aitape, 18th Army had not completed its major redeployment. Instead, its combat units were scattered along a 470-kilometer stretch of New Guinea coastline.

American and Japanese Operational Deployments

2

Hollandia and Aitape

The combined Hollandia-Aitape operation was the largest SWPA operation to date, involving 217 ships, nearly 80,000 men, and their supplies moving more than 1,700 kilometers to conduct three simultaneous amphibious landings (see map 7).[20] The multiple invasions caught the Japanese Eighth and Second Area armies completely unprepared, the former expecting an invasion of Rabaul, the latter an Allied landing near Madang. SWPA's successful deception effort thoroughly baffled the Japanese, who although warned by aircraft sighting reports of two Allied convoys moving north of the Admiralties, were unable to predict the exact objective of these armadas. On 21 April, one day before the landings, hundreds of American and Australian aircraft struck Hollandia, Aitape, and the Wakde-Sarmi vicinity. The magnitude of the strikes was such that local Japanese forces in each area believed that their sector was the main invasion target.[21] In addition to the obvious last-minute deception value of the air attacks, marauding Allied aircraft also destroyed the remnants of Japanese air strength in the region and guaranteed Allied air superiority throughout the subsequent campaigns.

The main American landings at Hollandia met only scattered Japanese resistance. At Aitape, Persecution Task Force, commanded by Brig. Gen. Jens A. Doe, landed more than 12,000 men, about 7,000 of them combat troops of the 163d Regimental Combat Team (RCT), reinforced. They encountered no resistance as the nearby Japanese rear service support troops fled into the jungle. By dusk U.S. troops had taken their primary objective, the three airfields at Aitape, known collectively as the Tadji Drome. Engineer troops who had accompanied the landing forces quickly set to work rehabilitating the airfields.

This was the first major landing in which units from the 3d Engineer Special Brigade participated. The 27th Combat Battalion, discovering no Japanese mines or booby traps, worked mainly on widening roads and strengthening bridges to support M-4 medium tanks.[22] Three Royal Australian Air Force mobile works (engineer) squadrons had a fighter strip operational

19

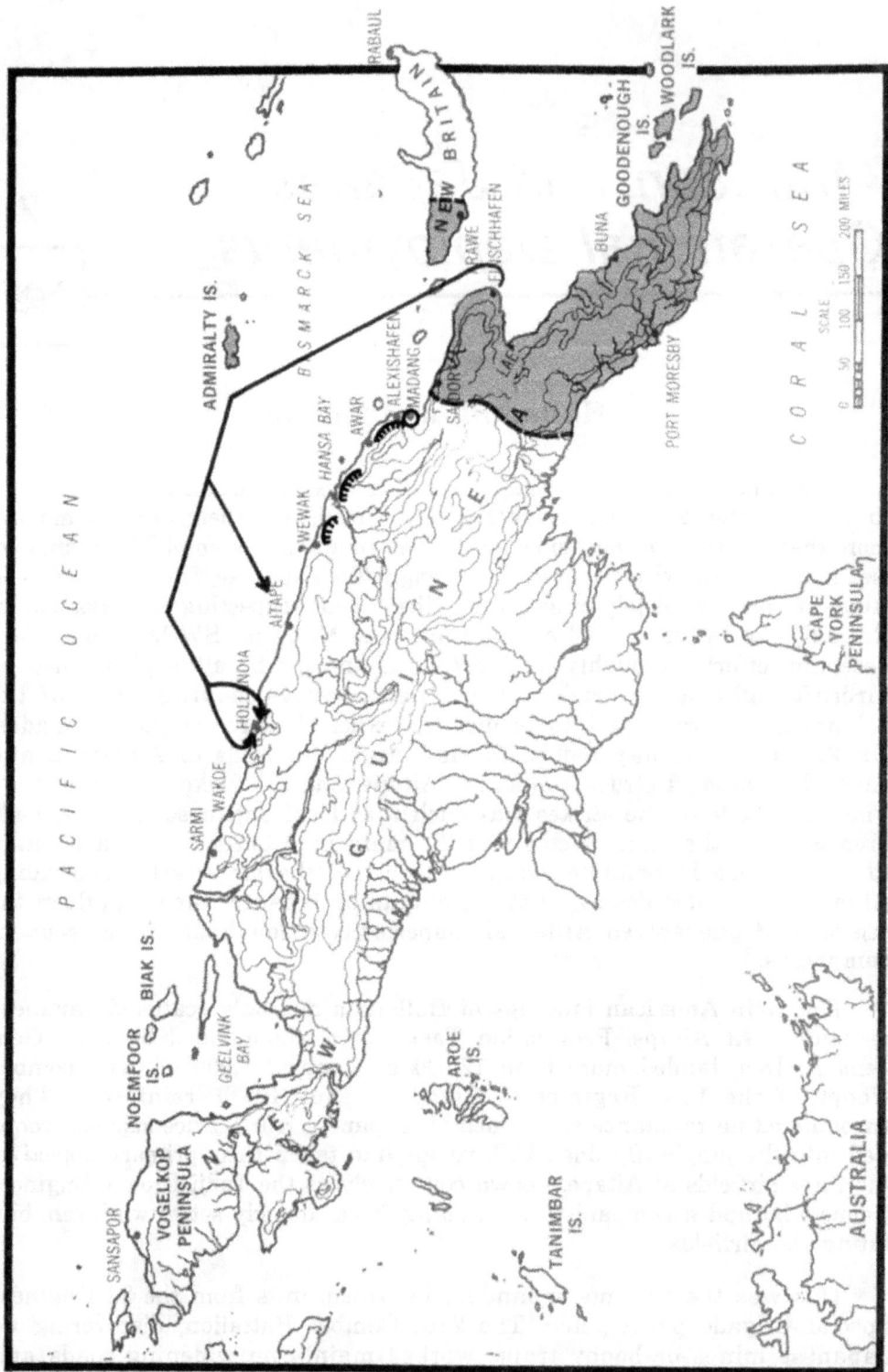

Map 7.   Allied landings, New Guinea, 22 April 1944

within two days of the landing, but heavy rains and poor drainage soon turned their labor into a quagmire. Work at a nearby bomber strip proceeded more slowly, even after the arrival in early May of the 872d and 875th American Airborne Aviation battalions. In fact the bomber strip was not ready for use until early July, by which time the need for it had been overtaken by events.

U.S. Army Signal Corps

1st wave, Aitape, Dutch New Guinea.

The engineers (40 percent of the invasion force) also unloaded seven Landing Ship Tanks (LSTs) the first day and began constructing roads. Unloading was slowed by the lack of Landing Craft Mediums (LCMs). Only eight LCMs and one Landing Craft Tank (LCT) were available to unload the cargo ship, auxiliary (AK) *Etamin*, which remained stationary, unloading its cargo near the beachhead.[23] On 28 April, a lone Japanese aircraft slipped through the air defense net and bombed and damaged the *Etamin*, forcing it to scuttle its cargo in order to remain afloat. Ordnance support units consequently lost all their tools and spare parts.[24] To add to the confusion, as their tension broke after the unopposed landings, the troops became very nonchalant about their personal belongings. Pilfering was common, and within twenty-four hours of the invasion, individual rations littered the entire beach. Soldiers discarded so many items of equipment and ammunition, especially hand grenades, that one officer later commented on their "strong lack of discipline" and the need for more guards and military police to maintain order on future beachheads.[25]

Moreover General Doe felt that the commander of the 163d Regiment was not moving quickly enough to secure his flanks. His tardiness ultimately led General Doe to recommend, and Lt. Gen. Walter Krueger, commander, 6th Army, to approve, the relief of the 163d's commander. He remained in command only until the 163d had been withdrawn to participate in the Wakde-Sarmi operation, 400 kilometers northwest of Aitape. General Krueger's Ultra-derived knowledge of Japanese weakness near Aitape might have facilitated his concurrence in the relief of the overly cautious regimental commander.

U.S. Army Signal Corps

Gen. Douglas MacArthur and Lt. Gen. Walter Krueger.

In any case, the 32d Infantry Division, veterans of the vicious Buna fighting, relieved the 163d RCT in early May. The 32d Division had trained and reorganized in Australia for seven months after Buna. Their training schedule stressed living in a jungle environment, individual combat training both day and night, basic and advanced amphibious training, and unit training, including night exercises.[26] The division's 127th RCT had landed at Aitape in late April, and the rest of the division, less the 128th Infantry Regiment, arrived on 4 May. The 128th remained in Alamo Force (6th Army) reserve at Saidor until 15 May, when it too went to Aitape. Maj. Gen. William H. Gill, commander of the 32d Division, also assumed command of Persecution Task Force. Gill, a Virginian and a graduate of Virginia Military Institute, was fifty-eight years old. He was a decorated World War I veteran with extensive staff and command experience and had commanded the 32d Division since March 1943. Gill dispatched elements of his 127th RCT to push eastward to uncover the whereabouts of General Adachi's 18th Army and to learn its intentions.* At the same time, other battalions from the regiment would patrol and prepare defensive positions. Minor patrol skirmishes aside, the first prolonged engagement fought between Company C, 127th RCT, and the Japanese 78th Infantry Regiment, 20th Infantry Division, erupted on 14 May near Marubian, about fifty kilometers east of the landing beaches. The inconclusive fight and the distance from potential reinforcements convinced General Gill not to push farther east.[27]

As the Americans probed the Japanese forces, the Japanese scouted American units. On 10 May, 18th Army sent four long-range reconnaissance platoons westward to gather intelligence about American dispositions, to obstruct American efforts to collect battlefield intelligence about 18th Army, and to reconnoiter American entrenchments and positions near Aitape.[28] These Japanese troops probably ambushed a U.S. ration train on 31 May and clashed with the 1st Battalion, 127th Infantry, near Afua in early June. As both sides stepped up their patrol activity, clashes were bound to occur. A particularly sharp battle broke out near Yakamul, about thirty kilometers east of the beachhead where, from 31 May through 6 June, casualties on both sides exceeded one hundred killed and wounded.[29] Increased sightings of Japanese patrols east and west of the Driniumor continued into early June, as it became abundantly clear that 18th Army was nearing Aitape in force. General Gill decided to protect the Tadji airstrip by establishing an outer defensive line, in the form of a covering force, along the Driniumor River.

Covering force doctrine defined the purpose of such a defensive line as to provide time for the main force to prepare itself for combat, to deceive the enemy as to the actual location of the main battle position, to force the enemy to deploy early, and to provide a deeper view of the terrain over which the attacker would advance.[30] If forced to withdraw, the covering force was expected to fight a delaying action against the enemy attacker. Covering force doctrine for jungle operations had languished. The 1944 version

---

*Ultra intelligence (identified as such) was not supposed to be disseminated below army level, and even there distribution was restricted. But 6th Army pointed out that in the Pacific theater, corps operated as armies did in the European theater and that corps in the Pacific could thus receive Ultra intelligence. Moreover 6th Army also disseminated Ultra-derived intelligence in sanitized (source concealed) form to army, corps, and division staffs via the SWPA G-2's so-called Daily Summary, a secret-level daily intelligence bulletin. See SRH-107, "Problems of the SSO System in World War II," 30–31, and Brief History, 18.

of the *Jungle Warfare Manual* restated verbatim chapters from the 1941
edition on retrograde movement and delaying action. That meant that the
112th Cavalry Regiment and the 32d Infantry Division were ordered to
conduct operations according to a doctrine that had officially remained
unchanged despite nearly three years' combat experience in jungle warfare.[31]
Nonetheless, Gill's decision was consistent with his principal mission, which
was to protect the Tadji airfields against Japanese attack. The inconsistency
lay in the doctrine and the small number of troops available to defend an
extended river line in jungle terrain.

By doctrinal theory, a rifle battalion in the defense would be assigned
frontage of 900 to 1,800 meters, depending on the defensive strength of the
terrain.[32] The depth of such a defense would vary from 720 to 1,260 meters.
In theory, the defense of a river line with extremely wide frontages cor-
responded to any defense on a wide front, depending on the type of terrain.
Again, according to the manual, if the terrain at the riverbank was unsuited
for close defensive fires, the main line of resistance might be withdrawn
from the river to obtain improved fields of grazing fire. In practice, on 7
June 1944 the 1st Battalion, 128th Infantry, held a 1,800-meter front running
south from the mouth of the Driniumor. The 1st Battalion, 127th Infantry,
defended a 3,300-meter front that extended north from the vicinity of Afua.
Patrols covered the approximately 2,700-meter gap between the units.[33] The
two rifle battalions were greatly overextended and, given the jungle terrain,
were in fact isolated. Japanese reconnaissance patrols easily infiltrated
through the porous American lines.

These Japanese long-range patrols were so successful at remaining
undetected deep behind the U.S. front lines that the Americans thought
that Japanese reconnaissance patrol activity near the Driniumor had slacked
off in early June. The stealth of the reconnaissance patrols contrasted sharply
with the bold activity of Japanese fighting patrols, whose ambush and
surveillance tactics proved singularly effective in preventing American
reconnaissance patrols from crossing Niumen Creek, about 2,700 meters east
of the Driniumor. Nevertheless, the combination of ground activity, patrol
reports, and aerial reconnaissance, combined with Ultra, revealed that 18th
Army was inexorably moving west. Sixth Army's May "Summary of Operations" noted the increasing Japanese pressure on Persecution Task Force's
eastern flank and warned that the enemy had "strong forces" moving towards
Aitape.[34]

18th Army Moves West

The 22 April Allied landings at Aitape and Hollandia naturally
provoked an immediate Japanese reaction. Lieutenant General Adachi
thought that if he attacked at Aitape with the entire 18th Army
immediately, he might be able to break through the American defenses
there and move on to seize Hollandia. Given the condition of his troops
and the enormous distances involved, it is doubtful that even Adachi

seriously believed such a grand scheme was possible. More likely he reasoned that, at the very least, a counterattack would retard the enemy's westward advance and thereby contribute to the overall operations of Second Area Army.[35] Adachi hoped to cooperate with Second Area Army, which could attack the beachheads from the west as 18th Army attacked them from the east.

General Anami, commander of the Second Area Army, already had ordered two battalions of his 36th Infantry Division, located near the Sarmi-Wakde area, eastward to check the Allied landing at Hollandia. When he received Adachi's signal outlining 18th Army's plan, Anami was receptive to the concept of a pincer attack against the invaders. Consequently, on the night of 24 April, Anami alerted the entire 36th Division for an attack against Hollandia. In the midst of these preparations, Anami transmitted his intentions to Southern Army at Singapore. Unless the Japanese could retake Hollandia, he warned, it would jeopardize Second Area Army's future operations.

Southern Army and IGHQ, however, disagreed with Anami's assessment and, rather than endorse the Hollandia attack, instead ordered Second Area Army to prepare against possible future Allied attacks in western New Guinea and the approaches to the Philippines and Palau, as well as against raids by Allied task forces against the western Caroline Islands. Moreover, because of Allied air superiority, IGHQ was reluctant to commit ground forces to the Hollandia counterattack without adequate air cover. The Imperial Navy Combined Fleet also opposed such an operation, deeming it "difficult to expect the Hollandia counterattack to succeed" because of enemy air superiority east of Sarmi, New Guinea.[36]

On 2 May 1944, in consonance with its strategic appreciation, IGHQ ordered 18th Army to move west "as quickly as possible" in order to link up with Second Area Army and thereby to improve Japanese defenses in western New Guinea. Simultaneously, IGHQ redefined Second Area Army's primary defense line as extending to the inner part of Geelvink Bay, Manokwari, Sorong, and the Halmahera Islands. The withdrawal of Second Area Army units around Sarmi increased the separation between 18th Army from Second Area Army and made it necessary for Adachi's troops to cover even greater distances to achieve a linkup. In effect, IGHQ had written off 18th Army. General Anami, however, had not. He continued to advocate a more active defense and took his case to Southern Army at Singapore, where during a two-day conference on 5 and 6 May, Anami pressed for approval of his plan to counterattack the Allied forces at Hollandia. Reinforcements en route could be used for that purpose.

IGHQ previously had ordered the 32d and 35th Infantry divisions then in the Philippines transferred to western New Guinea in order to reinforce Anami's command. On 6 May, however, U.S. submarines attacked this convoy just south of the Philippines, and the two divisions lost most of their artillery and infantry weapons in the attacks.[37] This latest disaster again forced IGHQ, Southern Army, and Second Area Army to reevaluate Japanese operations in the New Guinea theater.

Anami still wanted the survivors of the two ill-fated divisions sent to his command. IGHQ rejected this alternative because it remained unwilling to send the units to forward combat areas where the Japanese lacked air superiority. Instead, IGHQ again redefined the "primary defense line," this time to exclude Geelvink Bay, although the bay, Biak, and Manokwari were to be held "as long as possible" against Allied attacks. The decision pulled Second Area Army even farther away from 18th Army. MacArthur's 17 May landings at Sarmi, about 250 kilometers west of Hollandia, put Anami on the defensive, and he had to forsake any plans for a counterattack against Hollandia. Then, on 27 May, the U.S. 41st Infantry Division, less one regiment, stormed ashore at Biak (see map 8). The subsequent loss of Biak cut the last direct line of communication between Second Area Army and 18th Army.

With dogged determination, 18th Army was pushing slowly west. On 15 May, Adachi had one of his staff officers fly from Wewak to Davao to tell General Anami that he intended to attack Aitape.[38] The fall of Biak, however, had altered General Adachi's chain of command. Isolated from Second Area Army, 18th Army found itself, on 16 June, subordinated directly to Southern Army by IGHQ. IGHQ also limited Adachi's mission to conducting "a delaying action at strategic locations in eastern New Guinea."[39] That meant Adachi no longer had any military reason to attack Aitape.

Adachi's personal reasons, however, remained. To General Adachi's thinking, 18th Army's entire reason for being a fighting force was inextricably bound to the Aitape attack because of the deployment and the condition of his units. By late June his units had already begun to deploy for battle. The main elements of the 20th Division, for instance, had reached the Driniumor River on 18 June. They had started their two-month march through the jungle from Hansa, averaging ten kilometers a day. By the time they arrived at the Driniumor, they were making about half that distance daily. Their personal hardships on this trek exemplified the enormous difficulties Japanese units had to overcome during this overland move. Adachi could not concede that their hardships had been for naught.

A shortage of all classes of supplies and communications equipment also plagued 18th Army: a lack of expendable signal equipment, such as battery cells and tubes; shortages of wire cutters (essential for use against wire entanglements), antitank equipment, and hollow charge shells for the Type 94 mountain gun and the Type 92 infantry gun; only 300 trucks for the three divisions; and but twenty-seven landing barges to shuttle troops along the coast.[40] Furthermore, 4th Air Army could provide neither effective air defense nor aerial reconnaissance and aerial photographs to guide the

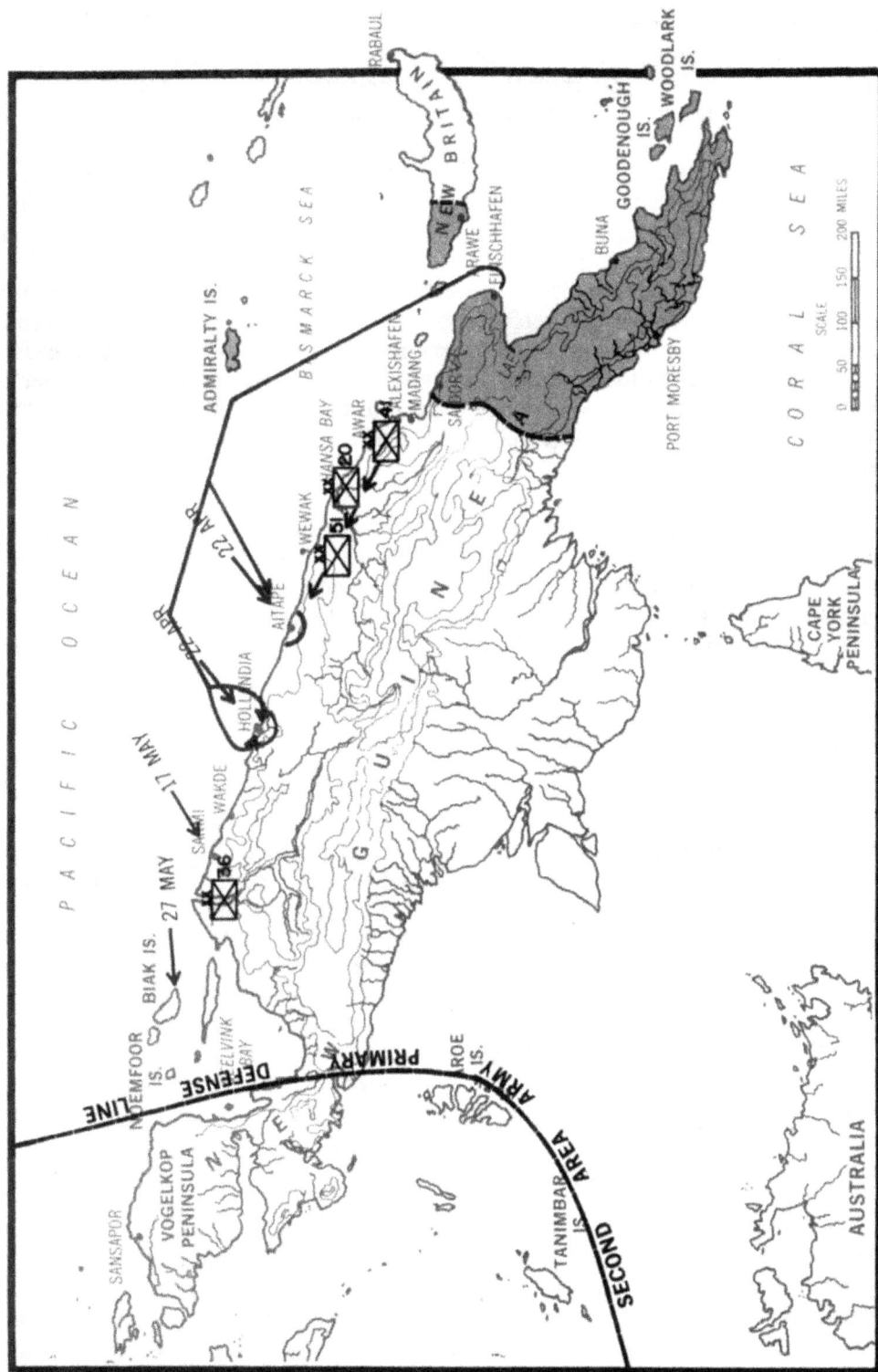

Map 8.   Allied landings, New Guinea, 22 April—27 May 1944

soldiers during their march. Following the destruction of 4th Air Army, the Allied air arms had switched their main efforts to attacking ground troops on the march and in their laager areas. Nearly 800 of the 2,600 tons of Japanese supplies were lost to Allied air strikes.

Individual formations likewise suffered. The 51st Division had only thirty trucks to move its equipment and supplies, leaving the division commander no alternative but to mobilize 1,700 of his combat troops as bearers to carry the division's baggage. Movement along coastal waterways became exceptionally dangerous as Allied aircraft, PT boats, and warships made numerous forays to interdict these transportation routes. Everyone realized that no major resupply convoys could be expected. Officers therefore ordered their men to take care of their equipment and clothing; in order to preserve their boots, troops were ordered to go barefoot in rivers and swamps and to wear *tabi* (thick-soled stockings) in camp instead of the precious boots.[41]

The move by the 2d Battalion, 80th Infantry Regiment, illustrated in microcosm the extent of 18th Army's problems. On 20 June the battalion neared the Driniumor and sent scouts to reconnoiter the so-called Paup Hamlets, four small native villages. About 1400, an American fighting patrol, numbering an estimated thirty to forty men, attacked the neighboring 3d Battalion's position. Later in the day, Allied aircraft bombed and strafed near the 2d Battalion's bivouac. The next day Allied aircraft continued to bomb and strafe randomly throughout the area. Allied artillery exploded a few hundred meters from the battalion area, but there were no casualties. On the twenty-fourth, patrols reported that the Americans had established outposts along the Driniumor, and other patrols clashed with American patrols, losing one man killed and another wounded. The 2d Battalion was readying an attack against U.S. positions in the Paup Hamlets for 29 June when it received word from division to postpone the assault because of the delay in moving supplies forward to support the other combat units involved in the operation.[42] On 27 June, around noon, Allied aircraft bombed and strafed near the battalion's positions, and about 0200 on 29 June Allied warships shelled the area. Neither incident caused casualties, but they were disruptive and unsettling. Yet all the 2d Battalion could do was dig in, block American reconnaissance patrols from moving through its area, and await further orders. Meanwhile, malnutrition and disease stalked the Japanese troops with deadlier effects than the Allied shelling and bombing.

Despite the hardships, 18th Army had little choice but to move west. Army staff officers estimated that with its normal organization and supply requirement it would be able to remain in the Wewak area until the end of September.[43] As 18th Army chief of staff, Lt. Gen. Yoshihara Kane, phrased it, the Japanese could die where they were or die advancing. Both ways were perilous, but the Japanese finally decided to carry out their duty to the nation. They advanced.[44]

As early as 5 May, preliminary intelligence reports about American forces at Aitape filtered into 18th Army. The reports, based on extensive Japanese patrolling in the Aitape vicinity, correctly noted that the Aitape airfields were the center of the American position and described a semicircular defensive perimeter about ten kilometers east of the airstrips. Probably because of the lethargic U.S. movement to establish flanks, Japanese patrols reported that the U.S. lines appeared anchored on the Nigia River, about halfway between Aitape and the Driniumor River. This, Adachi decided, was the defensive line he had to capture.

General Adachi's initial plan was simple, but risky. He planned to concentrate all available combat units on a narrow, 500-meter front, to echelon them in depth, and to launch a surprise attack that would penetrate the entire depth of the American defenses. Following their breakthrough of the American covering force, the Japanese attackers would regroup at Chinapelli and then attack Aitape from the south. Planners estimated that the entire operation would take three days.[45]

Confusion about the exact timing of the attack contributed to conflicting Allied interpretations of Ultra evidence. According to Japanese documents, the attack was to commence in mid-July. That date, however, originally seems to have referred to the second-phase attack planned against the Aitape perimeter after the destruction of covering force defenses. The Japanese initially had set a mid-June date for their attack against the U.S. covering forces supposedly on the Nigia River. Based on the recollections of an 18th Army staff officer, the attack was indeed to commence in mid-June, but the delays in moving men and supplies through the jungle necessitated several postponements because only about 10 percent of Adachi's forces were in their attack assembly areas by mid-June. The confusion and postponements paradoxically worked to 18th Army's advantage. Ultra provided so much information to 6th Army about the Japanese maneuvers that intelligence analysts might have been unable to see the forest for the trees.

Ultra and Operations

3

6th Army's Perspective

The German-born commander of 6th Army, Lt. Gen. Walter Krueger, was sixty-three years old and near the pinnacle of his career. His remarkable military life began as an enlisted man in the Spanish-American War, and he would cap his career in 1944 with a fourth star. In his memoirs, General Krueger wrote that increasing Japanese activity in June and the capture of enemy documents revealed that the enemy planned an intensive reconnaissance of the Aitape area.[46] Krueger could not then write about the role of Ultra in forewarning his command of Japanese intentions. SWPA's Central Bureau indeed provided a running intelligence commentary on the activities of General Adachi's 18th Army. Much of this Ultra information, in turn, appeared in sanitized form in SWPA's Daily Intelligence Summary, which was much more widely available to field units. Concealing the source of the precise information on Japanese activities, usually with the caveat "According to a Japanese PW," enabled SWPA G-2 to pass enormous amounts of Ultra-detected intelligence to its lower echelon units. The very volume of available intelligence information perhaps tended to confuse rather than to enlighten the intelligence analysts.

Without the complete Special Intelligence Bulletin (SIB) issued by SWPA, it is impossible to reconstruct with exactitude the Central Bureau's analytical process. The results of those labors, however, also appear in the Daily Intelligence Summary and, coupled with the Ultra information in the Magic Summary—Japanese Army Supplement, do show the unfolding intelligence estimate of 18th Army's situation. This tactical appreciation reveals Ultra in a far different light from its heralded strategic value. The Ultra-derived perception of the enemy came to rule the conduct of operations as a weapon whose tactical benefit was, at best, enigmatic.

Only two days after the Aitape landing, SWPA intelligence analysts first surfaced the idea that the Japanese would probably bypass Aitape in order to attack Hollandia. Exactly where this interpretation originated is unknown, but it colored General Krueger's perception of the Aitape covering force's role until late June and, perhaps, even later. Krueger feared that

31

Persecution Task Force might be contained within the main line of resistance (MLR) while the Japanese bypassed it and attacked Hollandia. During the next few weeks, for example, SWPA G-2's Daily Intelligence Summary reported that although a Japanese attack on Aitape was within enemy capabilities, it was not considered probable because the enemy "gains nothing." Allied troops at Hollandia would still be athwart 18th Army's supply lines (30 April—1 May 1944).

A few days later, G-2 reversed itself and suggested that an attack on Aitape would achieve more than one against Hollandia (3—4 May 1944), but shortly thereafter, it analyzed such an attack as diversionary in nature to allow the main body of 18th Army to slip around the south flank of the Aitape defenses (8—9 May 1944). The mid-May Japanese attack against Company C, 127th Infantry, at Babiang was initially believed to be the expected Japanese counterattack, and analysts thought that Japanese maneuver units would try to reach Aitape as quickly as possible (16—17 May 1944). Because the Japanese, however, did not follow up their attack, G-2 in late May again advised that all indications pointed to a Japanese attempt to bypass Aitape (25—26 May 1944).[47] When Ultra illuminated 18th Army's exact battle plans, overreliance on the Ultra sources blinded analysts to subtle shifts and variations in the Japanese scheme of maneuver.

The first Ultra-derived indication of Japanese intentions to attack Aitape appeared from the decryption of a 28 May message from Southern Army to Tokyo. Available to SWPA on 1 June, the message was a plea to rush supplies to Wewak by the end of June "due to the attack on Aitape by Mo [18th Army]."[48] This information, plus additional SWPA intelligence garnered from two letters written by Japanese officers of the 239th Infantry Regiment stating that their division would join the 20th Division in an attack against Aitape and Hollandia, appeared in the 2 June MSJAS.[49] The following day the more widely distributed Daily Intelligence Summary mentioned the possibility of a Japanese attack against the Aitape perimeter.[50] Around this time Ultra eavesdropped on the Japanese staff deliberations concerning operations against Aitape, and as the Japanese hammered out a consensus, Ultra provided SWPA all the Japanese options. It thus became more and more difficult to reconcile seemingly contradictory messages. A 7 May order, for instance, instructed 18th Army to use "aggressive tactics" during its withdrawal, but to attempt no "suicidal" moves. Other messages showed 18th Army hardly prepared for offensive operations, existing on reduced rations with only half the ammunition required for a major engagement. Beyond Ultra, SWPA depended upon the cumulative intelligence evidence, human intelligence (HUMINT), aerial reconnaissance, POW interrogations, captured documents, and patrol reports to piece together their mosaic of Japanese intentions. Amidst this welter of conflicting, incomplete, and sometimes contradictory evidence, it is not surprising that G-2, SWPA, clung to its original assessment that although the Japanese might be able to complete their attack preparations by the end of June, the attack would only be a cover for further withdrawals, with no "desperate" moves planned.[51] In short, they attributed their own rationality to their Japanese opponents.

Although the week of 11—18 June provided only minor contacts between roving Japanese and American patrols, on 17 June General MacArthur offered General Krueger the use of a regiment of the 31st Infantry Division to meet the impending Japanese threat near Aitape. Krueger, who by that time was planning his own "vigorous counteroffensive" against 18th Army, informed MacArthur that he preferred the veteran 112th Cavalry Regiment to a green unit from the 31st Division. Krueger's conviction that veteran troops could fight and kill the enemy better, faster, and with fewer friendly casualties was almost universally accepted among Army officers. Postwar studies, based admittedly on limited comparative data, lend support to this popular notion.[52] MacArthur agreed with Krueger's recommendation and, on 24 June, ordered the 112th Cavalry RCT* to Aitape. Although earlier Krueger had been reluctant to request reinforcements, that same day a 155-mm howitzer battalion was sent to Aitape to replace artillery sent to new operational areas in western New Guinea. Number 71 Wing, Royal Australian Air Force, simultaneously received orders to remain at Aitape. Krueger also reversed himself and ordered the 124th Infantry Regiment, 31st Infantry Division, to Aitape and a speedup in shipping the 43d Infantry Division from its New Zealand staging area to Aitape.[53] These reinforcements would bring U.S. forces near Aitape to more than two divisions, leading Krueger to form a corps-level headquarters. He selected Maj. Gen. Charles P. Hall to command this newly created XI Corps. Born in Mississippi in 1886 and graduated from West Point in 1911, Hall was a highly decorated World War I veteran and had spent nine of the interwar years at the Infantry School. Hall and his staff, however, had only recently arrived in New Guinea fresh from the United States and, according to General Gill, "didn't know anything about jungle fighting," being "untrained in this thing from the top down."[54] Krueger's instructions to Hall were:

> Recent information indicates that the Japanese are planning an all-out attack against our forces in the Aitape area. It is estimated that the enemy can concentrate in the area south and east of Yakamul, by 30 June, a combat force of 20,000. Additional units of a strength of approximately 11,000 are reported to be in the Wewak area.
>
> Missions assigned to the Persecution Task Force remain unchanged (defense of the Tadji Drome and other installations at Aitape). In carrying out these missions you will conduct an active defense, breaking the initial impetus of the Japanese attack against a flexible defense system and following up with a vigorous counteroffensive when the strength of your force and the tactical situation permits [sic].[55]

*The 112th's official designation was the 112th Regimental Combat Team (RCT). For the Aitape campaign, however, its 148th Field Artillery Battalion did not accompany the rest of the unit. So although identified as an RCT, the 112th at Aitape was in fact a dismounted horse cavalry regiment.

Persecution Task Force had evolved rapidly during May and June as additional reinforcements and support troops poured into the Aitape area.* Major General Gill, now placed in command of Eastern Defense Area, realized that any serious Japanese threat would develop on his eastern flank, and he therefore devoted his energies to strengthening that line. On 10 June, Gill's West Sector was held by the 126th Infantry Regiment (minus its 2d Battalion); his Center Sector was held by the 128th Infantry (minus its 1st Battalion); and the East Sector, by the 127th Infantry and the two battalions taken from West and Center, respectively. This reinforced covering force was commanded by Brig. Gen. Clarence A. Martin and designated Eastern Defense Command. Its defensive line was anchored on Driniumor's west bank, about thirty-five kilometers from the Tadji airfields (see map 9). This distance, most of it through jungle terrain, and the increased manpower required that logistic priority be given to the covering force.

U.S. Army Signal Corps

At the 32d Division command post at Aitape. From left to right: Maj. Gen. C. P. Hall, commanding general of task forces; Maj. Gen. William R. Gill, commanding general of 32d Division; and Maj. Gen. Leonard F. Wing, commanding officer of 43d Division.

See app. 2 for organizational charts depicting evolution of Persecution Task Force.

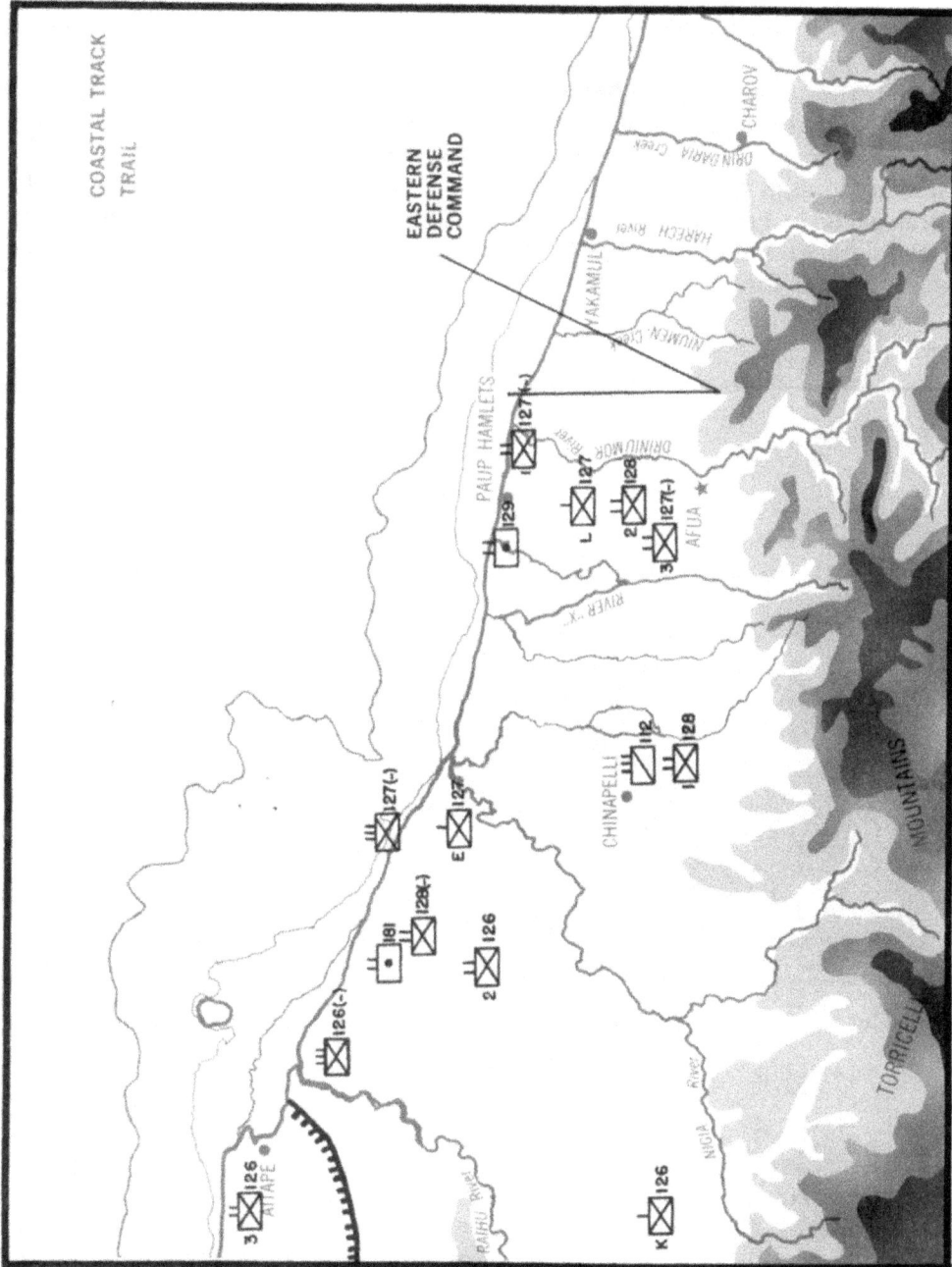

Map 9. U.S. Army dispositions, Aitape, June 1944

Resupply reached the units along the Driniumor through a variety of means. Small boats moved supplies along the coast, and native-portered ration trains carried provisions along the coastal track. Materiel destined for Afua moved south inland from the coast along the Anamo-Afua trail or, later during the campaign, over an inland track running from the Tadji airfields through Chinapelli and Palauru. After the Japanese ambush of a ration party in early June, the command resorted to air drops for resupply. A dropping ground about 2,000 meters north of Afua served as the main resupply point for U.S. units operating near Afua.

U.S. Army Signal Corps

Members of 128th Infantry Regiment, 32d Division, move up to the front along the beach at Aitape.

Units defending the Driniumor used radio to communicate with each other, but telephone to talk with higher headquarters. Radio range, however, was limited by the thick jungle vegetation, its impenetrable canopy, and atmospheric conditions. Most radio communications at night simply deteriorated into static. Telephone contact depended on easily broken wire. Friendly troops walking over it, artillery exploding on it, humidity rotting it, or, worst of all, Japanese patrols cutting it made wire communications as undependable as radio. Still, jungle trails and defensive perimeters were soon crisscrossed with telephone wires, because as the official historian notes, it was usually less hazardous to string new wire than to attempt to splice breaks in the line, particularly when the Japanese laid ambushes at those places where they had cut the wire.[56]

Artillery and air support at Aitape were also augmented as the Japanese threat loomed ever closer. After the original three P-40 squadrons of No. 78 Wing, Royal Australian Air Force, departed at the end of May, only the 110th Reconnaissance Squadron of the U.S. 5th Air Force remained. Then on 9 June, No. 71 Wing, RAAF, equipped with Beaufighters, arrived at Aitape and provided close air support throughout the campaign. The 5th Air Force A-20s and B-25s provided additional air support, staging first from Nadzab and later from Hollandia. Fifth Air Force C-47s, also flying from those two bases and occasionally from the Tadji strips, flew the aerial resupply missions that dropped rations and ammunition to U.S. troops along the Driniumor.[57]

The 181st Field Artillery Battalion's 155-mm howitzers reinforced the organic 105-mm howitzers of the 32d Division and provided artillery support.[58] Artillerymen worked under severe handicaps at Aitape because photomaps were too inaccurate to provide them a basis for a firing chart to enable them to plot accurately the locations of friendly troops. Air observation and numerous fire registrations partially alleviated, but never solved, the problem. To compensate for their deficiency in accuracy, artillerymen resorted to quantity. An Army historian described the "tremendous expenditure" of artillery ammunition, estimated by XI Corps to be the largest expenditure in any campaign up to that time in SWPA.[59] As will be seen, their profligacy would also require an enormous logistical effort just to keep the guns supplied with ammunition. In the defensive perimeter around Aitape, artillerymen positioned their batteries in diamond-shaped formations to obtain all-around fire. They located their batteries near the beach line to get minimum range necessary. All howitzers were dug in, and positions contained protective cover for ammunition and crews.[60] These guns would be decisive in disrupting one Japanese attack after another.

With reinforcements either in place or on the way, Krueger, though confident he could meet any contingency, believed that "the expected attack could not be met successfully by Aitape Task Force standing on the defensive."[61] Here, it seems, Ultra dictated his operational directives.* On 25 June the first translations of the "complete plan of attack by the 20th and 41st divisions became available."[62] Central Bureau had intercepted and decrypted a Japanese signal that announced that the attack against Aitape "is scheduled to begin about 10 July and to be made by approximately 20,000 troops, according to an 18th Army (HQ Wewak) message dated 20 Jun[e]." It should be noted that the signal made no mention of a flanking attack against Afua. Central Bureau apparently derived that perception from the analysis of Ultra together with captured letters, written by Japanese officers of the 239th Infantry Regiment in mid-May, documents captured on 31 May, and the reported disposition of the Japanese 78th Regiment. Nonetheless, the 27 June MSJAS paraphrasing SWPA's special intelligence reports described the plan outlined in the 20 June intercept as calling for the 20th

*See app. 1 for a sampling of pertinent Ultra-related intelligence assessments.

Division to attack west across the Driniumor, while the 41st moved south and attacked north and northwest toward the Aitape and Tadji airfields. Accompanying this information was a hand-drawn map illustrating the 20th Division's frontal attack across the Driniumor about three kilometers from the mouth of the river, concurrent with the 41st Division's envelopment of the southern U.S. flank, thence north towards Aitape. Such a plan of attack reflected Central Bureau's translators' and analysts' interpretation of the 20 June message.*[63] According to the original Japanese attack order, the final assault against Aitape would indeed originate from the south, but it would not involve a flanking maneuver. After both Japanese divisions broke through the center of the American covering force, the Japanese planned to envelop these American defenders from the rear, destroy them, and then regroup to attack Aitape from a southwest axis.

The very next day, SWPA reported that according to another intercepted message the Japanese intended to make a preliminary attack across the Driniumor on 29 June. This 24 June signal emanated from Headquarters, 20th Division, whose commander, Lt. Gen. Nakai Matsutaro, wanted his troops to drive back the American covering force "as early as possible" to facilitate the second, and main, Japanese attack against the American main line of resistance near Aitape. Nakai communicated his plans for such a 29 June attack to 18th Army. But because units of the 41st Division were unable to deploy properly by that date, he postponed the attack until 3 July and later was ordered to wait until 10 July.[64] The SIB for 27–28 June reported this development along with the facts that Japanese units were far understrength, suffering severe supply difficulties, and cut off from possible reinforcement. Furthermore, additional fragmentary intercepts revealed that the Japanese had expressed doubts about their ability to accomplish this mission on time. The cumulative evidence led SWPA G-2 analysts to conclude that "supply difficulties may force the date of the attack to be slightly delayed."[65]

The 24 June intercept, however, probably did prompt General Krueger to fly from Hollandia to Aitape on 27 June to confer with his new corps commander, General Hall.[66] Also present at the 28 June meeting was General Gill, now commanding the Eastern Defense Area. Gill voiced his concern over his force being overextended and thus unsupportable because of the difficulties in moving artillery and supplies through the jungle from Aitape to the Driniumor. Cognizant of the possibility of an imminent Japanese attack on the covering force, he requested reinforcements and permission to withdraw his force into the main defensive perimeter. Krueger not only rejected Gill's proposal, but also ordered General Hall to strengthen the Driniumor covering force and to take steps necessary to meet the Japanese attack

*The possible reasons for the interpretation are numerous: first, the ambiguity of the Japanese language; second, missing groups or "words" in the message; third, Ultra in combination with other intelligence sources altered perceptions; fourth, and not least, the intelligence analysts worked under tremendous pressure translating more than 20,000 intercepts in 1944 alone and did not have the leisurely retrospective powers time confers on historians.

with a powerful counterattack.[67] Because Ultra had indicated the possibility of a Japanese attack the next day, 29 June, perhaps Krueger meant that Hall should be ready to counterattack when the opportunity arose. Hall's G-2 revealed XI Corps's concern about the reliability of 6th Army's intelligence when he questioned the source of Krueger's detailed information about the impending Japanese attack. In reply, Krueger sent a top secret signal to XI Corps G-2 that explained that the Japanese scheme of maneuver and the objectives of the 29 June Japanese attack were "based upon further interpretation of ultra information."[68]

After 29 June had passed without a major Japanese attack, intelligence analysts reassessed their work and concluded that while the order of battle information in the 24 June message was accurate, the date of the attack had been postponed, exactly as they had foreseen. The 10 July date mentioned in the earlier 20 June intercept now appeared to be the day that the attack would commence. Further complicating the situation, on 30 June General Hall sent a priority message to General Krueger stating that a Japanese prisoner captured near Yakamul had reported an "attack to be made between first and tenth July" against U.S. lines along the Driniumor.[69] The Daily Intelligence Summary for 1–2 July, again resorting to the cover of a POW report, provided extensive details of the Japanese tactical order of battle for the impending attack, including the two-pronged plan of maneuver. The interpretation of a Japanese frontal assault to fix U.S. defenders, while the main force units maneuvered south around the covering force's flank, had taken on a life of its own.[70] Its origins may be found in the original SWPA assessments that 18th Army would try to bypass Aitape to the south. In short, overwhelming evidence indicating a Japanese attack was available, but the framework of analysis remained flawed.

As the Japanese maneuver battalions worked their way into their attack positions, their headquarters elements followed closely, negating the need for wireless communications between command echelons and reducing the number of Allied intercepts. In addition, atmospheric conditions and numerous breaks in Japanese landlines forced the Japanese to forsake both wire and signal communications and resort to runners to insure the delivery of critical orders. These factors influenced both the Japanese and American conduct of the battle, as a brief background of the situation demonstrates. On 30 June General Adachi and 18th Army Headquarters staff arrived at Charov, where a subsequent conference among Adachi and his division commanders eventually ratified his plan to conduct a frontal attack in deep echelon on a narrow front. No flanking maneuver was planned. After the initial break-through and destruction of the U.S. covering force, the Japanese would reorganize and press on toward Aitape. These verbal orders to division commanders naturally were unavailable to SWPA analysts who continued to think in terms of a two-pronged attack. Even more significant, runners hand-carried Adachi's final attack order, issued 3 July, to the respective division commanders resulting in two inadvertent consequences. First, it delayed significantly the receipt by Japanese units of their operational orders.

In the case of the 41st Division, for instance, orders did not arrive until the morning of 7 July and forced the division to deploy and attack over ground that it had no time to reconnoiter.[71] Second, with Ultra dried up, Central Bureau never did intercept the definitive Japanese plan of attack against Aitape.*

American patrols took up the Ultra slack and reported increased enemy activity.[72] Moreover, on 7 July so-called secret information, most likely distilled from the reevaluation of available intercepts and captured documents, reached the covering force. This information indicated that the Japanese planned to attack the Driniumor line on 10 July.[73] With four infantry battalions and one cavalry regiment deployed on or in reserve along the Driniumor, the covering force, alerted and prepared for an attack, seemed in perfect position to wreak havoc on any Japanese assault. In fact, however, the Japanese achieved tactical surprise, broke through the U.S. lines, and precipitated a bloody month-long fight for control of the Driniumor. General Krueger's own tactical decisions facilitated the Japanese breakthrough.

Krueger chafed at standing on the defensive. He perceived from Ultra that the Japanese intended to attack the Driniumor covering force, and he understood the pitiful supply situation plaguing the Japanese maneuver units. Furthermore, Ultra assessments led him to expect a two-pronged Japanese attack that would develop as a holding action to cover a Japanese envelopment of the covering force from the south. Simultaneously, Krueger's 6th Army was conducting major operations at Hollandia, Wakde, Biak, and Noemfoor and preparing for the Sansapor invasion. Krueger was under enormous pressure, and rather than let the Aitape situation linger, he decided that "it was desirable to develop the situation and bring matters to a head. Accordingly he ordered a reconnaissance in force to proceed to the Harech River and be prepared for further operations on Task Force order."[74]

The reconnaissance in force, ordered on 8 July, would proceed west along the northern and southern flanks of the covering forces. The northern force would disrupt any Japanese attempts to use the coastal road to transport supplies to their attack staging areas. The southern force would disrupt Japanese enveloping forces by forcing them into action before they were completely ready. The reconnaissance, however, required Krueger to strip away all reserves from the covering force, denuding, in Gill's words, "the pitiful force we had on the defense."[75] The operation began on the morning of 10 July. That night thousands of Japanese would storm the U.S. lines.

American patrols had been reporting increased Japanese pressure. But it had been strangely quiet in the Company F, 2d Battalion, 128th Infantry, sector, where only one patrol contact was reported between 29 June and 10 July. The absence of Japanese activity convinced the members of Company

---

*SRH-059, 026, argues that the 10 July attack followed the same pattern as the abortive 29 June plan. Although the plans were similar, the change of dates caused analysts difficulties in ferreting out Japanese intentions.

F that they were the target of an impending Japanese counterattack. They reasoned that the Japanese avoidance of the entire 2d Battalion sector suggested that the Japanese intended to attack there.[76] Japanese troops were active, however, in the 3d Battalion, 127th Infantry, sector, which bordered the 2d Battalion on the south. During the morning of 10 July, 3d Battalion patrols sighted several strong Japanese fighting patrols, but whether or not they reported these sightings back to Persecution Task Force commander remains uncertain. Even if they had, the reports probably would have made little difference.

At Task Force Headquarters, General Hall was not unduly concerned about an imminent Japanese attack. He had been expecting a Japanese attack since 5 July and had no reason to believe that the night of 10—11 July would pass any differently from those preceding it. General Gill felt that his G-2 had not impressed Hall sufficiently, and consequently his warnings of an imminent attack were disregarded. For instance, Hall would not believe the Japanese could bring mountain artillery through the jungle nor would he give total credence to intelligence estimates developed by the 32d Division G-2 section.[77] Hall signaled Krueger about 2330 that the reconnaissance in force eastward would continue the following day.[78] Maj. Gen. Charles A. Willoughby, SWPA G-2, was even more certain that the Japanese attack had again been postponed. On 10 July the MSJAS reported that 18th Army's attack

> which was scheduled to begin on that day had not been attempted and that there were no signs of the patrol activity which would be expected to precede the attack. G-2 SWPA suggested that the attack might have been postponed until urgently needed supplies could be received by submarine and plane and supplies in the forward area built up.[79]

The Ultra card, it seems, had been misplayed.

Part II

Tactical
Perspectives

112th Cavalry's Deployment to the Driniumor

Map 10 shows the disposition of U.S. forces along and across the Driniumor River about two hours before the Japanese attack. The headquarters map and its unit symbols were operational tools. They represented battlefield reality, the commander's operational deployment, and the enemy situation. They were ready reference aids for the commander and his staff. The artificial structure of battle necessarily imposed by higher headquarters could not accurately represent every event at the tactical unit level. The vast increase in human activity at the lower links in the chain of command precluded that. From the idealized solitary figure of the commander pondering his next order to the range of complex preparations of a rifle squad before patrol—and the squad was only a tiny fraction of a battalion—generalizations based on individual unit reports could place a patina of order on the chaos of battle. For instance, 6th Army Headquarters' knowledge of the location of its subordinate units was fairly accurate. The 32d Division, however, probably had a better grasp of the friendly and enemy situation near Aitape. Line units, like the 112th Cavalry, understood better than those two higher echelons the deadliness of the Japanese infantryman. Individual cavalrymen saw, heard, smelled, or fought their enemy. They were, conversely, almost totally ignorant of how 6th Army had structured the cavalrymen's fight. If order and precision were keynotes of command at the top, confusion and uncertainty over the larger picture were hallmarks at the bottom. To be confused was normal, and uncertainty bred the caution needed to stay alive.

Japan's 18th Army confronted similar circumstances. When General Adachi scanned a situation map, his reactions were probably quite similar to General Krueger's. Adachi knew that Japanese patrols had worked their way across the Driniumor and had observed, heard, smelled, and fought their American foes at close range. Along or near the Driniumor, small groups of armed men moved cautiously through a reeking jungle whose mangrove swamps and twisted roots made even walking an exhausting business. Small fighting patrols from both armies groped blindly in the primeval jungle for their enemies. When they found each other, higher headquarters could add or subtract another map symbol. Such was the grim

46

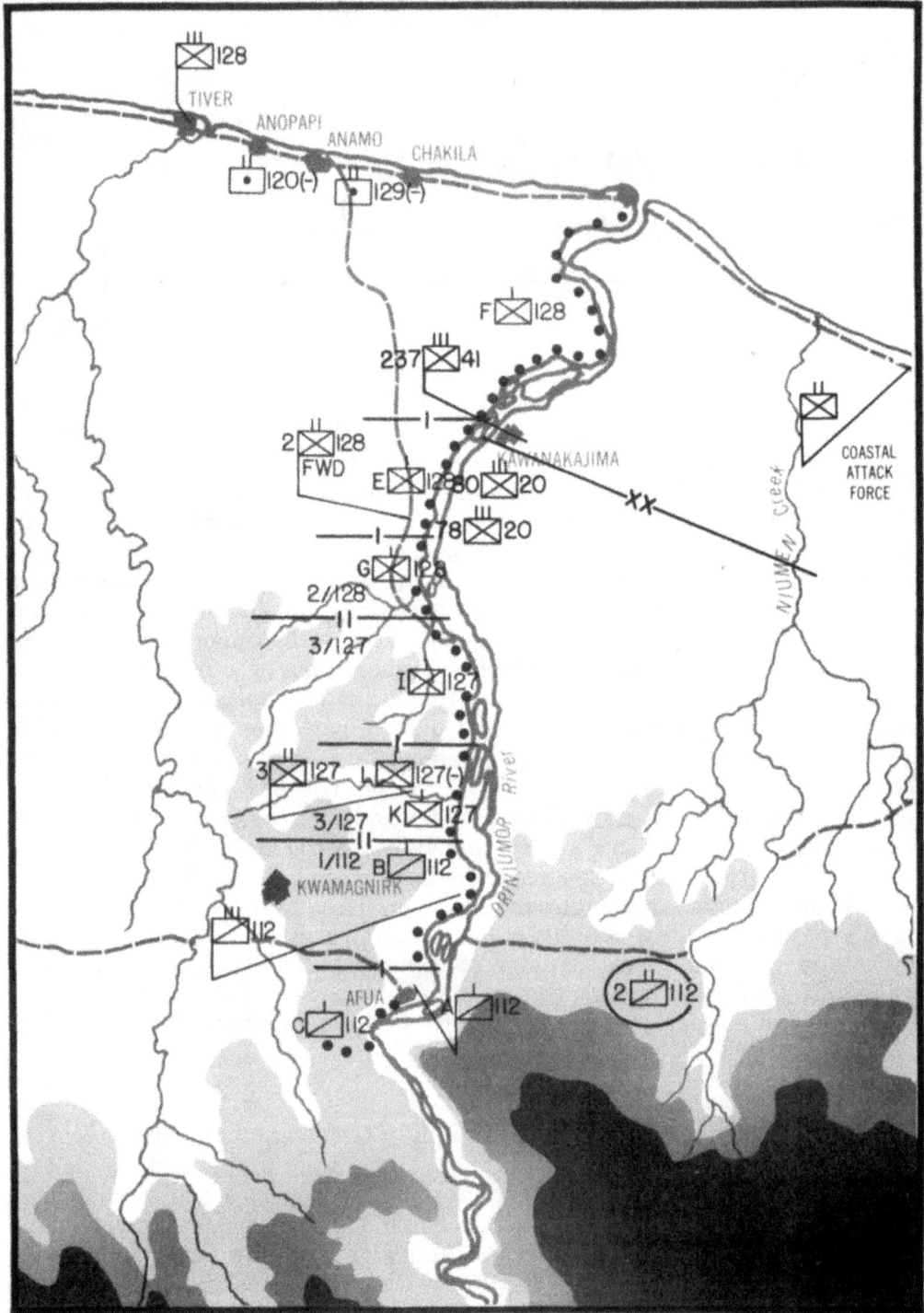

Map 10. Situation along the Driniumor, evening of 10 July 1944

reality behind the 112th Cavalry's symbol on the Aitape mapboard. That symbol, a snapshot of the present, said precious little about the soldiers who filled 112th's ranks.

112th Cavalry Regimental Combat Team

Three weeks earlier, on 21 June 1944, the 112th Cavalry RCT had received verbal orders to prepare for a move from its base at Finschhafen. According to the commander of the 112th Cavalry Regiment, Col. Alexander M. Miller III, members of the regiment knew that "something was in the works," perhaps even the invasion of the Philippines. Nevertheless, the initial information Colonel Miller received was purposefully vague, and the men in the unit had really no idea where it was going or what to expect once it arrived. Their only certainty was that they eventually "would contact the enemy and eliminate them."[1]

The 112th was a Texas National Guard regiment. When it was federalized in 1940, draftees from Brooklyn, New York, Chicago, Illinois, and Iowa augmented its ranks. When it received orders for a Pacific Ocean deployment at Camp Clark, Texas, the regiment had to search for a jungle warfare manual. Once a copy was discovered, Maj. Philip Hooper had to read it aloud to the regiment's NCOs assembled in a poorly ventilated orderly room on a sweltering Texas day. Page after page of the manual described the dangers of snakebite, insects, and tropical diseases. For men who had never been outside the United States and knew little, if anything, about the Pacific islands, it stimulated more fear than enlightenment about their assignment. Furthermore, the regulations dwelled on what could not be done in jungle terrain and unintentionally slighted what could be accomplished. So without much doctrinal assistance, the 112th shipped overseas in July 1942.

The officers and men did have the chance to become accustomed to the environment of New Caledonia, where they spent nine months of intensive training. Brig. Gen. Julian Cunningham's rigorous discipline and realistic training helped to make the members of the 112th physically tough and would enable them to endure the hardships of living and fighting in the tropical rain forest that lay ahead. The 112th had the time, nearly three years, to train and to prepare itself for combat.

Its first combat operation was an unopposed landing on Woodlark Island in July 1943. After occupying Woodlark for six months, the regiment moved to Goodenough Island, was strengthened by the 148th Field Artillery Battalion, and was redesignated the 112th Cavalry Regimental Combat Team. The 112th's next operation, 15 December 1943, was a diversionary effort to assist the U.S. Marines' invasion of New Britain and resulted in near catastrophe.

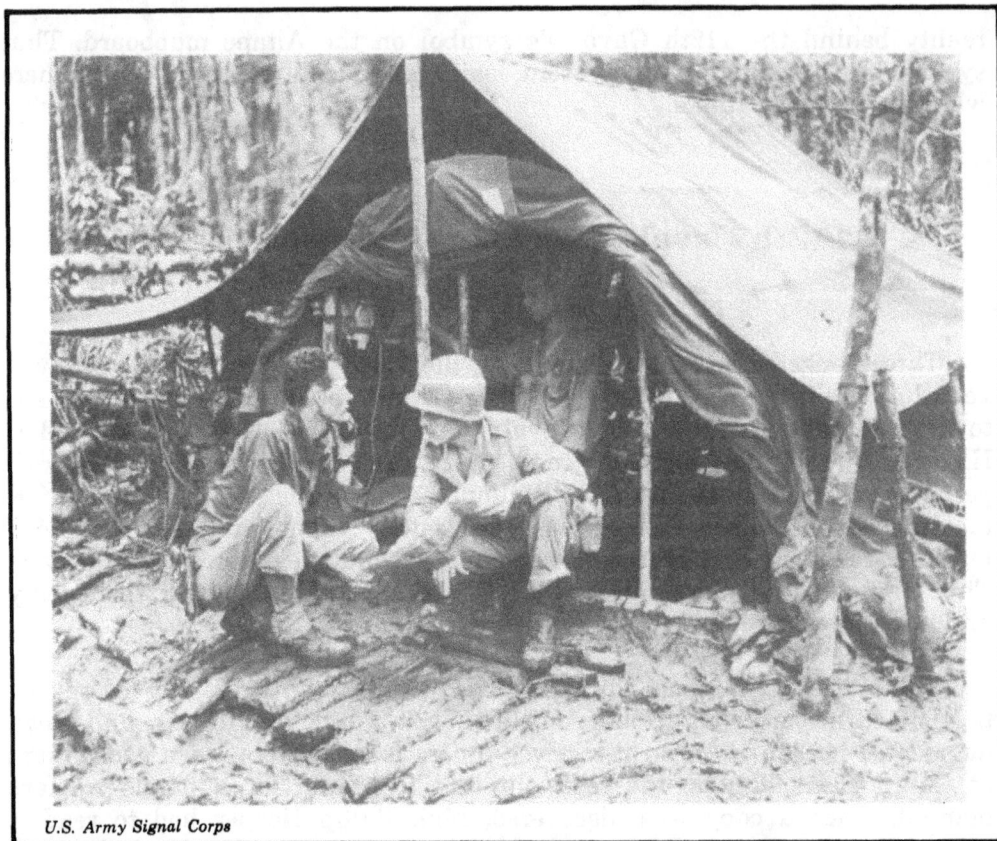

Lt. Col. Philip L. Hooper, executive officer, 112th Cavalry, telephones operational orders received from Brig. Gen. Julian W. Cunningham, commanding general, 112th Cavalry.

Troop A, 2d Squadron, attempted a forced landing at Arawe, New Britain, using rubber boats. Japanese 25-mm gunfire sank all but three of the fragile craft before they reached shore. Only the courage and willingness of the U.S. Navy minesweeper commander who sailed his ship into the cove and smashed the Japanese batteries with gunfire averted disaster. The survivors regrouped, eventually rejoined the 112th, and fought on New Britain for the next six months. The jungle fighting, sickness, and incessant enemy bombing whittled the units down to about 1,100 from their authorized strength of 1,728. In June 1944, the 112th finally received orders for rest and reconstitution at Finschhafen. That respite lasted only a brief two weeks. During that time, though, replacements and troops returning to duty increased unit strength to 1,458, or 85 percent of TO&E strength (see fig. 2).

A variety of circumstances molded the 112th Cavalry. The men who formed the nucleus of the outfit had known each other and soldiered together for a long time. By 1944 it was not uncommon for the members from the former National Guard regiment to have served with their unit for five,

(1,550 authorized)
(1,522 assigned)

1 NOV 1940

Rgt HQ & Band	HQ & SVC	MG	WPN	X2	
(35)	(206)	(159)	(142)	(944)	(63)
(29)	(206)	(159)	(141)	(940)	(47)*

(1,728 assigned)
(1,534 present)

1 JULY 1944

HQ & HQ TROOP	SVC	X2**	WPN		BAND
(210)	(178)	(1040)	(174)	(63)	
(229)	(184)	(1069)	(174)	(50)	(22)

SQDN (1940)
(406)

HQ	X3
(16)	(390)

SQDN (1944)

HQ	X3
(20)	(501)***

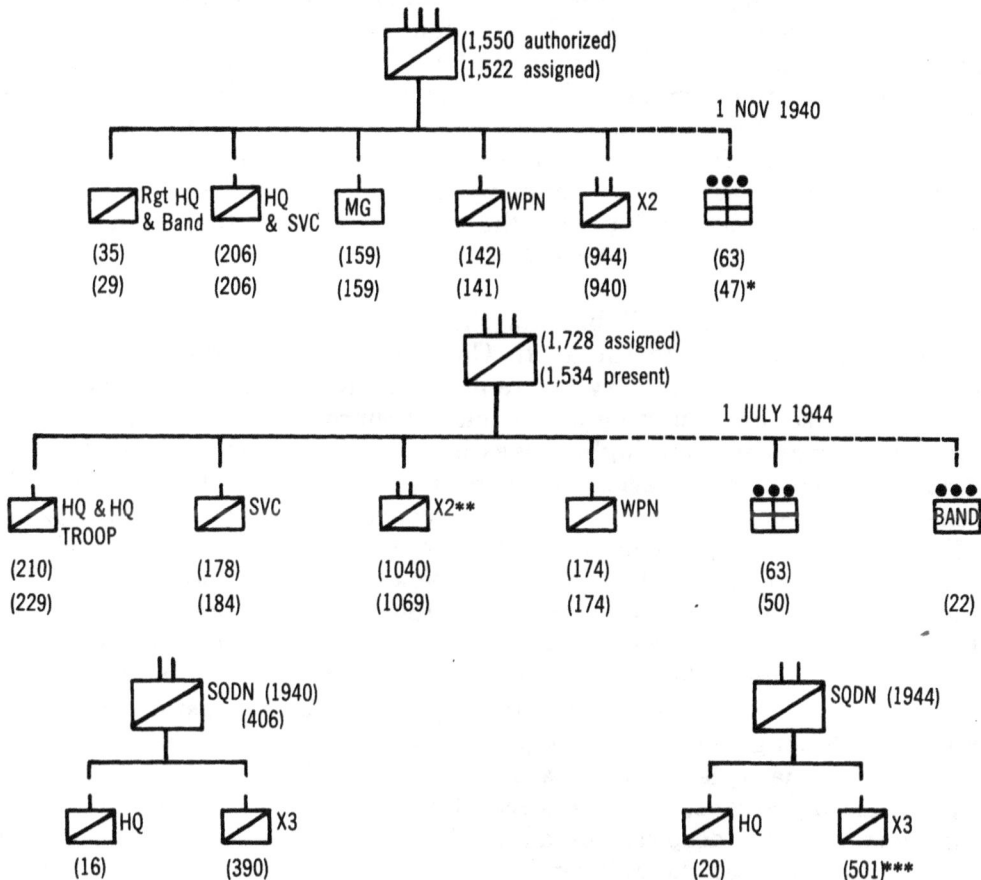

*Figures from 112th Cavalry Regiment troop manifest, 1942.
**Assigned strength in rifle troops varied from 166 to 177.
***Additional manpower drawn from disbanded MG Company.

Fig. 2. Evolution of 112th Cavalry Regiment

six, or even ten years. They knew, in the words of one veteran, whom they could count on and who were the deadbeats. Draftees were organized around this core of Texans. The veterans inculcated the new arrivals with their traditions and the esprit of a cavalry outfit. Pride in themselves and their unit developed naturally, and no artifice was involved. The distinctive cavalryman's uniform—breeches, knee-high boots, and cavalry hats—identified them as different, and therefore special, compared with other federalized National Guard units. The unit's longevity was its strength; it provided continuity, identity, and a sense of responsibility at a time when those qualities were much in demand. In addition, even after its mobilization, the 112th was a small unit, about 1,700 authorized officers and men, or roughly half the size of the standard TO&E infantry regiment. The identity neither of the men nor of the unit was overwhelmed by a vast influx of newcomers in the form of draftees or volunteers. Officers at regimental or squadron level knew their men on a first-name basis and bred identity, cohesion, and a sense of comradeship into the ranks. In short, the 112th Cavalry possessed a high degree of unit cohesion.[2]

Like any other unit, it had its share of problems. Brigadier General Cunningham commanded the 112th Cavalry RCT, but Colonel Miller had commanded the 112th Cavalry before it became an RCT. Their headquarters were collocated, and Cunningham would, at times, supersede Miller as regimental commander. Cunningham was a strict disciplinarian from the "Old Army" and was not the easiest commander to work with or for. The regiment relied on its company-grade officers for leadership, but at least one junior officer failed to carry out his combat assignment at Aitape for no apparent reason. Moreover, junior officer losses on New Britain had been heavy. Their replacements were either promoted from the 112th's enlisted ranks or sent fresh from the United States. Only a few of the original troop officers remained by June 1944, as the currents of warfare had taken their toll of young officers or pushed them into higher, more responsible, command positions. Among the ranks was petty jealousy over promotions or lack of the same. Some replacements responded to the indoctrination administered by the 112th veterans, but others resented the Texans' brashness. The men alternately feared, despised, or admired their officers. All felt that higher headquarters selected the unit for dangerous reconnaissance missions because of its cavalry designation, conveniently forgetting that the 112th was a dismounted cavalry regiment, in effect a half-strength rifle regiment. They had few illusions about ever going home before the war was won. No one doubted that they would win, but everyone knew that the price could be high. Most regarded their service as a job that someone had to do.

They lived in the open in an oppressive tropical climate that debilitated the health of even the strongest among them. But that condition was only incidental to their mission to track down and kill other men in the jungle. Those exposed to the greatest danger, the riflemen and machine gunners on the front line, received the least rewards. As a postwar report noted, the infantryman "can look forward only to death, mutilation, or psychiatric breakdown. He feels that no one at home has the slightest conception of the danger his job entails or of the courage and guts required to do one hour of it."[3] Added to this was the constant fear. Most were afraid all the time, but at least their fear kept them alert and probably made some of them fight. There were those few whom S. L. A. Marshall described as "natural fighters," and they excelled in combat. But, for most, it was a constant strain to check their natural inclination for self-preservation. Given their dismal prospects for survival, why would they fight? Self-preservation motivated them as did the fear of severity of court-martial. The essential motivations that kept these men going were "pride (self-respect) and the strong bond with [their] fellow soldiers."[4] They fought by themselves for themselves, and little else beyond that mattered.

To the Driniumor

On 24 June, three days after the verbal alert, the 112th received formal orders to embark for Aitape. Two days later General Cunningham and his staff arrived by air at the Tadji strip. The 112th, less its rear echelon of about 100 officers and men, embarked aboard twelve Landing Craft Infantry (LCIs) on 26 June. The unit was understrength, averaging between 140 and 150 men per troop of an authorized 162-man strength. The men were coming off a two-week "rest" at Finschhafen, which meant that they lived in company tents, ate communal meals, and remained exposed to the elements and exotic diseases of New Guinea. But at least they were not shot at by the Japanese.

As they embarked, the troops carried individual equipment and weapons, five days' ten-in-one rations, one unit of fire, kitchen equipment, and a small amount of canvas.[5] These items were the infantryman's basic survival kit, so it is worthwhile to examine their contents. The ten-in-one ration was meant to feed ten men for one day, providing, in theory, about 3,660 calories per man per day.[6] The ration held a breakfast, lunch, and dinner meal, given variety by different dehydrated cereals, meat, and vegetables. About one soldier in three considered the food sufficient, but another third did not like it.[7] The popularity of the ten-in-one ration resulted from its sundries, packs of cigarettes, matches, toilet paper, halazone tablets, and a can opener in each ration—luxuries to the combat soldier. The other basic ration was the K ration, with three meals separately wrapped in waxed paper or cellophane, making it lighter in weight and more compact, allowing the soldier an easier time carrying his food supply. Unfortunately, it was not packaged for the tropics, where after three days, the boxes would come apart in the high humidity. Troops in the 112th also "had a tendency to carry too much equipment for personal comfort," and their officers worried that the soldiers might discard essential articles to compensate for the load.[8] Men, for example, generally kept their ponchos to ward off the rain, but occasionally discarded blankets or half-blankets and spent the chilly tropical night shivering. To sum up, on any given night a rifleman's lot was to be afraid, perhaps hungry, probably wet, and surely cold.

The dismounted cavalryman's weapon was his most important tool for survival. His uniform could be in tatters and his boots rotting away, but the working parts of his weapon had to be spotless. The high humidity of the rain forest, coupled with the varieties of dirt, sand, and bugs that could work their way into a weapon and jam it, forced the men to spend extra time and care cleaning their weapons. Browning automatic rifles (BARs) and carbines required special care. Each man carried his ammunition, a unit of fire. This varied from 750 rounds for a .30-caliber BAR operator to 150 rounds for a rifleman. Machine gunners obviously required more ammunition and thus had teams to carry the gun and its ammunition, 2,000 rounds for a light machine gun and 1,200 for a water-cooled heavy machine gun. The 60-mm mortar crews of the 112th Cavalry had fifty rounds per mortar. To lug these weapons and their accompanying ammunition through the jungle in the sweltering heat was exhausting labor. The men compensated by reducing their loads—that is, by not carrying complete units of fire.

The 112th's voyage to Aitape was uneventful, and the RCT, less its artillery battalion, landed there on 28 June. Japanese scouts of the 1st Battalion, 237th Infantry Regiment, 41st Infantry Division, observed some phase of these landings and reported to 18th Army that "many enemy transports and LSTs" were active near Aitape.[9] Japanese patrols, however, could get no closer and, thus, were unable to identify the 112th, a deficiency for which they would later pay heavily.

The evening of the next day, Brig. Gen. Clarence A. Martin, commander of the Eastern Defense Command, ordered the 112th to join the covering force along the Driniumor River. Its mission was "to delay the enemy to the maximum extent possible without sacrifice of troops." Martin also instructed the 112th to assume responsibility for the defense of Afua, the southern anchor of the Driniumor line, and assigned to General Cunningham's command the 3d Battalion, 127th Infantry Regiment, plus attached medical personnel.

There was little time for sleep, for most of the men spent the night preparing for the move inland. Two men per troop (twelve total) and a portion of the Service Troop remained near Aitape as a rear echelon. Regimental bandsmen became litter bearers. All heavy weapons (81-mm mortars, 37-mm antitank guns, and rocket launchers) were left behind. The antitank platoon, Headquarters Troop, instead carried heavy machine guns and functioned as a machine gun platoon. The 81-mm mortar crews from the Weapons Platoon converted to ammunition bearers and served as an oversized rifle platoon. Riflemen, BAR operators, and submachine gunners carried a modified unit of fire; machine gunners, a unit; and 60-mm mortarmen, a half unit. Everyone carried three days' ten-in-one rations in their packs.[10] Replacements carried ammunition and supplies so that the experienced combat veterans could be put on the firing line.[11] Their lowly status as porters was not lost on the replacements. Native bearers also transported supplies.

The regiment moved by truck from Aitape on the morning of the twenty-ninth and dismounted at the Nigia River, where an engineer ferry boat transported the troops across the river (see map 11). The limited fifty-man capacity of the ferry made the crossing a slow affair. From the river, Eastern Defense Command expected the 112th merely to make a five-mile forced

53

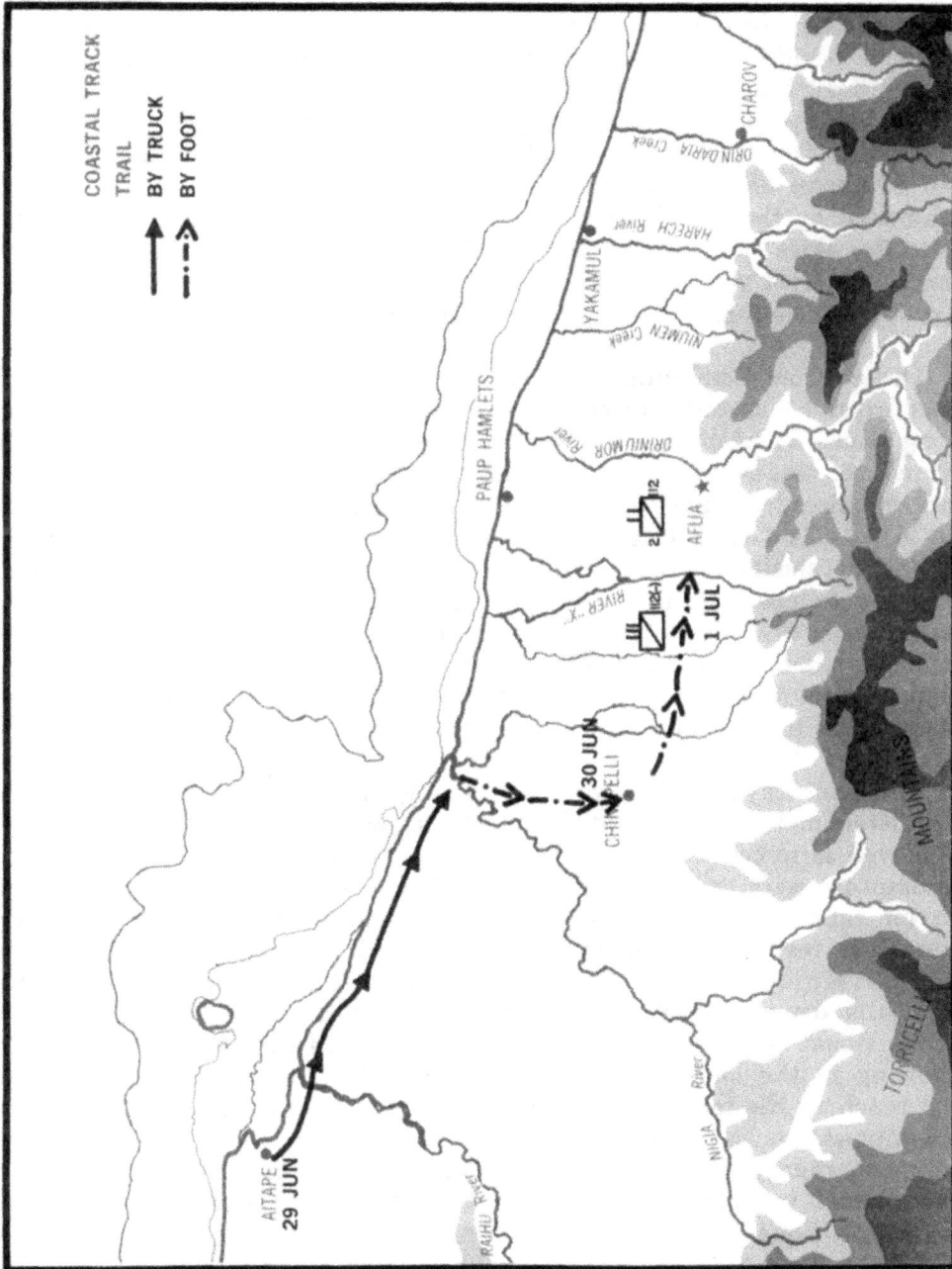

Map 11. Move of 112th Cavalry to Driniumor

march through no-man's-land and, after reaching Chinapelli, to establish a defensive position there. A tropical rainstorm made this "normal" activity more difficult than usual. Shoes muddy, heads down, carrying thirty to forty pounds of equipment, the men plodded though the downpour toward Chinapelli. Torrents of rain washed over the long column and over the men who were slipping and sliding through the now deep mud of the trail. Exhausted by the march, they still had to form their defensive perimeter. After the skies had cleared, a C-47 flew over and dropped provisions at Chinapelli. Cold rations, wet clothing, and a night in the jungle were the cavalrymen's reward for their first day in the field at Aitape.

Orders from Persecution Task Force directed the men to continue their eastward move in order to establish defensive positions and a patrol base along River X, which ran parallel to and about 4,100 meters west of the Driniumor. Meanwhile, the 2d Squadron would advance to the Driniumor and organize defensive positions near Afua. Their deployment would allow the 3d Battalion, 127th Infantry, then occupying the Afua positions, to shorten its line by closing to the north.[12] General Martin's 32d Division G-3 had prepared careful tactical plans for the 112th Cavalry premised on the assumption that the 112th was equivalent to a full-strength infantry regiment.[13] Instead of the 3,000 men he expected, Martin found himself with slightly more than 1,500 men to cover a frontage originally designed for two or three times that number (see fig. 3). They would have to do.

The next day's march was even worse than the first. A seventy-five-man detachment remained at Chinapelli to patrol between there and River X, as well as to cover the Palauru-Afua trail. In addition, they were expected to maintain wire communications from River X to the rear, a dangerous job, for Japanese patrols would cut the wire and wait in ambush for repair crews. The rest of the men marched to River X in another downpour. The hilly terrain crisscrossed by many small streams made this trek more physically demanding than the previous day's. The first few men up an incline would strip off the vegetation, and the constant tramping by those following in the long column would soon reduce slopes to muddy slides. Just reaching the top of such a slope burdened with thirty or forty pounds of equipment on one's back required the use of every muscle and expended enormous energy. But there were no stragglers, except for two sick men who returned to Chinapelli shortly after the 112th's departure. The regiment, less the 2d Squadron, which had pushed ahead toward the Driniumor, put up a defensive perimeter along the west bank of River X. After two days of exhausting marches in heavy rains and mud, eating cold rations, and sleeping in wet clothes, Persecution Task Force moved the 112th's unit symbol to River X. In peacetime, this feat alone would have been considered an accomplishment; now it was merely a prelude to bitter days ahead.

The 2d Squadron spent the night of 30 June southeast of River X and the next morning moved to the Driniumor. Under scattered clouds and intermittent showers they relieved the 3d Battalion, 127th Infantry, at 1100,

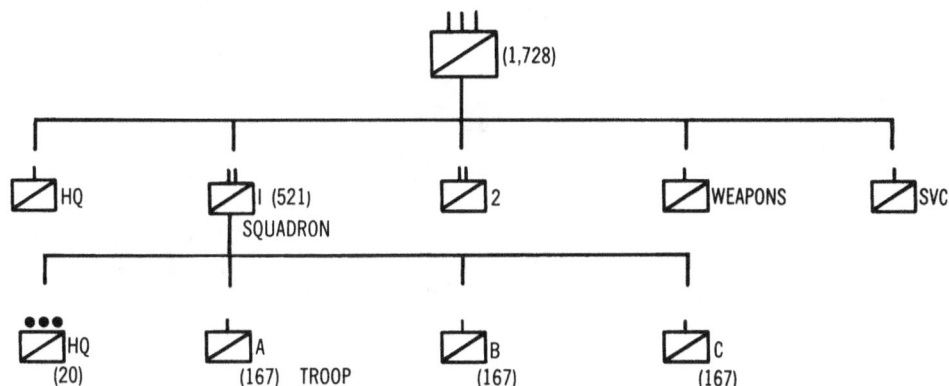

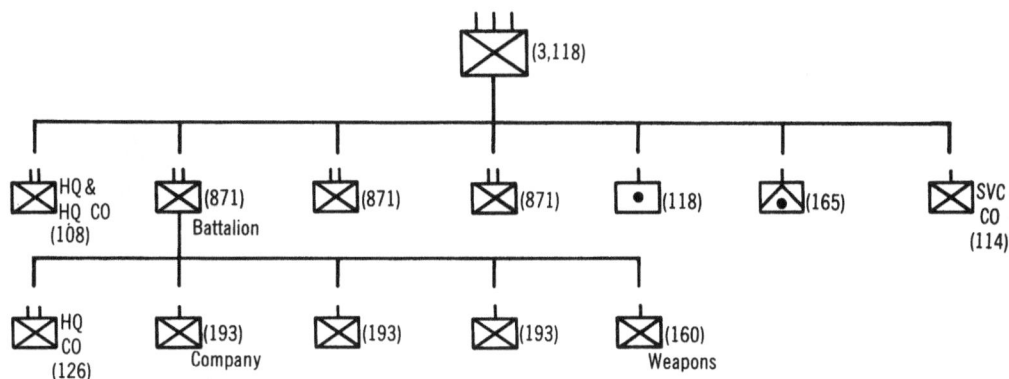

Fig. 3. Comparison of U.S. cavalry regiment and infantry regiment

placing Troops E and F forward on the riverbank and Troop G in reserve, the approved "two up—one back" configuration, despite the rugged, close terrain. Everything was quiet, and no patrols were sent out. Regimental headquarters, however, did dispatch four patrols to check the security of the 112th's flanks. After the 3d Battalion had moved out to the north, the 2d Squadron was alone anchoring the covering force's south flank. Its isolation, in part, was a function of the jungle terrain features that fragmented large formations into scattered pockets remote from one another. The men knew what was within a few yards of their particular entrenchment and little more. As for the enemy situation, they depended on their patrols,

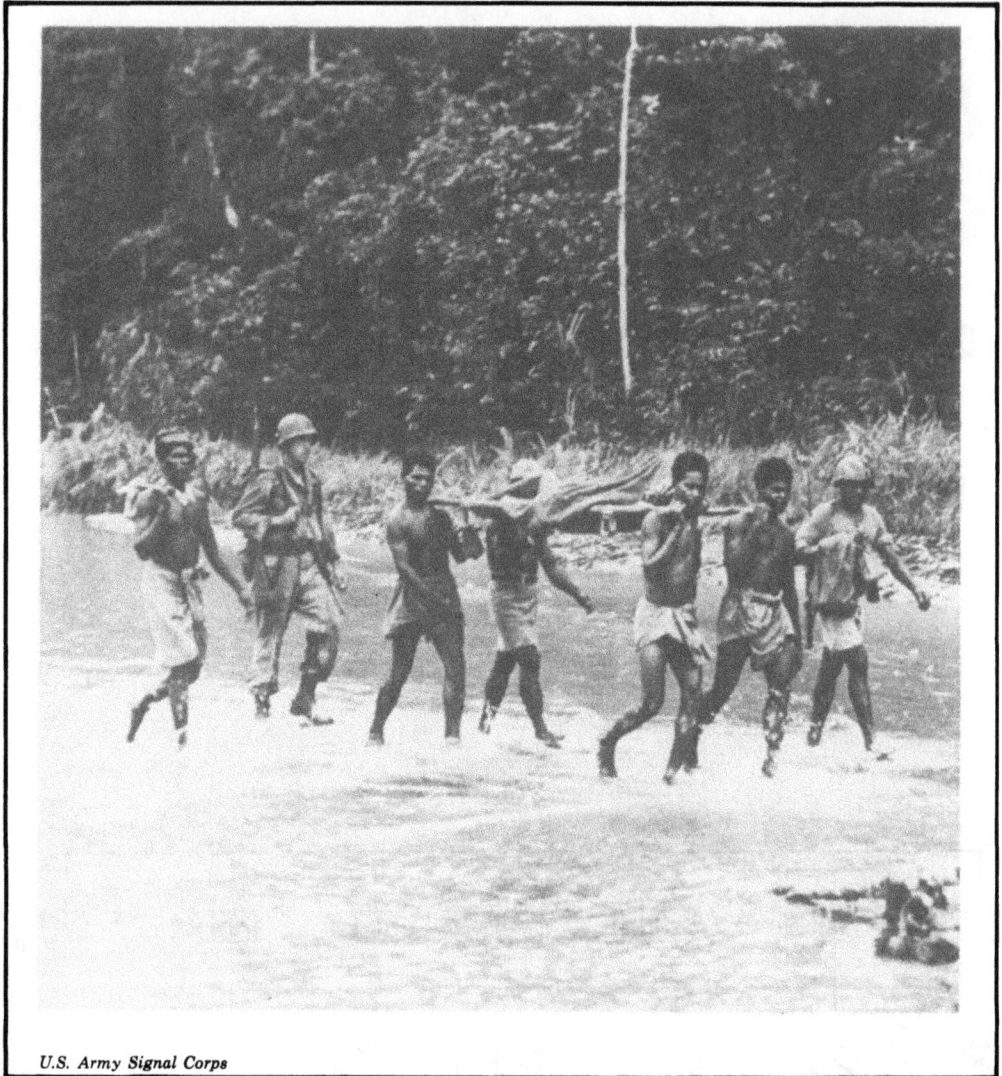

U.S. Army Signal Corps

Native bearers, with soldier escort, evacuate a casualty across the Driniumor River near Afua Village. Note the shallowness of the river.

the reports sent by wire from neighboring units, and those transmitted from higher headquarters. The so-called big picture of the campaign did not interest them. Their concern was more basic: to stay alive.

Members of 2d Squadron spent their first full day at Afua constructing a defensive perimeter, improving fields of fire by clearing the kunai grass from the small islands or sand spits in the river as well as cutting jungle vegetation on the flanks and rear of their perimeter. They established telephone communications with the main body of the 112th. A liaison party from the 120th Field Artillery Battalion joined regimental headquarters. The 2d Squadron then proceeded to register artillery and mortar fire on locations in front of both River X and the Driniumor.

Meanwhile 1st Squadron and the rest of the 112th worked feverishly on their defensive positions near River X. Generally speaking, troops engulfed in jungle fighting had no shelter. The only efficient protection combat troops had was the "jungle poncho" (a rubberized cloth about five by six feet), which was thrown over the back and head and strapped under the chin.[14] In place of rain, the men now worked on 3 and 4 July under a broiling sun that burned and blistered their exposed skin. Mosquitoes, insects, worms, and leeches latched onto their sweating bodies as the soldiers excavated the pits that would be their crude shelters and fighting positions. Besides the work on entrenchments, twenty-five men cut a trail through the jungle vines and ferns from the command post toward the Tiver River for use as a medical evacuation route. An Australian and forty natives arrived at River X to assist in evacuation and supply efforts. Although the extra labor was helpful in stockpiling supplies at the 112th's base, the natives' blissful disregard of the 112th's sanitary regulations within the perimeter made their presence a mixed blessing. The 112th's small buildup continued as the troops laid ground panels on dry portions of the riverbed to identify a drop zone for aerial resupply. The original site proved too rocky, and about half of the air-dropped supplies broke on impact. Yet another nearby drop zone had to be cleared by machetes of brush and vegetation. Meantime, the original drop zone became so contaminated, smelled so bad, and became so thick with flies that a third drop zone had to be constructed. Air resupply then functioned better and provided ten-in-one rations, blankets, mail, and new boots for the troops. Officers had to badger some of the men about sanitation and digging proper latrines. Troop commanders handed out Atabrine, salt tablets, and halazone to the unit. Threatening court-martial, they ordered troops not to use kunai grass for beds or shelters because of the danger of bush typhus.* The concern was as much practical as humanitarian. A sick man would have to be evacuated, and that meant fewer combat soldiers available to fight. Losses from disease most affected rifle companies, which seldom had more than two-thirds of their authorized strength at any one time, so every man was precious.** Paradoxically these same men had to live in the harshest natural surroundings and were exposed to the greatest danger in combat. They compensated by building themselves what amounted to a primitive fortified village, which a time traveler from the Middle Ages would probably have recognized as a defensive hamlet.

After 2 July, intensive patrolling north and south along the Driniumor, east to Niumen Creek, and west along the trail to River X characterized the 112th's activity. Patrol leaders were under orders to observe the enemy, not to fire on them.[15] These patrols had a dual purpose. The obvious, stated goal was to collect intelligence about the enemy and, if possible, to capture

*During the entire campaign, a total of 279 typhus cases resulted in sixteen deaths.

**For example, of an authorized 152 officers and 3,100 men, the 128th Infantry Regiment had 121 officers and 2,649 men present for duty on 29 June 1944. The 127th Infantry counted 117 officers and 2,861 men available. On 1 July the 112th Cavalry's six line troops had 46 officers and 885 men present of an authorized 48 officers and 972 men.

a prisoner. Likewise, patrols provided terrain information unavailable on the inadequate maps issued to the units. A third, but unstated, purpose of patrolling was to build the men's confidence, to familiarize them with the terrain, and to train replacement officers and enlisted men in overcoming their initial fear of the unknown. But patrolling was dangerous work. The stress and tension of men on patrol never slackened.

The 112th, like other American units fighting in the Pacific, did not believe in taking Japanese prisoners. Prejudice tinted the American soldier's view of the Japanese and increased the savagery of combat. If the sneak attack on Pearl Harbor brought the cauldron of anti-Japanese feeling to a bubble, U.S. military and civilian propagandists continued to stir the witches' brew in order to foment a hyperpatriotism they believed would be beneficial to the war effort. Japanese atrocities, such as using captured 112th troopers for bayonet practice on New Britain, served to confirm stereotypes of the Japanese as subhuman creatures who had to be killed. This refusal to take Japanese prisoners had important operational ramifications. In the 32d Division's G-3 Journal for 4 July 1944 appeared the entry that "*1 unarmed Jap* killed on E bank of Driniumor River." Appended to this entry was the following handwritten note:

> Another prisoner that could have told us if the 41st (Division) had arrived. What effect our bombing had had, possibly when the attack was expected, where were what units. These troops seem to want to fight this war the hard way, they won't take a prisoner.[16]

The savagery went far beyond the 112th Cavalry. It infected troops of both nations.

So the patrols went out daily to find the enemy and to kill unwary opponents. On 2 July, a Troop E patrol was the first from the 112th to spot the enemy when it saw six Japanese crossing the Driniumor 540 meters south of Afua, but the Japanese soon vanished into the deep jungle. The same day the 112th suffered its first casualty, a band member who accidently shot himself.

During the next few days, patrols gradually extended their range and their fighting strength. For example, on 6 July a forty-eight-man patrol from Troop B, led by two officers, left Afua to destroy a suspected Japanese radio installation near Charov. According to their maps, Charov appeared just west of the Drindaria River, but it was actually on the east bank. By staying close to the Torricelli foothills and scouting only the west bank, this fighting patrol inadvertently sidestepped the Japanese 20th and 41st Infantry divisions, which were then massing about halfway between Afua and the coast for their planned 10 July attack. The inaccurate maps probably saved the men's lives. The terrain was so rugged and thick with vegetation that the Americans could pass undetected near hundreds of Japanese troops and return to their base unharmed. Other patrols reported evidence of Japanese activity, but no sightings, probably because of recurring showers,

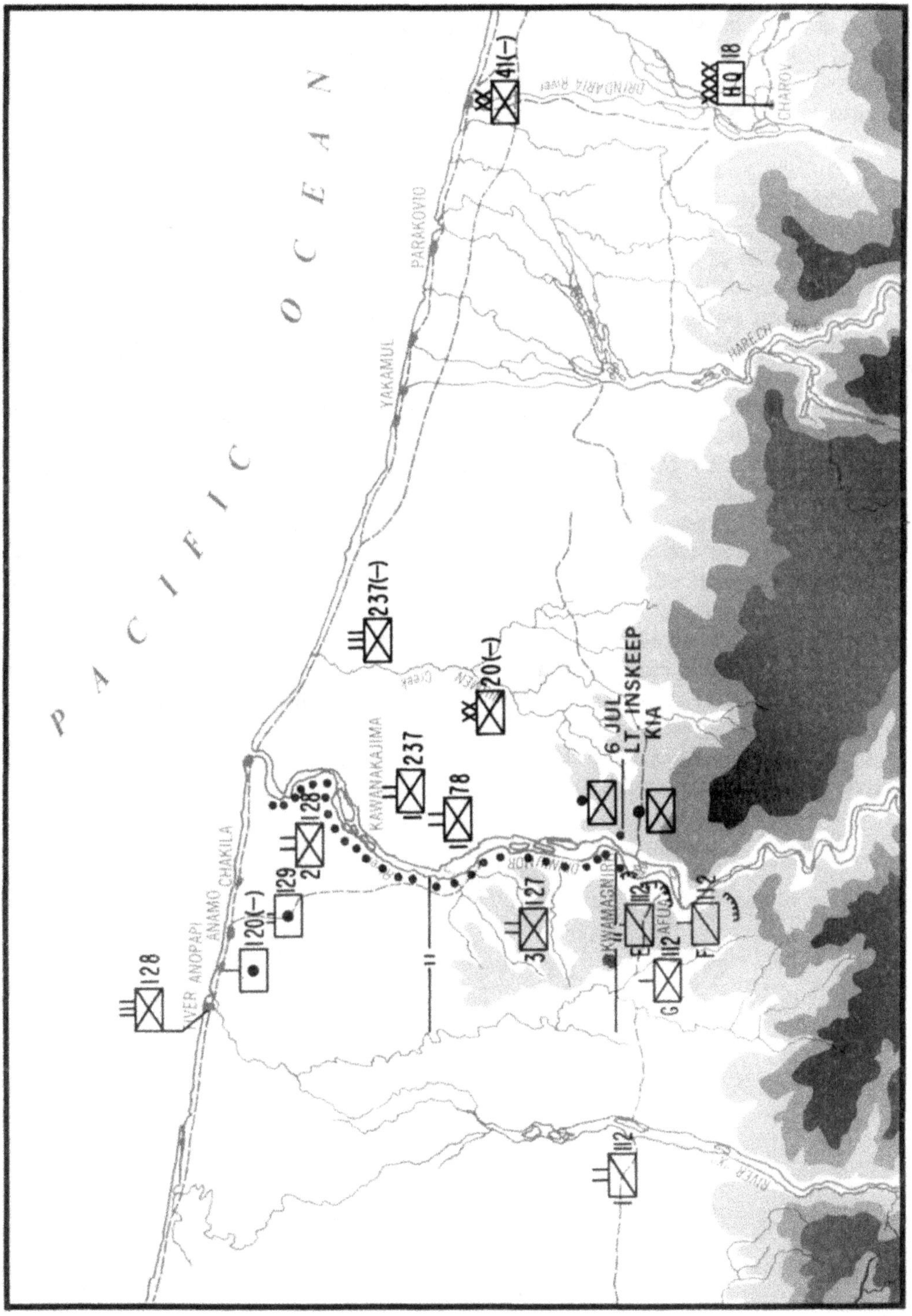

PACIFIC OCEAN

DRINIARIZ River

PARAKOVIO

YAKAMUL

CHAROV

HARECH

XXXX HQ 18

41(-)

237(-)

20(-)

237

78

KOEN CREEK

KAWANAKAJIMA

6 JUL
LT. INSKEEP
KIA

28

29

2

20(-)

128

RIVER ANOPAPI

ANAMO

CHAKILA

3

27

DRINIUMOR

KWAMAGNIR

AFUA

13

N-2

112

E

F

G

112

RIVER

Map 12. Dispositions along Driniumor, early July 1944

which further masked enemy activity. By about 6 July, the cumulative patrol reports had suggested that the Japanese were forming counterreconnaissance screens along the Niumen Creek vicinity, where 112th patrols met determined Japanese opposition for the first time during the campaign.

On 6 July, about 1,000 yards northwest of Afua, a platoon from Troop F walked into an ambush triggered by dug-in Japanese troops supported by machine guns (see map 12). The Japanese probably were a screening force for units of the 41st Infantry Division, which had arrived in the area that same day. Troop F's men blindly exchanged gunfire with the Japanese, but could not penetrate or flank the Japanese trail block. The patrol leader, Lieutenant Inskeep, was killed, after which the Americans withdrew. Two days later a patrol led by Lt. Ray A. Titus again tried to penetrate the Japanese screening force to retrieve the body. The Japanese had set another ambush on a heavily jungled bank overlooking the ravine. Again there was a sudden outburst of gunfire followed by initial terror and confusion. Two American enlisted men were shot and wounded, but they claimed to have killed one Japanese soldier. Nevertheless, Titus's patrol could not retrieve the body. This minor skirmish typified the hazards of jungle patrols. Sudden ambushes triggered at close range meant a high incidence of gunshot wounds. The abrupt stutter of a light machine gun or bark of rifle fire was followed by shouting, screaming, confusion, initial panic, and then more gunfire or a muffled grenade explosion as both sides reorganized. More likely, after the first gunshots, one side or the other (sometimes both) would run back into the thick vegetation for safety. This type of small unit action occurred over and over as the American patrols brushed against the Japanese screening forces who were covering the assembly of the main Japanese units.

Breakthrough
on the Driniumor

5

18th Army Prepares to Attack

As more and more Japanese soldiers were arriving daily along the Driniumor, long-range Japanese reconnaissance patrols were also sending detailed reports on the American defenses west of the Driniumor. On 19 June, for example, Japanese officer scouts provided precise information about U.S. positions along the Driniumor. Based on that intelligence, Col. Ide Tokutaro, commander of the 80th Infantry Regiment, already deployed near the Driniumor, suggested that his men infiltrate deep into the American position rather than make a potentially costly frontal assault. General Adachi was thinking in other terms.

Eighteenth Army had correctly estimated in mid-June that three U.S. Army infantry battalions were defending the Driniumor, thinly stretched out from the coast to Afua. Adhering to his original May plan for a penetration that would carry all the way to the airfields, Adachi decided to commit the 20th Division and available units of the 41st Division to a frontal attack against the center of the American covering force. Around 30 June, Adachi and his staff arrived at Charov to coordinate final attack preparations with the 20th Division's headquarters staff. One of Adachi's staff operations officers, Maj. Tanaka Kengoro, had preceded Adachi to Charov in order to conduct a firsthand staff appraisal of the situation. After he had reported his evaluation of the U.S. covering force along the Driniumor and the enemy situation at Aitape to Adachi, Tanaka wondered aloud if the attack against Aitape should be reconsidered. Would the intangibles of battle like morale, unit esprit, fighting spirit—the qualities the Japanese relied so heavily on to compensate for materiel deficiencies— suffice to see them through a successful frontal attack on the Aitape defenses? Adachi said nothing, but asked his assembled staff officers to consider the matter. Next morning Tanaka again told Adachi that the attack should not be launched as planned. Adachi replied that he had not changed his mind. He would not allow radical alterations in tactical planning to negate the efforts each Japanese unit had made just to reach the Driniumor.[17] Furthermore, the general's personal notion of officership dictated the attack.

General Adachi's concept of battlefield leadership had its roots in his understanding of the heroic Japanese military tradition. Death in battle was sufficient reward for faithful service to the emperor. Like most Japanese officers, he was imbued with the spirit of the offensive and therefore always looked for opportunities to attack. Rather than watch his army rot and disintegrate in a passive, defensive role, Adachi felt that even in unfavorable circumstances the more aggressive commander could emerge victorious. He fully understood that the odds against reaching Aitape were heavily against his understrength, poorly supplied troops. But he also was convinced that if troops followed his high standards of leadership and capitalized on enemy mistakes to exploit their initiative, 18th Army could severely damage the U.S. forces near Aitape.[18] Already having asked much of his men, Adachi was about to demand more.

The Japanese infantrymen who figured so prominently in General Adachi's plan were nearing the end of their remarkable endurance. Compared to the Japanese soldiers' existence, the 112th Cavalry troopers, for all their hardships, lived in luxury. In early July, 18th Army had perhaps 55,000 personnel, including about 3,000 hospitalized. About 15,000 were in the forward combat area, with approximately 5,000 frontline combat troops, 1,500 in the rear echelon, and the remainder filtering into their assembly areas (see fig. 4). They were weary, dirty, and hungry. Rations were meager. Men of the 3d Battalion, 80th Infantry Regiment, subsisted on rations of less than 330 grams per man per day, supplemented every two or three days by biscuits and once every ten days by cigarettes—three cigarettes to be exact. For additional nourishment and starches, Japanese ate sago palm leaves. A general lack of essential condiments, especially salt, debilitated the Japanese soldiers in the heat. Malnutrition cases became alarmingly commonplace. Medicines were also in short supply, although a few daring transport pilots did fly night missions across the Celebes Sea to drop quinine and surgical alcohol to the beleaguered army.[19] Ultra had, of course, alerted General Krueger to 18th Army's plight, perhaps leading him to underestimate the tenacity of his opponent.

Compounding the materiel deficiencies, a command and control problem arose when the staffs of the 20th and 41st divisions were killed during their approach to the Driniumor. On 10 May Lt. Gen. Katakiri Shigeru, 20th Division commander, and his staff departed Hansa Bay for Wewak. Just before their gasoline-powered landing barge reached Wewak, it struck a floating mine, and all aboard perished. Shortly thereafter, six staff officers attached to Headquarters, 41st Division, died in an Allied bombing attack. Both of Adachi's frontline divisions had to plan and fight with reduced staffs that lacked the extensive planning experience of their late predecessors, a severe impediment to smooth operational planning for the Aitape attack.[20]

Isolation from normal resupply channels accounted for 18th Army's pitiful condition. Capricious weather and rugged terrain further complicated

Japanese TO&E

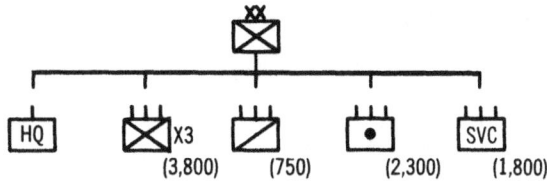

**Actual Japanese TO&E
Driniumor River Operation**

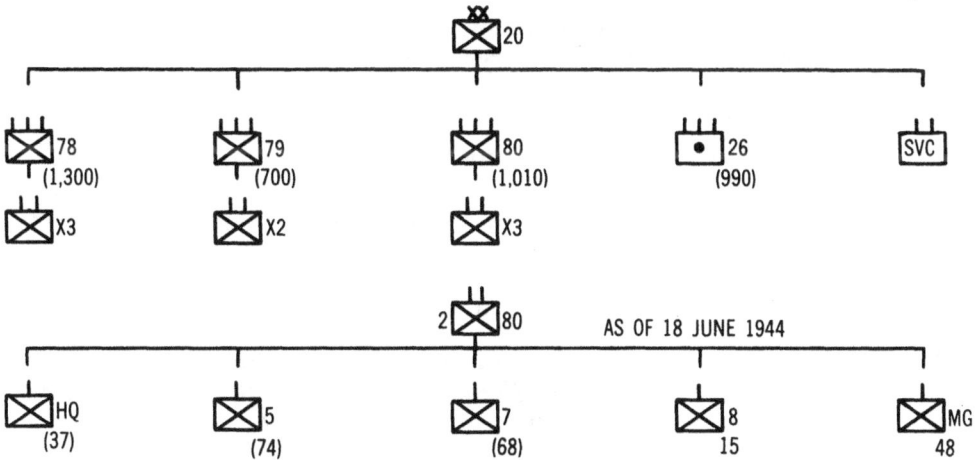

406 assigned, 138 on sick call, and 28 used as porters.
Total of 242 available for duty.

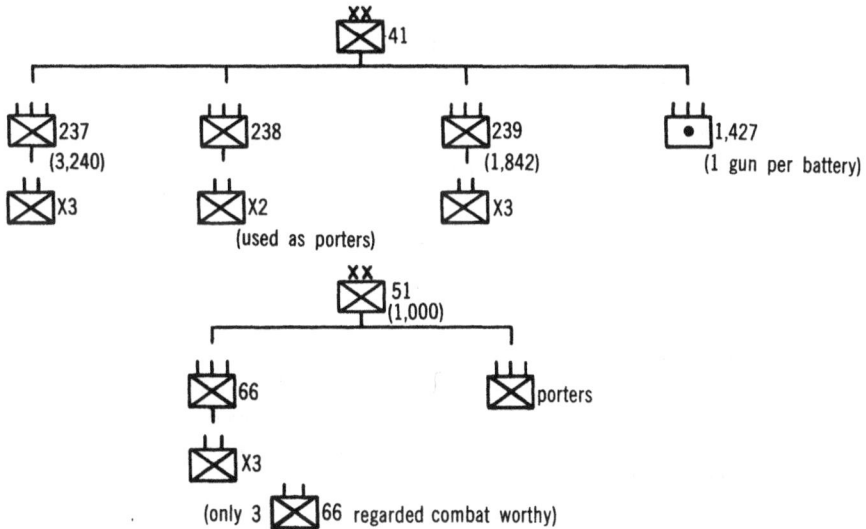

Fig. 4. Japanese TO&E

the situation. To supply combat forces attacking the Driniumor positions, Adachi had planned to construct a dirt road from Wewak to Aitape, about 130 kilometers, and to employ landing craft to ferry provisions as far west along the coast as Allied interdiction operations would permit. His idea foundered as tropical rainstorms turned the track into a quagmire. The sea route lacked suitable ports and shelters. Beyond those functional concerns, Allied floating mines, PT boat attacks, and air strikes preyed on Japanese coastal traffic. Finally, Adachi had to resort to human porters, including his precious infantrymen, to manhandle 18th Army's supplies through the jungle. General Yoshihara later estimated that it took six porters per one combat soldier just to maintain the trickle of supplies.[21]

Adachi proceeded with his plan, determined that human spirit could overcome physical obstacles to victory. At 1500 on 3 July, he issued the attack order, the gist of which was:

1. The 18th Army will attack the enemy occupying the Driniumor River, drive back the enemy in the Paup and Afua vicinities, and then advance to the Nigia River to prepare for the next or main attack against the enemy's main positions.

2. The attack will begin at 2200 on 10 July.

3. The 20th and 41st divisions will attack in column formation, cross the Driniumor, annihilate the American defenders on the covering force, and complete the operation by 12 July.

4. Both divisions will finalize their preparations for the main attack against Aitape by 15 July.[22]

Adachi selected the sector his men would attack based on scouts' reconnaissance reports. It was about 2,700 meters inland from the coast, across three small islands in the Driniumor, the largest of which the Japanese called Kawanakajima* (literally, Island in Middle of River). A patrol report of 1 July outlined the positions of Company L, 127th Battalion, in detail. Scouts estimated that perhaps fifty Americans with one field artillery gun, misidentified as a 105-mm howitzer, held the outpost line. Japanese scouts even pinpointed foxholes occupied by American NCOs on that line.[23]

A situation map accompanying Adachi's 3 July attack order dramatically revealed the efficiency of Japanese patrolling. In early July, 18th Army had a fairly accurate picture of U.S. defenses not only along the Driniumor, but also to Chinapelli and beyond. The key Japanese assumption was that three American infantry battalions held the Driniumor line (see map 13).

*The name also evoked martial sentiments because the Kawanakajima Battlefield in Japan was as well known to Japanese as Gettysburg was to Americans.

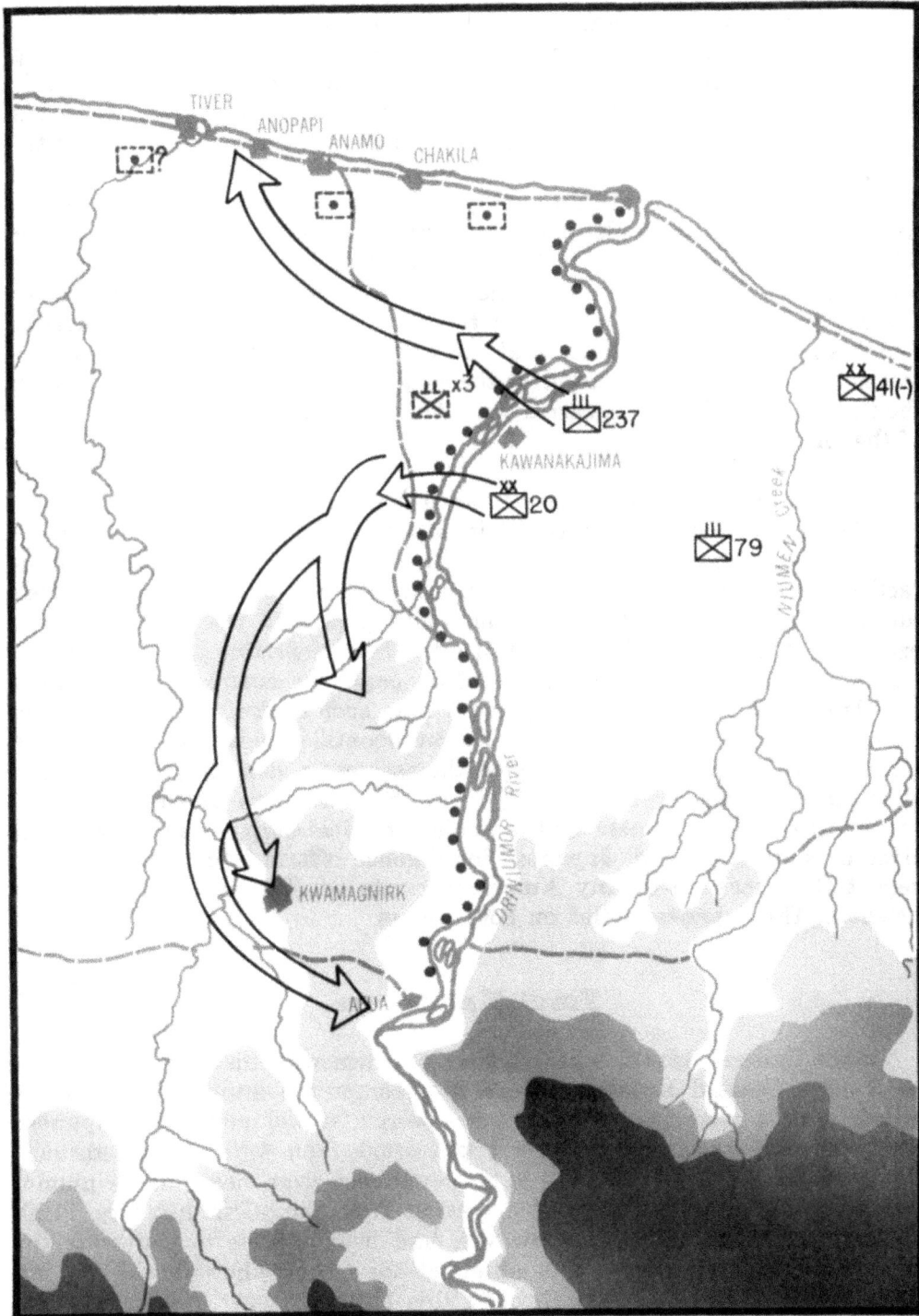

Map 13. Japanese plan of attack and estimate of U.S. situation, 1 July 1944

The two divisions that would make the attack, the 20th and 41st, adapted their tactics to conform to 18th Army's original concept of breaking through on a narrow front, regrouping, and continuing the attack towards Aitape. The division staff officers, however, privately wondered whether a breakthrough in the center of three widely dispersed enemy infantry battalions would enable them to destroy those foes. The extreme frontage of the U.S. defenses could conceivably isolate the Japanese attackers in the narrow corridor of their planned penetration. At least one operations officer felt that an attack south against Afua would be a better alternative, because the Japanese could then outflank the U.S. defenders and drive them toward the sea.[24] The new commander of the 20th Division, Maj. Gen. Miyake Sadahiko, however, said flatly that the worsening physical condition of his troops made it difficult to conduct the long and arduous march entailed in the flanking attack. He concurred with Adachi's plan to attack at the center of the enemy line.[25]

There were other advantages to such a straightforward plan of attack. The Japanese expected to mass their battalions on a very narrow, 300- to 500-meter front, regiments abreast in three-deep echelonment. This simple tactical formation allowed them to concentrate the limited firepower of their understrength infantry battalions and also permitted the commanders to exercise better command and control over their respective units. An attack on an extended frontage would preclude Japanese company commanders (let alone those at battalion or regiment) from such control of their maneuver elements. The inherent risk of the narrow frontal attack was that massed infantrymen crossing a river offered themselves as densely packed targets that alert defenders could hardly miss. Success thus depended on two factors. First, the Japanese had to achieve tactical surprise by crossing the river in silence. Second, Japanese intelligence efforts had to identify and report the presence of any American units reinforcing the Driniumor defenses. The Japanese failed on both counts.

Final Maneuvers

While General Adachi urged on his tired men with his fiery instructions on 6 July, General Krueger decided to preempt the anticipated Japanese attack with a reconnaissance in force, which would make the Japanese reveal themselves so that Krueger might crush them with a counterattack. He knew from Ultra sources that the Japanese were near the Driniumor and preparing to attack. American patrols from the 127th Infantry, 112th Cavalry, or 128th Infantry, however, had been unable to penetrate the Japanese infantry screen that shielded the exact whereabouts of 18th Army's formations. To break through this blind, Krueger ordered a reconnaissance in force along the northern and southern flanks of the Driniumor covering force. Moreover, General MacArthur's pressure on Krueger "to hurry up and get through this New Guinea thing" caused a ripple effect throughout the command. Each subordinate commander in turn found himself subjected to orders "to get the job done." Thus, while Generals Gill and Martin wanted to delay the reconnaissance, Krueger and Hall, anxious to please MacArthur and to end the campaign, insisted that the operation go forward.[26]

In the north, the 1st Battalion, 128th Regiment, drew the assignment, and in the south, the 2d Squadron, 112th Cavalry, was designated (see map 14). On 9 July at 1700, General Martin ordered 2d Squadron to move forward on the following morning to the Harech River, 7.7 kilometers east of Afua. This operation required, in turn, a redisposition of U.S. forces to cover the positions about to be vacated. Troop A, 1st Squadron, would replace the 2d Squadron. At 1700 Troop A departed and took a little more than an hour to cover the two plus miles from River X to Afua. They had to move rapidly to reach Afua before nightfall, for after dark anything moving was considered unfriendly and likely to be shot. Commanders simply expected that Troop A would cover the distance and be in position to guard Afua until the rest of the regiment could reach them next morning. In the unthinkable event that Troop A did not carry out its mission, the entire south flank of Persecution Task Force's covering force would be exposed to Japanese envelopment.

At 0730 the next day, the remainder of the 112th Cavalry set off for Afua in a long column, Troop B leading and Troop C bringing up the rear. Thirty-minute intervals between each of the six units* in the order of march stretched the column almost the length of the march. It took the command group nearly three hours to reach Afua. As soon as they arrived, 2d Squadron began to move forward to conduct its lonely mission. First Squadron prepared its defenses with Troop A on the right, Troop B to the left, and Troop C behind the Squadron Command Post located at Afua. Regimental Headquarters and the Weapons Troop moved about 1,400 meters north, nearer task force headquarters. Patrols from Troop A were dispatched to reconnoiter in front of the position, and in late afternoon, a squad patrolling toward Niumen Creek surprised several Japanese absorbed in setting an ambush. The ambushers became the ambushed as the cavalrymen shot and killed two Japanese and claimed to have wounded several others who ran into the jungle. The American squad then searched the Japanese corpses and withdrew quickly, fortunate to have suffered no losses. Elsewhere along the 1st Squadron's front, two- and three-man teams established listening posts across the Driniumor before dusk.

Meanwhile, the 2d Squadron underwent its own ordeal. After fording the Driniumor, the men had to hack and cut their way with machetes through the thick jungle vegetation. They were moving in the deep jungle, where no sunlight broke through the canopy and where the stench of rotting vegetation and human sweat filled their nostrils. Even more lonely was a

---

*The order of march was Troop B, 1st Squadron Headquarters, Command Group, Headquarters Troop, Weapons Troop less detachments, native carriers, Troop C.

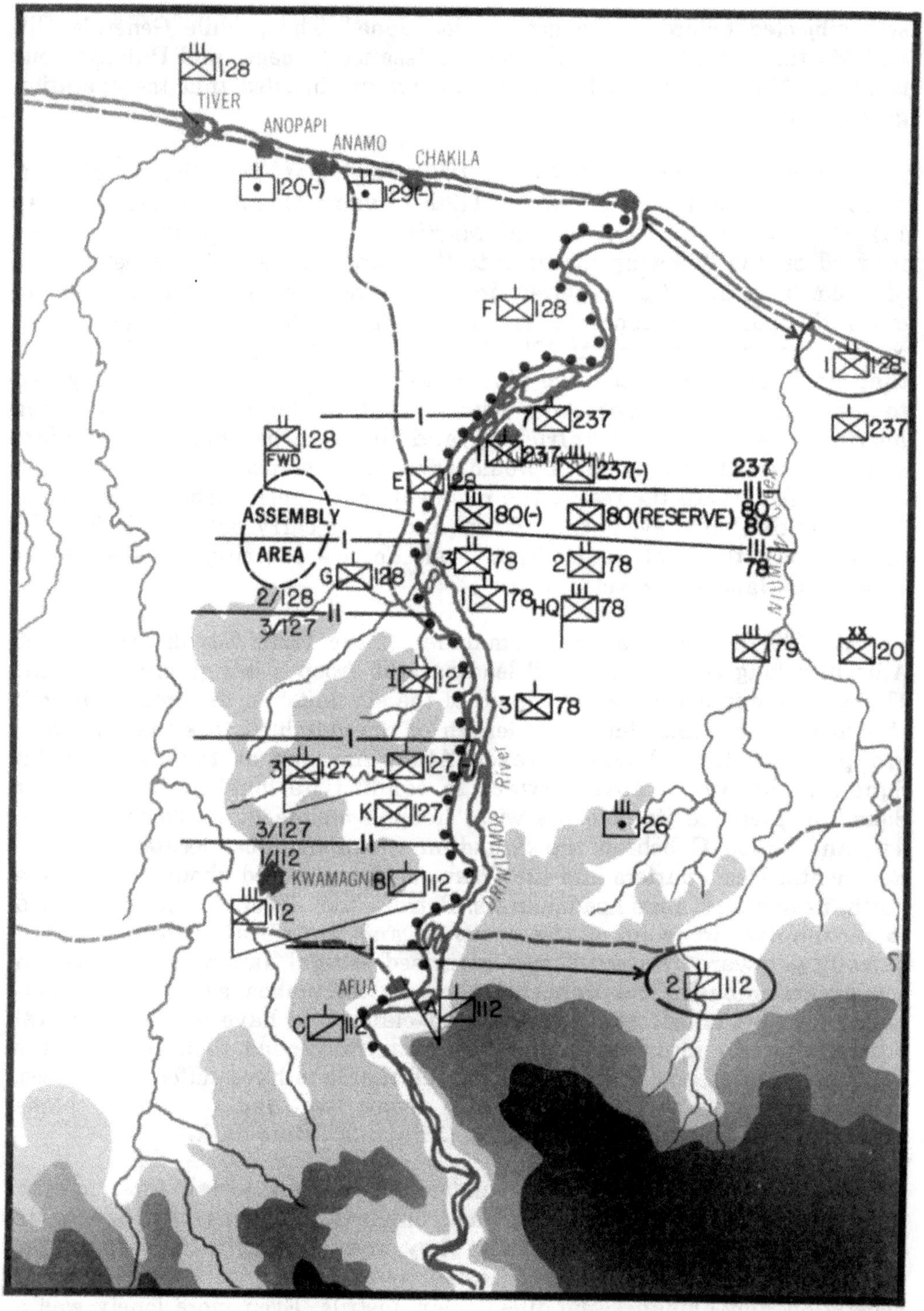

Map 14.   Reconnaissance in force, 10 July 1944

Troop G platoon that had to move parallel and about one kilometer south of the main column in order to provide flank security. To the physical strain was added the mental stress of not knowing what danger might suddenly appear from the tangled bush that they were laboring to cut through. It took their single file column several hours to "march" about one and one-half kilometers east through the virgin jungle. It was a grueling and draining effort. When they finally found a defensible, high-ground position anchored on the Torricelli Mountains, they settled in for the long, black night. Their communications failed as usual at night, so the 2d Squadron spent the night of 10—11 July alone and isolated in the jungle.

The men used tactics they had learned in combat on New Britain, two men per foxhole, one always awake. No one left his hole at night, or he risked being shot by his own comrades. This particular night the squadron formed a "doughnut defense," with the command position in the middle and the three troops encircling it.[27] Besides the exhausting march, cold food, exertion from digging a foxhole, and no communications, every man on that perimeter had to face the isolation and darkness seemingly alone.

The black jungle night made it impossible to see anything, even the man sharing the foxhole. Yet, their senses magnified every jungle noise. Palm leaves brushing together became objects of menace. The effect was cumulative and infinite, yet the energy and stamina of the men were only finite. They had expended enormous energy just to get to their night laager, and now they had to call on even more to stay alert. Then shortly before midnight, they got a shot of adrenaline as artillery and heavy machine gun fire broke out to their north. Everyone was tense, but alert, fearful the Japanese might overrun them at any moment.

Breakthrough

In the few hours remaining before the Japanese attack, American front-line troops were apprehensive about the possibility of such an assault, as was their commander, Brigadier General Martin. Despite this unease, there was no uniform stage of readiness among U.S. units covering the river; no reinforcements came from the MLR; no reserve moved east of the Nigia River to replace those troops used for the reconnaissance in force. Lt. Col. Edward Bloch's 3d Battalion, 127th Infantry, "certainly expected some action during the night." The 1st Squadron, 112th Cavalry, on his south flank, merely recorded a 7 July alert from the commander, Eastern Defense Command, about increased enemy activity near the north center of the Driniumor line. The 2d Battalion, 128th Infantry, believed that the Japanese would attack sometime between 1 and 15 July and that its sector would be the target.[28]

Until 9 July, the 2d Battalion's sector had about a 1,600-meter frontage, with the 1st Battalion, 128th Infantry, and the 3d Battalion, 127th Infantry, covering its northern and southern flanks, respectively. When General

Krueger, through Major General Hall, ordered the 1st Battalion to conduct a reconnaissance in force, 2d Battalion had to occupy the line vacated by the 1st Battalion. In order to accomplish this, the 2d Battalion committed its reserve, Company F, to hold the 1st Battalion's former line, about 2,700 meters long. Company E, with one heavy machine gun platoon attached, extended its north flank an additional 900 meters, which made the company responsible for a 1,600-meter defensive frontage, normally a battalion-size sector. Such extended frontages and the many small islands covered with dense foliage in the Driniumor made an adequate defense impossible.[29]

Orders, though, were orders, so during the day of 10 July the men of Company E dug their individual fighting positions. The company commander, Capt. Thomas Bell, placed three or four men at those places he felt were most vulnerable, although everyone realized they were incapable of stopping a determined Japanese attack. The four-man fighting positions also allowed one man to stand guard while the three others slept at night; yet should the enemy attack, the men could disperse to their nearby fighting holes for the battle. On Company E's south was Company G, which occupied a front about 500 meters south along the river. There Capt. Ted Florey, Company G commander, had his men string a single strand of barbed wire from rock to rock all over the riverbed. It was little more than a trip wire, but it was all that he had available. On the night of 10 July, 2d Battalion found itself defending almost 4,500 meters of river line in jungle terrain without any reserves to plug a possible enemy breakthrough (see map 15).

The Japanese also had problems. The 237th Infantry was to spearhead the attack across the Driniumor against Company E's sector. Col. Nara Masahiko, the regimental commander, echeloned his three battalions in column. On his left, the 80th Infantry, 20th Division, lined up for its assault. On its left, the 78th Infantry had its 3d and 1st battalions on line along the riverbank. The 6th Company, 2d Battalion, 237th Infantry, and the 1st Mountain Artillery Battalion would create a diversion against Company F along the coast. The 26th Field Artillery Regiment would support the 78th and 80th regiments' offensive.

But the plan was already unraveling. The 237th Infantry did not reach the Driniumor until the afternoon of 10 July because of the delay in hand-carried orders reaching its parent 41st Division. With the exception of the 237th's 1st Battalion, no other Japanese had even seen in daylight the ground that they had to attack over in darkness in just a few hours. Although there were guides and trail markers to lead them to their assembly areas, moving forward after nightfall further confused soldiers unfamiliar with the terrain. Moreover, the Japanese would launch their attack believing that they faced three U.S. infantry battalions. Only later did they learn that their previous reconnaissance had missed the arrival of the 112th Cavalry, and consequently, they could not know that the Americans had shortened and strengthened their line.[30] The attack plan

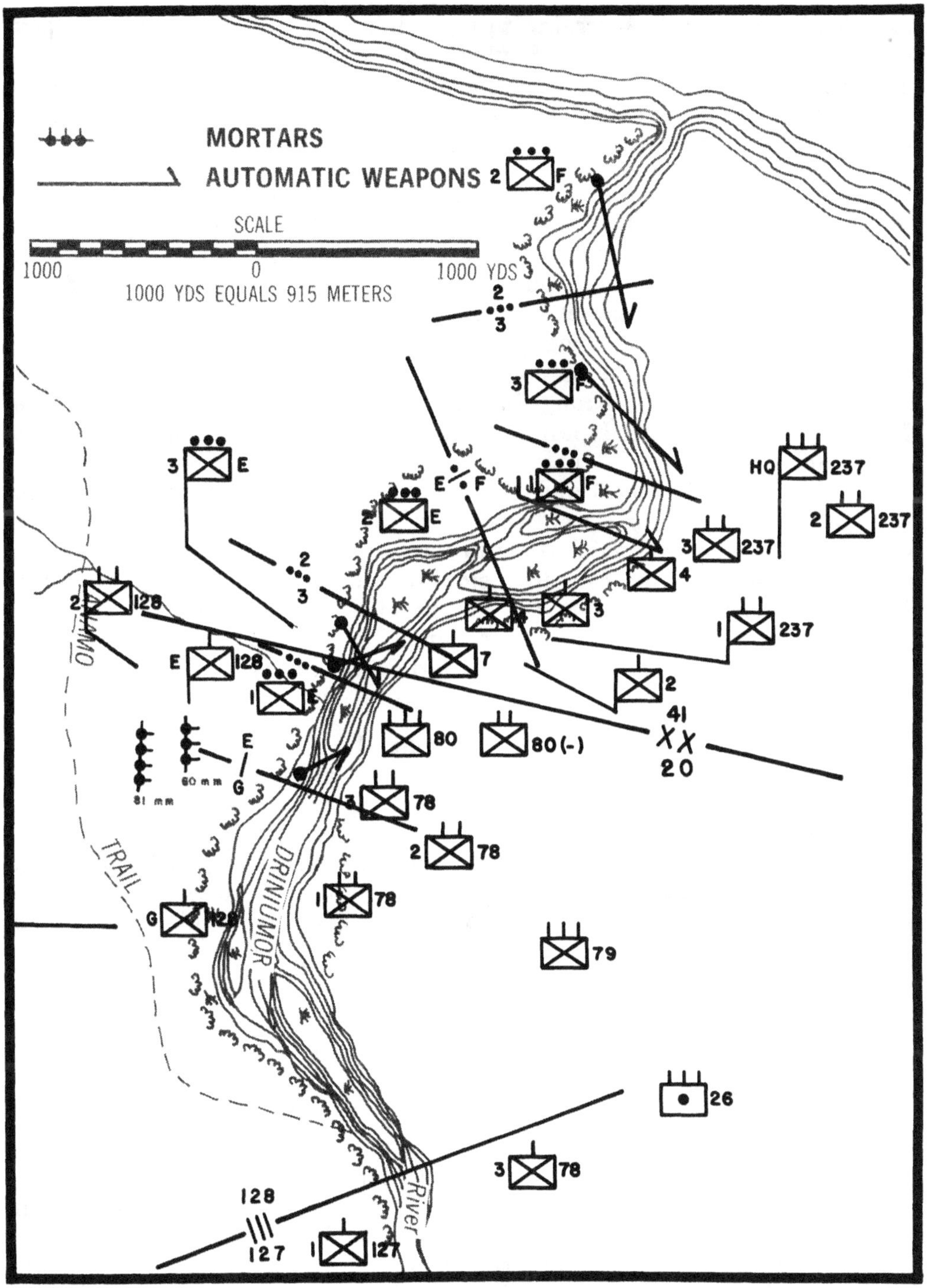

Map 15. Tactical situation, night of 10—11 July 1944

had also been revised. According to the original plan, the Japanese attack would begin at 2200, about thirty minutes after moonrise, but this was changed to provide for a ten-minute artillery and mortar preparation to start at 2150 and to continue to the time of assault.[31] Not all the Japanese units, however, received word of this important alteration.

As the American reconnaissance in force advanced along the U.S. northern and southern flanks, they moved past the assembly areas of six Japanese battalions, five infantry and one artillery. The reconnaissance in force, as well as American patrols operating on the east side of the Driniumor, also missed the arrival of the 237th Infantry Regiment during 10 July, although an "unknown number of Japanese soldiers" were reported two miles southwest of the mouth of the Driniumor, and the sergeant who sighted them felt that a strong Japanese attack was imminent.[32] Opposite Company E's front, the Japanese were less than ninety meters from the Driniumor's east bank. Along this sector, the width of the Driniumor riverbed varied between 70 and 120 meters, with a meandering stream 30 to 50 meters wide. The water was waist deep with a slow current. The stream bed was rocky and shallow in normal weather, but the banks were steep; the west bank (the American side) was about one to two meters high. Reeds or canebreaks grew to the height of a man's head and extended forty-five meters inland from either bank. These were major obstacles to men whose strength had so greatly deteriorated during their march to the Driniumor.[33]

Maj. Yamashita Shigemichi, commander, 1st Battalion, 237th Infantry, was about to lead the advance elements of these units across the Driniumor. He later recalled that, at the time, he and his men were so hungry that they were thinking more about breaking into the American positions to seize American rations than they were about the possibility of being killed. Yet Yamashita realized the crossing might be a costly, difficult attack. The afternoon of 10 July he confessed his misgivings to his regimental commander. Colonel Nara simply told Yamashita, "It's an order. Let's get on with it."[34]

Maj. Kawahigashi Moritoshi's 1st Battalion, 78th Infantry, would spearhead the 20th Division's attack. His battalion had about 400 effectives, one 70-mm battalion howitzer, and four heavy machine guns, making it the strongest of the 78th's battalions. Unlike the 237th Regiment's predicament, Kawahigashi enjoyed detailed reconnaissance information about the terrain he was about to fight on. It was, however, too much to ask the exhausted, nearly spent troops who subsisted on short rations during a two-month jungle march to conduct a silent night attack. The attackers had left their assembly area and even crossed the river in comparative silence, but the cumulative fatigue finally overwhelmed them. Along the east bank, the weary troops could not climb up the two- or three-foot bank without excessive slipping, sliding, and banging of equipment. Muffled threats and curses to keep quiet did no good. Their limit had been reached, and they could do no more.

Several men of Companies E and G heard noises from across the river, but they remained crouched in their foxholes and passed no word of the sounds to their comrades. What these Americans heard was Major Kawahigashi's men moving across the Driniumor. Finally, an American defender from Company E or G fired, and then a hail of small arms and automatic weapons fire lashed the struggling Japanese soldiers. The volume of deadly fire stunned Kawahigashi's officers and men, who, based on previous reconnaissance reports, thought that they would need little firepower support to force the river. Consequently, their battalion machine guns had not been sited for firing, because the battalion, like the division, like the army, had anticipated an easy crossing. The battalion's 70-mm gun had only two rounds of ammunition brought forward—in part, because Japanese artillery doctrine insisted on conserving ammunition with a one-round-one-hit philosophy. Under heavy fire, the men of the 1st Battalion, 78th Infantry, fired their grenade dischargers all along their attacking line and charged forward to Company G's defenses.

Major Kawahigashi led his men in the attack. In the moonlight he could see forty or fifty meters, about halfway across the river. His men had crouched along the eastern riverbank for about five minutes before they heard a battalion gun open fire. Into the riverbed they went, and suddenly a tremendous roar of artillery fire crashed around the battalion. The artillery fire splintered trees like matchsticks along the east bank, and the sheared limbs and trunks plummeted to the ground, crushing or pinioning Japanese troops in the forward platoons of the second echelon who had not dug themselves into the earth.[35] Screams, explosions, and noise punctured the darkness. Once the firing had erupted, the three or four Americans sharing a single large foxhole rapidly fanned out, running or crawling to their individual emplacements, and began shooting into the densely packed Japanese infantry.

The American defenders in Company G who had time to look across the river saw the astonishing sight of hundreds of Japanese soldiers screaming and waving their arms as they lunged through the shallow water or pulled themselves up the riverbank. Artillery explosions had stripped away the canes and reed cover, exposing massed targets for American machine gunners and BAR men. Machine gun barrels turned red hot from constant firing, and still the Japanese charge would not be stopped. Kawahigashi's men then ran into barbed wire strung low to the ground just in front of Company G's perimeter. Many were entangled, slowed, and killed as they struggled to free themselves. The attack by the 78th and 80th regiments hit near the company boundaries of Companies G and E, so the fighting spilled over to E's sector, where an intrepid BAR operator fired twenty-six magazines, more than 500 rounds, in a period of fifteen minutes into the massed Japanese attackers. Even when his weapon overheated, this anonymous infantryman continued to fire single shots into the Japanese troops. According to his company commander, this one man was instrumental in breaking up the first two enemy attacks against Company E.

Friendly artillery was falling so close to the American positions that men on the firing line would instinctively duck their heads as the shells flew overhead. Shrapnel, rocks, and pebbles from the explosions showered the American lines. When the Japanese first echelon finally did break into Company G's perimeter, American automatic weapons fire killed the Japanese captain commanding the battalion machine gun company leading that last-ditch charge. The Japanese attack broke, and the survivors retreated to the east bank. Of the 400 men who had started across the Driniumor, only ninety remained.

To the left of the 1st Battalion, 78th Infantry, the regiment's 3d Battalion soldiers watched horror-struck as the American artillery blasted Japanese soldiers along the Driniumor. Maj. Koike Masao, the battalion commander, saw Kawahigashi's men advance into the sheets of flame spurting from the American positions. Then it was Koike's turn, and he led his battalion across. Again artillery fire ripped into the Japanese ranks, shredding limbs and torsos. Despite the carnage, the 3d Battalion managed to get across the river in Company E's sector and pass through holes in the American line shortly before midnight. The rest of the 78th Infantry Regiment followed, except for the pitifully few survivors of the 1st Battalion, who tried again and again to break the Company G positions. Their otherwise futile attacks might have distracted Company G just sufficiently to permit the 3d Battalion to reach the west bank.

Farther to the north, near Kawanakajima, Major Yamashita was also leading his 1st Battalion, 237th Infantry, into the river. Two machine gun squads had arrived just one hour before his attack, but he had no idea of the whereabouts of his battalion artillery and its crews. Regardless, he had to get his troops across the Driniumor. Along the densely packed, 100-meter front, the three companies of the Japanese first echelon were halfway across the river when the second echelon began its passage. The second wave of Japanese, two infantry companies, drew scattered tracer rounds from Company E's positions. One by one, Japanese machine guns began to lay down suppressive fire for the skirmishers. Suddenly, from the south, where Yamashita knew the 20th Division attack was underway, came the thunder of artillery explosions. The Americans seemed to remember that a bugle sounded, but that is doubtful. Then everyone seemed to open fire. Japanese artillery hit just to the rear of Company E's thinly held lines. Japanese blue tracers streaked across the Driniumor, appeared to converge with the red and yellow tracers fired by the Americans, and then split off on their deadly paths. Flares burst over the river.

Company E's commander, Captain Bell, thought that the Japanese had fired the flares because they burst directly over his command post and company mortar positions. Major Yamashita, conversely, believed that the Americans had fired the flares to illuminate his attacking forces, which were now exposed massed in attack. Under the eerie light, which caused shadows to flicker and dance, turning trees and bushes into enemy soldiers,

American artillery shattered Japanese formations. The men of Company E struck the screaming Japanese with small arms and automatic weapons fire. Four Japanese heavy machine guns, in turn, raked the American lines, concentrating their fire on Company E's now revealed machine gun and automatic weapons positions.

Major Yamashita heard Japanese soldiers shouting that their machine guns were running low on ammunition. The pandemonium reached a crescendo as human screams, shouts, curses, and crashing artillery accompanied by the popping and banging of small arms fire combined to create acoustics for the tracers and flares. During a brief lull, as flares temporarily flickered out, Yamashita heard more reports of small arms fire to his north and realized that his 6th Company had engaged the Americans.

The roar resumed. Trapped under the massed American firepower, Yamashita's 4th Company veered south, the wrong direction (see map 16). The din of battle was too loud for them to hear other Japanese soldiers screaming to turn back. The unlucky 4th Company reached Kawanakajima and began to cross the little island. Company E defenders loosed another sheet of small arms fire that knocked down almost the entire 4th Company and turned the island's pebbles blood red under the brightly burning flares. Yamashita still heard reports of heavy firing from the south, which meant to him that the 20th Division had not reached its objectives.

After the destruction of 4th Company, Company E defenders believed that the Japanese attack had then shifted to their north, but in fact, that had been the original Japanese plan. Yamashita led the remnants of his 1st Battalion across the Driniumor and over its western bank. The rest of the 237th Infantry followed shortly thereafter. As American artillery and mortars shifted their fires to repel these breaches, Japanese troops from the 78th and 80th Infantry regiments again struck Company E's southern flank. Visibility deteriorated as the flares were nearly used up, and smoke, debris, and dust from artillery explosions drew a grayish pall, stinking of cordite, over the river. The distance between Company E's strongpoints was too great to cover all the gaps. Their small arms ammunition was depleted, artillery fire had shifted to other targets, and although firing at ranges down to 135 meters, the company's 81-mm mortars alone could not stop the renewed Japanese assault. Company E was overrun (see map 17).[36]

Japanese infantrymen broke through Company E's line, rushed into and through the American command post and mortar positions, and then started to regroup in order to move inland to the high ground southwest of the main attack sector. The 1st Battalion, 78th Infantry, suffered terrible losses, 290 men out of 360 effectives, and altogether about 600 men of the 78th Infantry died in the breakthrough. The 237th Infantry had also picked its way through openings in Company E's extended front and worked northwest toward the Americans' rear. Badly mangled by American artillery, the 237th attackers' efforts to regroup in the jungle at night, after such a

NOTE: In breakthrough sector, O.P. #1 held 5 men;
O.P. #2, 4 men; BAR position, 3 men.
O.P. #1 & O.P. #2 were about 100 yds apart,
with BAR 30 yds left of O.P. #2.

LEGEND
RAIN FOREST & JUNGLE
CANE BRAKES
STONEY RIVER BED
NOT DRAWN TO SCALE

NORTH
(APPROX.)

"C" Sector—Infiltration
in force—approx platoon

"B" Sector

237(-)

4

—550 Meters—45 Meters—14 Meters—35 Meters—55 Meters—

237

E 128

2 128

60 mm

81 mm

BAR

O.P. #2

O.P. #1

"A" Sector—Where main
breakthrough came.

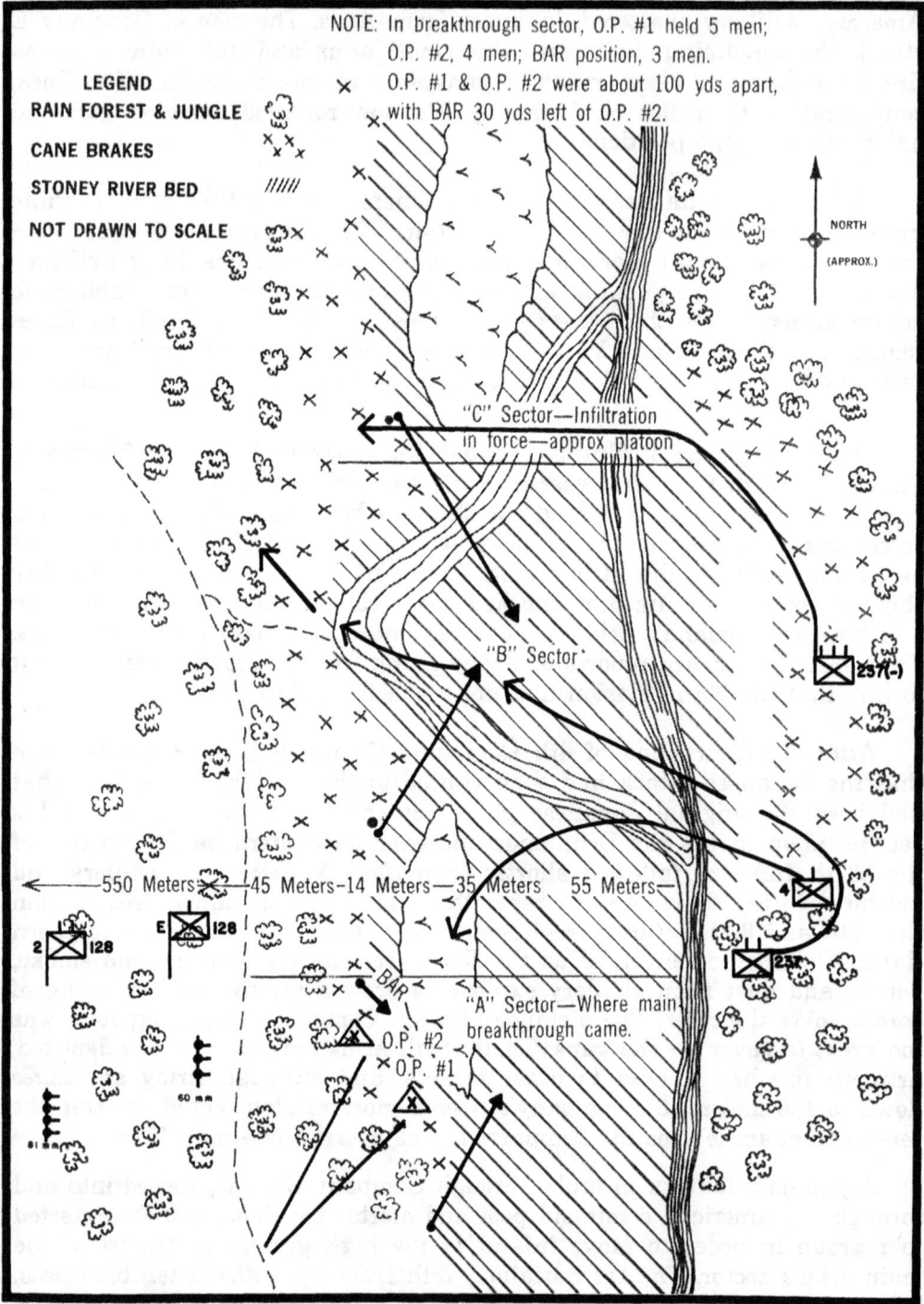

Map 16. Destruction of Japanese 4th Company

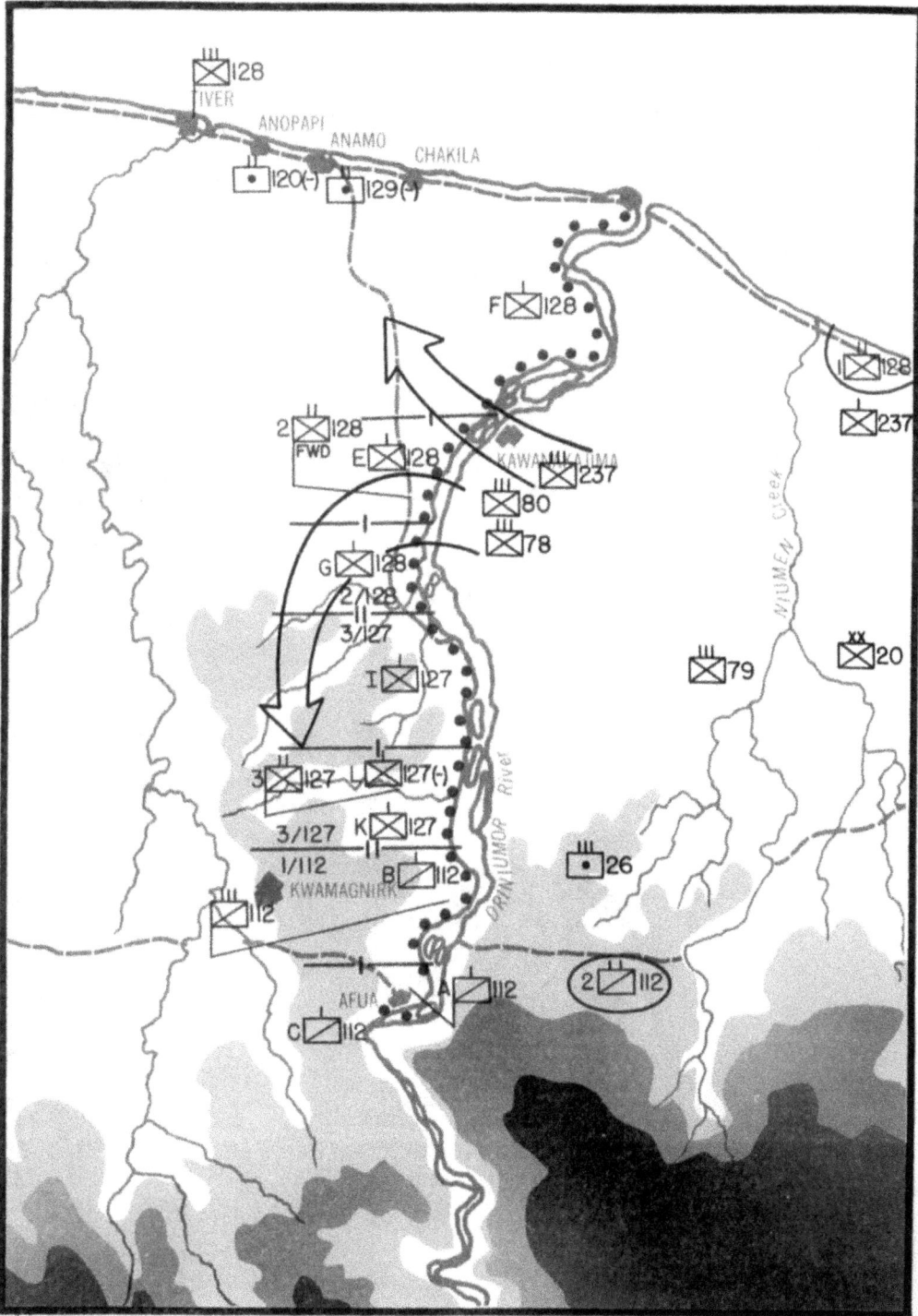

Map 17. Japanese breakthrough, 10—11 July 1944

78

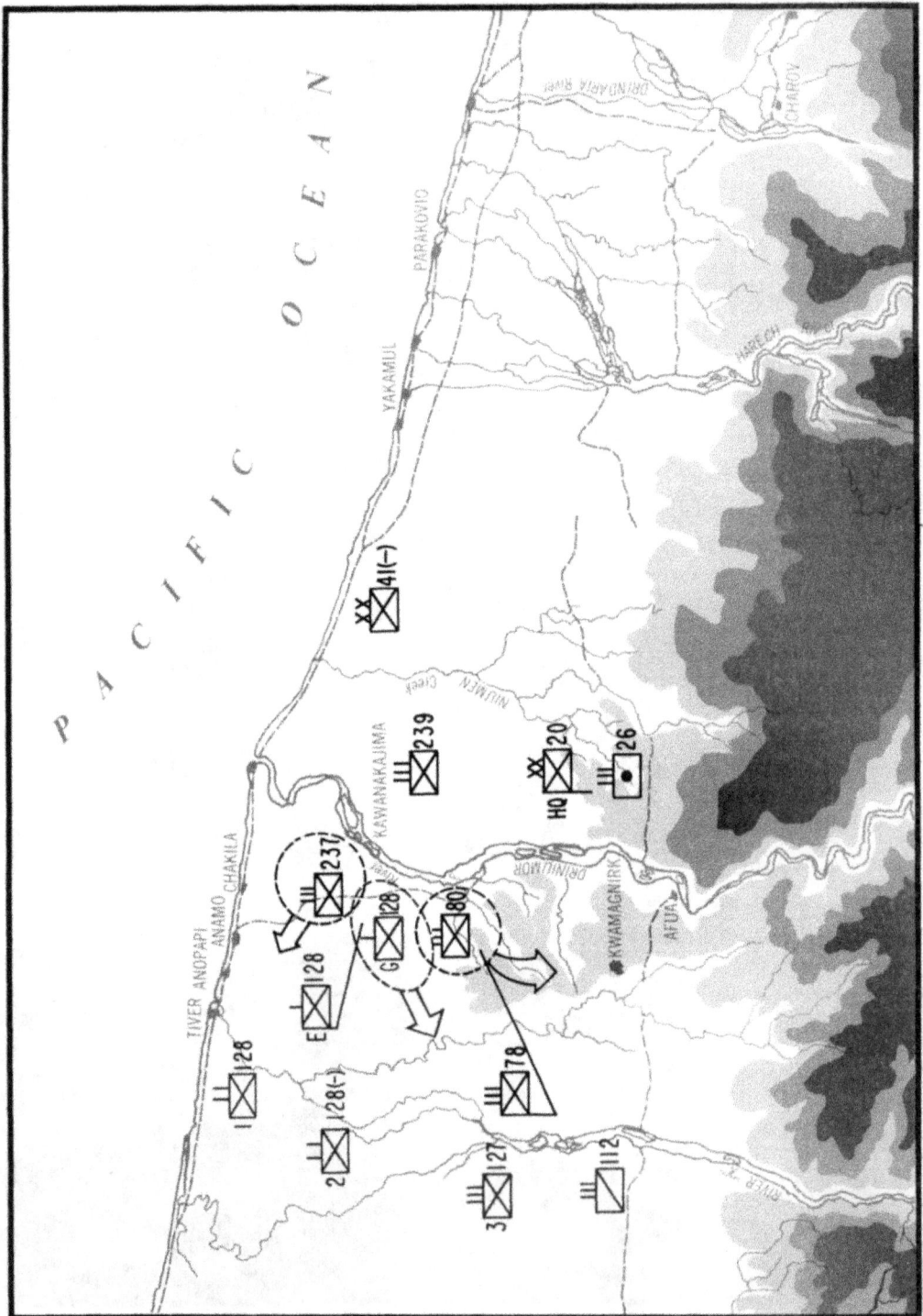

Map 18. Situation, 12 July 1944

ferocious hour-long battle, proved beyond them. Instead, small groups of Japanese and American infantrymen isolated or encircled one another in turn along a 1,100-meter-wide opening that a few hours previously had been the front line for Companies E and G.

Company E lost perhaps ten killed and another twenty wounded before it exhausted its ammunition and pulled back from its defensive positions. Its contingency withdrawal plan was impossible because of the chaos, darkness, and lack of communication. All land lines had been severed an hour before, either by U.S. artillery or by Japanese troops. Suffering about 30 percent casualties and overrun, Company E was thoroughly scattered and, as far as higher headquarters could determine, had ceased to exist.[37] The disintegration of Company E meant that Company G's left (north) flank was wide open. The company commander, Capt. Ted Florey, thus put his reserve platoon on the open flank to continue his makeshift line back to the battalion mortar positions. Until 0400 on 11 July, heavy enemy small arms fire and irregular mortar or artillery fire struck the Americans, but after that, quiet ensued. About 0200 Company G lost contact with higher headquarters, but could communicate through the artillery liaison officer's radio. Shortly after dawn, with "no reserve to restore the break in the line," General Martin ordered Florey to withdraw to River X, about 4,500 meters to his west (see map 18). Company G, plus assorted units and remnants of Company H, spent the next three days marching and fighting those 4,500 meters.[38] They were alone, exhausted, and afraid. The Japanese 78th and 80th regiments were in similar straits, and their officers and NCOs were urging them to move southwest to mop up the rest of the American covering force. That Japanese enveloping maneuver brought them into contact with the 112th Cavalry near Afua.

Counterattack

6

Afua

As for the cavalrymen of the 112th, they knew only from the heavy sustained volume of fire to their north that a large battle was in progress. The XI Corps commander, Major General Hall, knew about as much. Hall contacted General Gill for an assessment of the fighting. American Tech. Sgt. Serph Smigiel, who was monitoring the communications equipment to insure circuits were not in use during a cutover procedure, overheard Gill say that although the "Japs" had broken through, the overall situation was all right. Gill's flanks were holding, and his reserves were intact. Hall told Gill to carry on and that he, Hall, was going back to sleep.[39] The men fighting and dying on the line did not quite share Gill's sanguine appreciation of the battle.

The sergeant then contacted regimental signalmen closer to the covering force, because many of the infantrymen were from his home town, and he was anxious to learn their fate. He heard that the Japanese indeed had smashed through the covering force, even using their weapons as clubs against the American defenders. No one knew exactly what was happening, but ominous reports were filtering back that Company E had been overrun and annihilated.[40]

Meanwhile, on the periphery of this confusion, the 112th Cavalry had its forces divided. Half its units were east of the Driniumor and completely out of contact with the regiment at this critical time. The 1st Squadron along the Driniumor was not under attack, but it did receive scattered artillery and small arms fire, possibly some of the latter from its own understandably nervous sentries. Sometime between midnight and 0300 on 11 July, the 112th Headquarters command post learned that the Japanese had broken through the 3d Battalion's sector, when the neighboring battalion commander called for artillery fire through the 112th command post to cover his withdrawal.[41] Later a preliminary report reached the 112th that about fifty Japanese had broken through the 2d Battalion's sector. That grim news meant that the Japanese were in the 112th's rear and that the unit might already be cut off.

At higher headquarters as well, the progress of the battle was still unclear. The "G-2 Estimate of the Enemy Situation" of 11—12 July reported that "At 0430 hours, 11 July an estimated battalion (but possibly a regiment) penetrated our covering position." It recounted that the first two Japanese attacks had been repulsed, but that Allied units, after suffering heavy casualties, were ordered to withdraw (see map 19). Ultra added nothing substantial to clarify the situation. Based on their own preconceptions reinforced by a patrol report from the 112th Cavalry, G-2 estimated that the 78th Infantry Regiment might have crossed the Driniumor south of Afua. In other words, G-2 concluded that the long-awaited, two-pronged Japanese attack was underway and planned its operations accordingly.[42]

The morning of 11 July the 112th had to discover whether any Japanese troops were nearby and reestablish contact with the 2d Squadron. At first light, 1st Squadron dispatched patrols from Troop A south and southeast to search for enemy formations on the 112th's flank. Lieutenant Boyce and twenty men were about 2,700 meters southeast of Afua when they heard an enemy column approaching them. The Japanese were marching in columns of two's, closed up, laughing, and talking loudly. Boyce quickly deployed his men in ambush and waited until the Japanese were within twenty-five meters before springing it. He saw eight Japanese troops topple as his patrol's submachine gun and light machine guns fired into their column. More Japanese fell screaming as they ran for cover. Boyce and his men then took advantage of the enemy's confusion to withdraw and beat a hurried retreat to Afua, where they arrived at 1300.[43]

Earlier that morning, another 112th patrol, this time from Troop C, under Lieutenant Smith, was resting at a waterfall about 1,800 meters south of Afua, when the men spotted an eleven-man Japanese patrol marching up the river straight toward them. Smith also set a hasty ambush and waited until the first six Japanese were within three meters of him before firing. He personally killed two Japanese with point-blank rifle fire, two more Japanese died in the explosion of a white phosphorus grenade, and two others were wounded. The survivors fled into the jungle. Smith continued his patrol and about 500 meters west of the river discovered what he thought was a large Japanese bivouac. He reported his news back to Headquarters, 112th Cavalry, shortly after noon.

Another patrol to the northwest, this one from Troop B, reached Niumen Creek, where the men discovered fresh boot tracks and heard Japanese talking. At one point, the men in the patrol had the chilling experience of feeling sure that Japanese were trailing them, but they managed to return around noon without incident. All these patrol contacts indicated to General Cunningham that large numbers of Japanese were attempting to outflank his exposed position from the south. Later that afternoon, reports of large numbers of Japanese crossing the Driniumor south of Afua seemed to confirm it. His perception, in turn, colored SWPA G-2's estimate that the 78th Infantry was conducting a flanking operation southeast of Afua.

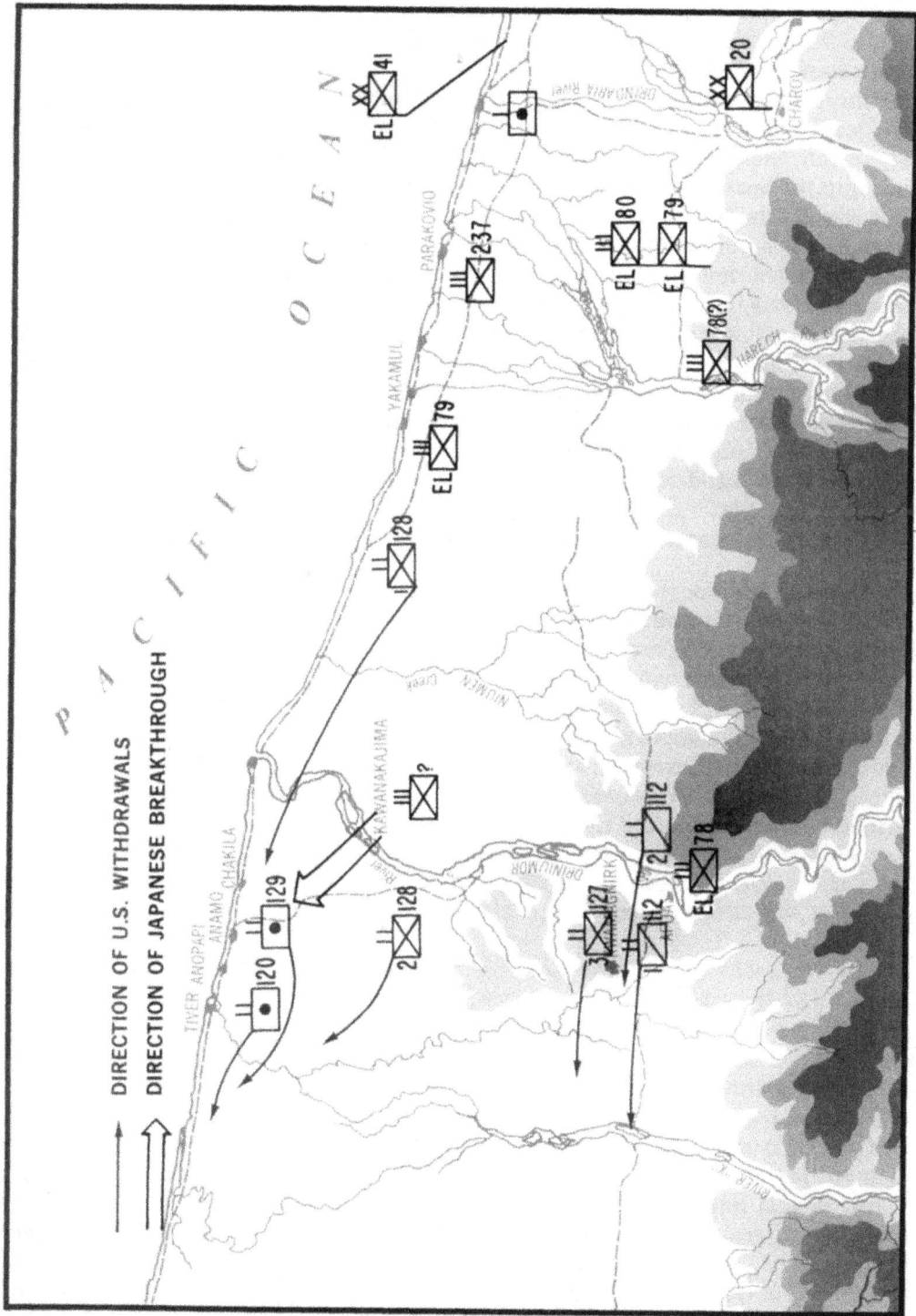

Map 19.   SWPA G-2 estimate of enemy situation, 11—12 July 1944

In the meantime, telephone communication with 1st Squadron Head-quarters failed because of a fault in the line, thus delaying until 0730 orders for the immediate return of 2d Squadron from east of the Driniumor. About two and one-half hours later, as 1st Squadron waited the arrival of 2d Squadron, General Hall contacted the 112th's command post and ordered the unit to destroy supplies and equipment that the men would be unable to carry in their withdrawal to River X.* Supply sergeants ordered the men to bury all supplies in foxholes before moving out, and the men destroyed what could be neither buried nor carried. Everyone worked in haste, fearful that each passing moment gave the Japanese time to tighten their grip on the unit. To this point, except for scattered small arms fire during the night of 10—11 July, the 112th had not been engaged in the fighting. Nevertheless, their perception of that battle rested on the fragmentary reports they had received, and the so-called fog of war had produced extreme apprehension. Thus, while General Martin approved General Cunningham's request to withdraw at 1100 instead of the scheduled 1500, he did so only after emphasizing that the mission of the covering force was to delay the enemy, not to give up ground without resisting.[44]

General Martin faced a series of decisions he had to make on the basis of incomplete information. He had no forces left to plug the breakthrough because the reconnaissance in force operations along either of his flanks required all his reserves. He judged, correctly, that the Japanese were across the Driniumor in force and were threatening his rear. General Krueger did not agree with Martin's estimate of the seriousness of the situation. As limited as his information was, Martin did realize that there were no U.S. forces between the Japanese and the American main line of resistance near Aitape, and consequently he ordered a general withdrawal to River X, where he would reorganize his forces to combat future Japanese attacks.[45] A signal from the Japanese 80th Infantry put it more bluntly, "Under our eyes the enemy is retreating in boats and along the trails."[46]

As General Cunningham led the first echelon of the 112th in retreat to River X, 2d Squadron finally appeared at Afua. Fear propelled the Americans as they covered in an hour the same distance that had taken them most of the previous day. Everyone pushed himself at an exhausting pace or risked being left alone in the jungle again that night. By 1200, 2d Squadron had replaced the 1st at Afua, and the 2d, in turn, withdrew three hours later. Native bearers helped carry the squadron's baggage, particularly by dismantling and portaging the 5th Portable Hospital, then assigned to the 112th. The 2d Squadron's luck again failed as a torrential downpour punished them all afternoon. The heavy trail and slippery going slowed the native bearers, who, in turn, retarded the column's progress. So, near midnight the 2d Squadron, less Troop F, wearily reached River X. It had been a physically exhausting and mentally terrifying ordeal. Troop F, whose men brought up the rear, did not close with the main column and, fearful of crossing the River X in darkness, spent the night alone. The night march

*Similar orders were issued to the 2d/128th and the 3d/127th.

over a narrow jungle trail was later described in the unit history as "a great hardship." Litter bearers got lost in the black maze, requiring the column to halt until they could be found. After that, men caught hold of the belt or shoulder of the trooper in front of them and led each other in a procession of darkness. The men stumbled along, and when they tripped and fell over slippery roots or bush on the trail, it caused a chain reaction as several beltholders crashed down together in the mud. Weapons were consequently covered with mud and not in firing condition. The 2d Squadron was no longer a fighting unit, and the men were too exhausted to care. They were too fatigued even to eat. Only a day's rest and refitting would reconstitute the unit.

Both combatants needed time to regroup and reorganize. The 112th's troopers were drained not from fighting, but from the physical demands of making a hasty withdrawal during a tropical deluge, as well as from the mental strain from a night and day of unrelieved tension. The 3d Battalion, 127th Infantry, had not participated in the fighting either, but it too was scattered in retreat. Farther north, Companies E and G were in disarray somewhere in the heavy jungle between the Driniumor and River X. Nearer the coast, small groups of men from Company F were fighting Japanese soldiers from the 237th Infantry. The Japanese 78th and 80th Infantry regiments had swung southwest after their breakthrough, but both had suffered dreadful personnel losses. Their turn south was too late to cut off the retreat of the 112th. In short, despite the initial Japanese breakthrough and severe losses on both sides, the fighting so far had been inconclusive. Once again the respective commanders had to make the operational decisions that would set in motion another desperate melee in the New Guinea wilds.

General Krueger at 6th Army still refused to believe that Martin's retreat from the Driniumor had been necessary. On 12 July, he ordered General Hall to drive the Japanese back eastward across the Driniumor. General Hall, in turn, ordered General Martin to retreat no further, except before overwhelming odds, and he forbade the withdrawal of any unit not in actual contact with superior enemy forces. To emphasize the point, later the same day General Martin was relieved of command of the covering force and assigned command of Eastern Sector. Major General Gill assumed command of Persecution Covering Force.[47] Gill's Field Order Number One, Persecution Covering Force, directed a counterattack on 13 July to restore the Driniumor line. For operational purposes, two clusters of units, designated North Force and South Force, would attack east to the west bank of the Driniumor, where they would turn south and north respectively in order to join forces, thereby sealing the Japanese penetration (see map 20).[48]

At 18th Army, General Adachi believed that the battle was developing favorably. According to the preliminary reports he had received on 12 and 13 July, the 20th Division was southwest of Afua, and the Americans were in full retreat. Regimental staff officers reported that the Americans had suffered "many casualties," but darkness prevented a detailed account of

86

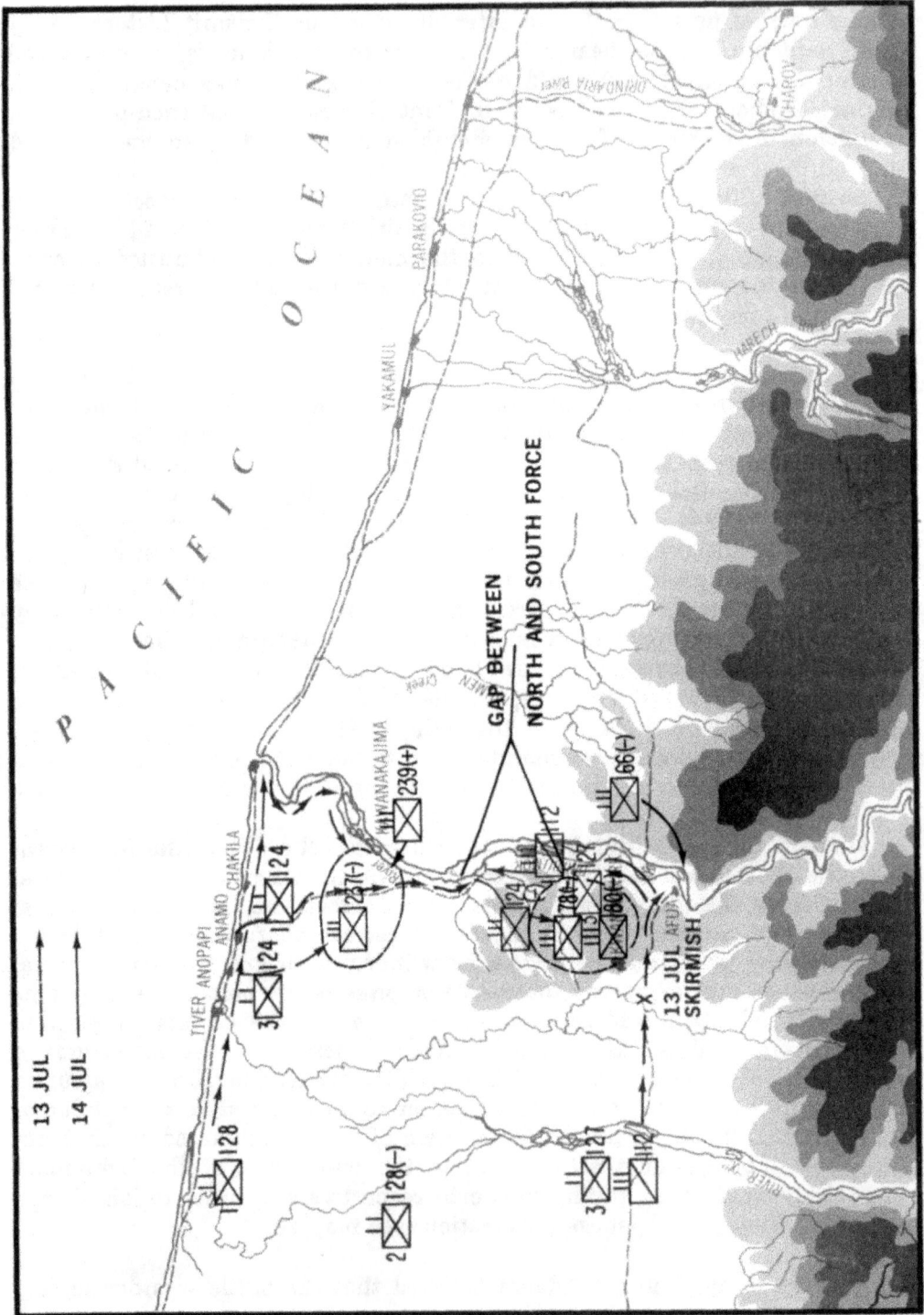

Map 20. Sealing the gap, 13—14 July 1944

enemy dead or captured equipment. Japanese losses were given as twenty-five dead and fifty-nine wounded.[49] Adachi concluded that his initial attack had succeeded and that his next attack towards the airfields at Aitape could continue according to plan.

On 12 July the 112th Cavalry was sorting itself out in anticipation of imminent fighting. Patrols had no success in locating the Japanese, but everyone dug in, expecting yet another Japanese attack that night. About twenty men laid out an escape trail, and others reestablished communications between the 112th and the 3d Battalion, 127th Infantry, also regrouping after being scattered during its retreat. Then at 1750, in accordance with 6th Army's orders, General Martin ordered the 112th Cavalry to reoccupy its former positions on the Driniumor the following morning. Commanders' meetings and coordination conferences with the 3d Battalion, which would advance on the 112th's left flank, occupied the early daylight hours. During this time, General Cunningham also coordinated air and artillery support for the 112th Cavalry, should it encounter Japanese resistance. Similar preparations were repeated to the north, where the 1st Battalion, 128th Infantry, would simultaneously attack towards the Driniumor.[50] Rested and refitted, the 112th was ready to be committed to battle again. At 0800 an advance guard platoon moved from River X eastward to the Driniumor.

In three hours during intermittent showers the advance guard platoon from Troop B had covered about 2,000 meters, making very good time over the jungle trails. Then the point men bumped into perhaps seventy-five Japanese soldiers from the 20th Division near a stream crossing. As one American veteran recalled, "We just walked up on what looks like about fifteen Japs out in the river. They were great big Japs, looked like he was six feet tall and with one of our ponchos on his back."[51] Both sides recovered from their initial shock and surprise and sprinted for cover. A sharp fire fight flared, punctuated by bursts of light machine gun fire, thunks of Japanese grenade dischargers, and rifle shots. The Americans wisely waited for the main body of the 112th Cavalry and its additional fire support. For the next three hours, 1st Squadron cautiously deployed forward, with Troop B in the center, A on the right, and C on the left, until all had reached the creek. Most of their firing was unaimed, because the thick vegetation precluded seeing much farther than a few meters, and men were reluctant to expose themselves for aimed fire. Another pause occurred as requests were made for artillery fire against the Japanese. Finally at 1400, after artillery fire had fallen on the suspected Japanese positions, the entire 1st Squadron made a rush across the stream. Their spectacular charge went for naught, however, because the Japanese had realized early in the engagement that they were outnumbered and outgunned and had fled deeper into the jungle. So the 112th Cavalry crossed the nameless stream, and by 1530 lead elements had reached Afua without opposition. The 112th was back on the Driniumor.

Squadron defensive deployments were textbook: two up, one back. The 1st Squadron deployed Troop B on the river's west bank as the squadron's south flank with Troop C to its north and Troop A in reserve. The 2d Squadron moved downriver from Afua and took up positions north of 1st Squadron with Troop F's lines tied to C, Troop G holding the north flank, and E in reserve. The impression that the defenses were laid out in neat and orderly "lines" was misleading. Afua had already been hit with an air strike, and the American soldiers had to dig in amidst the rubble. It was too late in the afternoon to prepare elaborate entrenchments, so they used bomb craters and artillery shellholes that pitted the area as foxholes or outposts for minimal protection against potential enemy fire and the elements. The heretofore constantly booming artillery fire slackened by early evening after General Hall had warned artillery officers to conserve ammunition or risk exhausting their stocks. For the next ten days, harassing fire was limited to not more than ten rounds per gun per night.[52]

Troop G's sector was the most active that night. Throughout the night, sentries heard and occasionally, when the clouds parted, caught fleeting glimpses in the moonlight of Japanese soldiers crossing the Driniumor and moving southeast, away from the American lines. These Japanese probably were scouts or guides sent to find the exact whereabouts of the 20th Division, at present somewhere southeast of the river and Afua, but two of whose regiments were now northwest of Afua.

Pvt. William Garbo had arrived at Troop G that day as a replacement and promptly became an ammunition bearer. After dark he found himself in a machine gun pit, about the size of a dining room table, covered with ponchos and logs. Although he had listened to everything the veterans had said, nothing had prepared him for a night in a pit so black that he could not see his hand in front of his face. It was so still that he could hear the Driniumor flowing past, but more menacing sounds of five Japanese infiltrators soon followed. A Japanese soldier climbed onto the logs covering Garbo's dugout and hurled a bundle of dynamite onto the startled machine gun crew. Only the detonator caps exploded, deafening the Americans and covering them with sulphur powder. Grenades, followed by American small arms fire, killed two of the infiltrators, and the surviving Japanese escaped into the jungle darkness. While the rest of the night passed quietly in the 112th's area, once again came the sounds of small arms and heavy artillery fire to the north. Although the men of the 112th could not know it, what they heard was fighting among the American 1st and 3d battalions, 124th Infantry, and the Japanese 1st and 2d battalions, 237th Infantry. They had the vaguest idea that someone besides themselves had the misfortune to find Japanese troops. It was probably fortunate that the 112th troopers did not know that the 78th and 80th Infantry regiments at that moment were about 2,500 meters northwest of Afua, in the rear of the 112th's defenses, and preparing to attack. All the cavalrymen knew for certain was that in the morning it would be their turn to attack.

On a situation map everything was clear. The Japanese had broken through the center of the American lines. The U.S. forces even now had launched a counterattack to seal off the gap. On 14 July South Force (the

112th Cavalry and the 3d Battalion, 127th Infantry) would attack north as the 124th Infantry Regiment, minus one battalion, would attack south. The axes of attack were parallel and west of the Driniumor. The objective was for the Americans to join forces, thereby destroying the Japanese units operating west of the Driniumor. The more one was removed from the actual fighting and terrain, the clearer the situation seemed. No one at any echelon realized that two Japanese regiments were readying an attack from northwest of Afua.

In the 112th Cavalry, everyone was tense and nervous, checking their weapons before their attack on the morning of 14 July. No one knew exactly where the Japanese were silently waiting for the American approach, but everyone knew that Japanese ambushes from the thick, lush, green vegetation could erupt at any moment and spray them with deadly small arms fire. Leading the advance patrols was as nerve racking and potentially lethal. But without patrols, the squadrons were blind.

Shortly before 0800, a squad-size patrol from Troop F crossed to the Driniumor's east bank in front of its troop sector. Almost immediately, Japanese machine gun fire struck the patrol, wounding one man. The squad was temporarily pinned down, but covering fire from Troop F's machine guns and mortars kept the Japanese gunners' heads down and gave the patrol time to escape back across the river. Then tragedy struck. As the artillery liaison officer tried to adjust the 120th Field Artillery Battalion's 105-mm fire on the Japanese ambush site, four shells landed short, exploding just in front of the south flank in Troop F's sector. Friendly fire killed one American and wounded three others. It was a portent for the 112th Cavalry that day.

The 1st Squadron pushed north, parallel to the Driniumor's west bank, preceded by squad-size patrols. Screening patrols, one squad from each troop sector, took up positions about 600 meters east of the river and remained there during the day to protect 1st Squadron's flank. The mission of 1st Squadron was to link up with the 124th Infantry, operating somewhere—no one seemed to know where—to the north. Cavalry patrols, however, advanced 1,500 meters downriver without finding any trace of either American or Japanese units. Moreover, the commander of the 124th Infantry, who was supposed to be clearing Japanese troops along the Driniumor by a southern advance, reported that his troops had reached the Anamo-Afua trail junction. The 2d Squadron, however, was occupying these positions at present, which meant that the 124th Infantry was lost.* As if to exacerbate the already muddled situation, Australian fighter aircraft mistakenly strafed the 2d Squadron's sector, wounding one cavalryman. Close air support was a continual problem, because the Americans and Australians operated on different radio frequencies, which meant that the ground troops could not

*Gray, "Aitape," maintains that there were two Afuas—an old Afua and a new, the latter 1,500 meters upstream—so both commanders were correct. The terrain map of Aitape issued to the troops shows only the one village.

contact the pilots and identify themselves. In addition, in the midst of preplanned American artillery concentrations, Japanese artillerymen would sometimes also fire a round or two near the area. This led to confusion among the Americans over whether or not friendly artillery was falling on their heads. Also that afternoon, Companies G and H, 128th Battalion, after wandering and fighting for two days in the jungle, arrived at the 112th's rear echelon at River X, where they helped to man the perimeter that night on Persecution Task Force's orders.

The picture for 14 July, then, was one of American regiments and battalions segregated by the jungle terrain into squad- and platoon-size formations which, relying on inaccurate maps, were milling around thick jungle on either side of a spur of the Torricelli chain, which stretched irregularly about 3,600 meters north of Afua between the Driniumor and Koronal Creek. The Japanese, simultaneously, had two understrength infantry regiments consolidating positions on that very spur near Kwamagnirk Village. Conceivably, squads of Americans and Japanese passed within a few meters of each other, but enclosed and muffled by the great trees and expansive vegetation, they passed unaware of the presence of the other. Had they even glimpsed another patrol several meters away, the jungle had reduced all their uniforms and national identities to a sameness.

The Japanese infantrymen had picked up numerous pieces of American clothing and equipment, probably after overrunning Company E and forcing G to withdraw. A 2d Squadron security patrol, for instance, saw four Japanese near River X wearing American packs and clothing. As early as 29 June the Persecution Task Force S-2 warned all units that the Japanese were wearing U.S. uniforms and equipment and to be careful "not to identify the enemy by clothing alone."[53] Members of the 112th were reduced to the fatigues they wore on their backs. Clothes and boots rotted away, because in the harsh priorities of combat, they were less essential to survival than ammunition and food. The 112th would spend the next three weeks fighting along the Driniumor. The only relief was for the seriously ill or the wounded. The living and the dead stayed on the line.

That night, General Hall declared a full alert because a Japanese prisoner had claimed that a major attack was imminent. The 112th had special cause for concern because a few hours earlier Persecution Task Force Headquarters had informed them by message that approximately two Japanese regiments were about 3,600 meters northwest of the 112th's right rear.[54] The anticipated attack never materialized, and only light small arms fire was audible to the north.

Another reason that American patrols encountered so few Japanese on 14 July was that the Japanese were still regrouping. The 78th and 80th Infantry regiments, which had suffered such terrible casualties on the night of 10—11 July, amalgamated themselves under the command of Maj. Gen. Miyake Sadahiko and henceforth were known as Miyake Force. Also on 14

July, 18th Army Headquarters apparently realized the serious losses incurred to date. General Adachi then recognized that the Americans had reoccupied the original Japanese crossing point on the Driniumor, that strong enemy units were advancing along the coast against his 237th Infantry, and that for the first time to his knowledge, Americans were appearing in strength on the Afua front. He responded to the new situation by ordering the 41st Division to destroy the Americans near the Driniumor crossing and along the coast. Meanwhile, he directed the 20th Division to annihilate the enemy near Afua.[55]

The 112th Cavalry was in the midst of its counterattack, but the men could account for little but frustration, confusion, and needless death from "friendly fire." Persecution Task Force was dissatisfied with the 112th Cavalry's seemingly slow and overly cautious advance. General Hall wanted the gap in the U.S. lines closed. At 2300 on 14 July, he ordered General Cunningham to move Troop E north to fill the opening, although he did agree to a request that the move be delayed until first light. At dawn on 15 July, the men of Troop E started north to find the 124th Infantry. About one hour later they passed Company L, 127th Infantry's left (north) flank, which rested on the exposed gap (see map 21). Afterwards, they used the Anamo Trail and had proceeded north perhaps 2,700 meters when the lead scout, Pfc. Carlos A. Provencio, heard a Japanese dragging a weapon along the trail. Provencio waited for the man to appear on the trail and, when he did, shot at him. The startled Japanese turned and fled. The point man moved after him, and as he turned another twist on the jungle path, he almost ran into another Japanese soldier, whom he promptly shot and killed. The troop reacted quickly, moved forward firing in support, and killed six Japanese soldiers.[56] Private First Class Provencio then caught sight of a Japanese machine gun emplacement, so instead of going straight along the trail towards the gun, he led the troop on a detour around its right flank. The Americans then resumed their march and reached the 124th Infantry's command post by noon. Shortly thereafter, Troop E sent a message to General Cunningham reporting this linkup, but it never arrived, leaving the general to wonder what had happened to his men. The cavalrymen spent the rest of the afternoon exchanging stories and food with 3d Battalion, 124th Infantry. At 1700, that battalion received orders to attack south to close the gap, but with darkness fast approaching, a request to postpone the attack until morning was granted.

While Troop E made its way north, patrols from the 112th Cavalry reported numerous sightings of small parties of Japanese south and west of the regiment's positions near Afua. General Cunningham, in some distemper, readjusted his lines northward to cover the void created by Troop E's departure.[57] Other cavalrymen improved defenses around Afua, sweating under the tropical sun. Three C-47s flew over and dropped rations and ammunition, for Japanese ambushes had made ration trains too dangerous or too prohibitive in terms of the men needed to guard the trains, which of

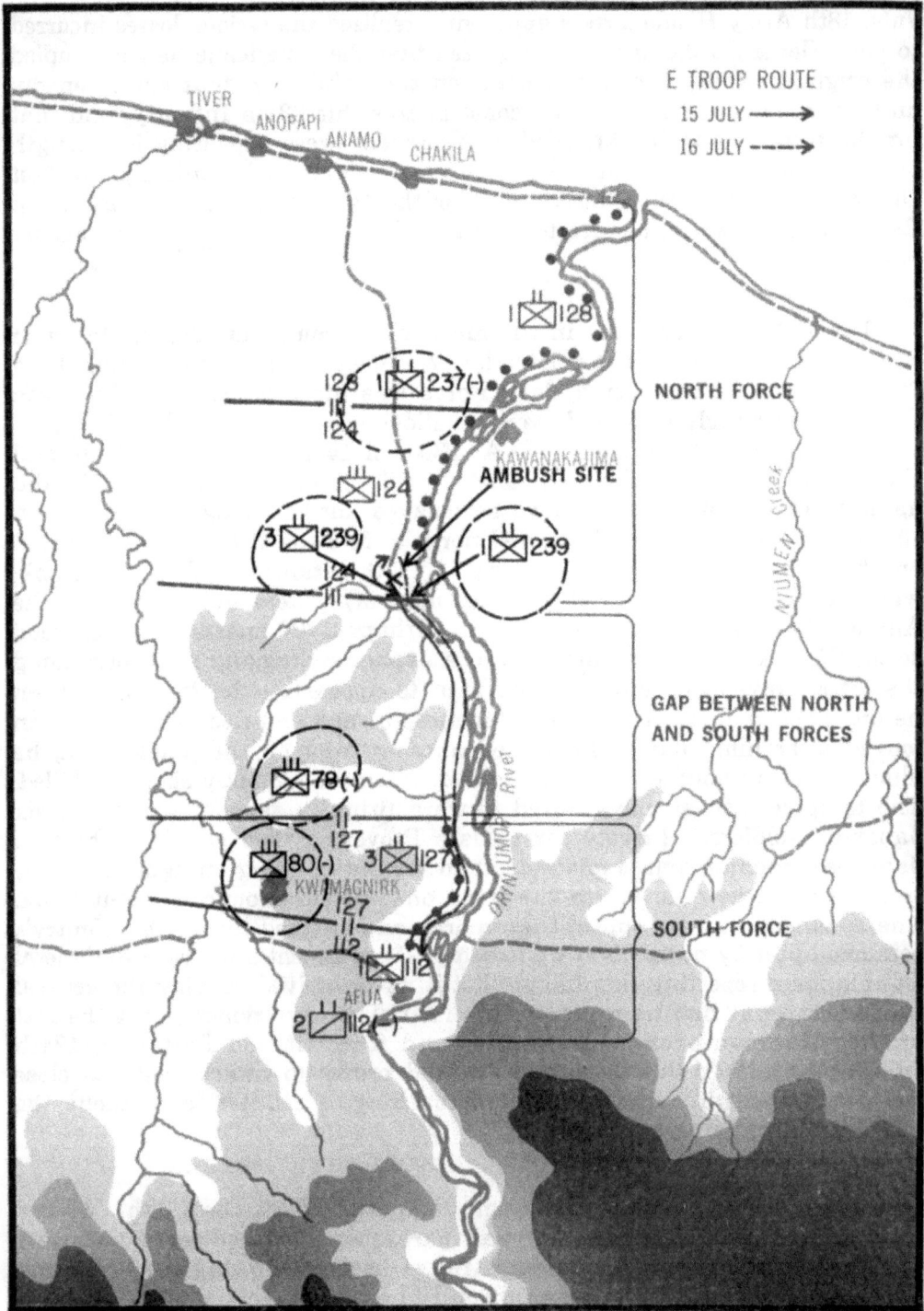

Map 21.   Sealing the gap, 15—16 July 1944

necessity moved slowly along the easily ambushed jungle trails. Usually the airmen dropped ten-in-one rations, but for one three-day period, the cavalrymen on the ground had to subsist on K rations alone.[58]

Members of the 112th's Service Company like T-5 Albert Earl Gossett volunteered to ride in the C-47 ration planes and to kick supplies out the doorless side of the aircraft. It was the kind of effort that could easily be overlooked, but without resupply the combat troops would be unable to function. An idea of the magnitude of the airdrop may be gained from the statistics that 5.1 tons of supplies were air-dropped on 22 July to the 112th at Afua, and just two days later, another 3.1 tons were parachuted to them.[59] Kicking out supply pallets was dangerous work, because in the excitement of the few seconds one had to kick the supplies out, it was deceptively simple to get tangled in the parachute static lines and pulled from the aircraft. On the ground, after eating, 112th personnel settled in for the night. It passed quietly with only desultory firing heard to the north. But there was always potential danger. A friendly artillery battery firing a routine night interdiction mission had one stray shell explode in the riverbed about fifty meters in front of Troop G's sector, killing a trooper who had decided to sleep above ground that night.

On 15 July the Japanese 20th Division reported that in its sector "almost all" the enemy had retreated and that its troops were "pursuing and mopping up" the Americans. Evidently, the 78th and 80th Infantry regiments of the 20th Division had as little notion of the whereabouts of the 112th Cavalry, 127th Infantry, and 124th Infantry as the Americans had of Japanese locations. That day, General Adachi decided to send the previously uncommitted 66th Infantry, 51st Division, to expand the 20th Division's gains. Concurrently, he ordered the 41st Division's 239th and 237th Infantry regiments to attack west and east, respectively, in order to hold the original Japanese breakthrough corridor on the Driniumor.[60] While Troop E and the 124th Infantry would be attacking south and the 112th Cavalry and 127th Infantry pushing north, the convergence of Americans and Japanese units from all points of the compass would create a unique tactical situation and make a collision unavoidable. It happened the morning of 16 July.

Troop E spent the night of 15 July with Company I, 124th Infantry. Supply Sgt. Frank Salas recalled that the 124th's men were "very happy" to see fellow Americans. The 124th Infantry had had no combat experience, and the sight of the 112th Cavalry men, veterans of New Britain, calmed the understandably nervous green troops. The Company I commander distributed E troopers throughout his unit, which occupied the right (south), or exposed, flank of the battalion. He acknowledged the "steadying influence" of the cavalrymen the next morning, when he told Lieutenant Campbell, then commanding Troop E, that it was the first time Company I's soldiers had not opened fire at shadows and noises during the night.

In the still cool morning, some of the cavalrymen and infantrymen were sitting around cleaning their weapons for the upcoming attack. An advanced detachment from Troop E began moving across a clearing. In the jungle vegetation on the south side of the clearing, about fifty Japanese troops from Major Harada's 1st Battalion, 239th Infantry, lay in ambush. As the Americans approached, a nervous Japanese machine gunner tripped the ambush too soon. Machine gun fire raked a knoll just below the feet of the surprised E troopers. No Japanese could be seen, but puffs of smoke and rifles were visible in the jungle foliage. The new men stood frozen in amazement that live Japanese could be only twenty meters away, but the 112th veterans ran back into the perimeter and opened fire.

Manning weapons belonging to the 124th Infantry, Cpl. T. D. Clark and Pvt. Jasper Fortney fired into the thicket. Clark used a machine gun, and Fortney fired a 60-mm mortar without a site. About ten meters closer to the Japanese, another E trooper adjusted the mortar fire because he could see movement in the trees. The mortar shells seemed to go straight up to apogee and then plunge back to earth. The firing continued for about thirty minutes, and then the surviving Japanese rushed the Americans, who promptly shot them down.[61]

Troop E searched the bushes for any Japanese survivors. Discovering none, they spearheaded the 3d Battalion's push south. Meantime, the Japanese 3d Battalion, 237th Infantry, attacked the rear of the 3d Battalion, 124th Infantry, temporarily separating it from Troop E. Nevertheless, the cavalrymen pushed slowly south against only occasional sniper fire and contacted Company K, 127th Infantry, at 1245 and then proceeded on to the troop bivouac near Headquarters, 2d Squadron. During their battle, forty-five Japanese infantrymen were killed, including Major Harada. The 112th Cavalry miraculously suffered no casualties. This action of 16 July forced General Adachi to reconsider the forces arrayed against him.

Attrition

7

American resistance and Japanese supply difficulties made Adachi forsake his original plan to destroy the U.S. covering force and then to regroup for a main attack against the Allied defenses near Aitape. He now threw his reserves and available support troops into the battle raging along the Driniumor. Ordering a "temporary suspension" of preparations for an attack against the main American positions, Adachi directed "all available" force be used to strengthen the frontline units engaged with the Americans. Bolstered by these reinforcements, the 41st and 20th divisions would continue their attacks against the estimated five U.S. battalions on or near the Driniumor. The 79th Infantry Regiment would advance simultaneously against Afua from the southeast. A fragmented version of this signal was later available to SWPA via Ultra.[62]

Not privy to the gleanings from Ultra until several days afterward, General Hall at Persecution Task Force Headquarters still did not comprehend that the entire 20th Division was moving on Afua. Hall was, however, thoroughly dissatisfied with General Gill's seeming lack of progress, and he made his feeling explicit in the following message to Gill.[63]

> 16 July 44 0005
> TO: GILL, CG, PCF
>
> FOR EYES OF GENERAL GILL
>
> CAREFUL ANALYSIS OF YOUR SITUATION DISCLOSES AT YOUR DISPOSAL 127, 128(-), 124(-), 112th, SOME TD'S AND ENGINEERS. CONFRONTING YOU WEST OF DRINIUMOR IS AN UNDETERMINED NUMBER OF JAPS BUT CERTAINLY NOT YOUR EQUAL IN EITHER NUMBER OR FIRE POWER. IT APPEARS TO ME THAT WITH THE FORCES AT YOUR DISPOSAL IF THE PROPER OFFENSIVE ACTION IS INSTITUTED AT ONCE YOU SHOULD BE ABLE TO CLEAR THE AREA WEST OF THE DRINIUMOR WITHIN 48 HOURS. TROOP MOVEMENTS HAVE BEEN DELAYED AND I CANNOT PROMISE YOU ANY REINFORCEMENT. I DO NOT ATTEMPT TO TELL YOU WHAT MEASURES TO TAKE TO COUNTER AN OFFENSIVE FROM THE EAST AND AT THE SAME TIME CLEAN UP THE SITUATION WEST OF THE DRINIUMOR. IT CANNOT BE DONE BY DEFENSIVE ACTION. I EXPECT YOU TO TAKE ALL OFFENSIVE MEASURES NOT ONLY TO CLARIFY THE SITUATION BUT TO ERADICATE THE ENEMY WEST OF THE

DRINIUMOR. YOU MUST DO IT WITH YOUR OWN FORCES WHICH ARE CONSIDERED ADEQUATE FOR THE PURPOSE. WE CANNOT WASTE TIME BY DILATORY TACTICS. WHILE ITEM APPRECIATE THAT SOME OF YOUR TROOPS ARE TIRED I KNOW OF NO BATTLE WHICH WAS ENTERED INTO WITH FRESH TROOPS. PLEASE GIVE THIS YOUR PERSONAL ATTENTION AND PUSH IT TO A CONCLUSION IN ORDER THAT INCOMING TROOPS MAY BE USED TO FINISH UP THIS SITUATION OUTSIDE OF YOUR AREA.

HALL

Hall's directive must be understood in a strategic rather than a tactical context. In late spring 1944, Washington planners reconsidered the idea of bypassing the Philippines in favor of an attack against Formosa. The Combined Chiefs conference in London in early June endorsed the Formosa plan, and a JCS notification to MacArthur on 12 June stated that in order to expedite the Pacific Campaign, "presently selected objectives" (read Philippines) would be bypassed in favor of an invasion of Formosa. MacArthur attempted to rebut the JCS note in an 18 June message, but by this time General George C. Marshall also was leaning toward the Formosa plan. Nevertheless, MacArthur had his plan to retake the Philippines ready by 10 July, and this was the strategy he tried "to sell" to President Franklin D. Roosevelt when they met in Hawaii from 26 to 29 July. In this light, it seems logical that MacArthur was pressuring his subordinates to conclude the Aitape campaign rapidly in order to demonstrate the efficacy of his strategic concepts and thereby win presidential endorsement for his Philippine plan. Strategic decision making directly influenced the tactical conduct of the Aitape fighting and, in large measure, accounts for the enormous pressure from above that General Gill described. Tactics, however, did not exert a reciprocal influence on strategy, because Gill could not finish the campaign in forty-eight hours. Nor did the Hawaii meeting clarify U.S. Pacific strategy to the degree MacArthur desired.[64]

The immediate impact on the 112th was that Gill rejected General Cunningham's plea for an additional rifle battalion. Higher headquarters' apparently cavalier disapproval infuriated Cunningham, who compensated by shortening his line, bending his south flank back from the Driniumor along the Afua-Palauru trail, and stationing Troop A on the high ground guarding the western extremity of his new position.[65]

He was convinced that a numerically superior enemy force was outflanking the regiment from the south. He also had unsettling reports of Japanese troops to his west and northwest, where a Japanese roadblock prevented overland resupply at River X, and was uncertain about his routes of withdrawal, should the necessity arise. For all Cunningham knew, the 112th Cavalry might already be surrounded. The men could only dig deeper, improve their defensive positions, and distribute ammunition dropped by plane. Their fate had become intertwined with that of the Japanese soldiers in Miyake Force, who spent 17 July slowly maneuvering into their assembly areas north and northwest of Afua for the attack on the 112th Cavalry.

Area of the 112th Cavalry command post, showing rugged conditions at Aitape.

Miyake's screening patrols were in position by daybreak on 18 July. Shortly afterward, one of these patrols, operating about one mile west of Afua, ambushed a squad-size 112th Cavalry patrol that was reconnoitering the trail to River X. A point-blank burst of machine gun fire killed one cavalryman and scattered the Americans, who ran for cover in the jungle. Two or three Japanese light machine guns peppered the cavalrymen, but their officer had made radio contact with Troop A, which sent reinforcements. The Americans pinpointed the Japanese ambush positions and called for artillery and mortar fire. After the high explosives saturated the Japanese-held jungle, wrecking trees and cratering the area, Troop A assaulted the Japanese positions and killed six of the enemy. The remaining Japanese had already escaped east and north into the jungle. At the other end of the trail near River X, a detachment of cavalrymen proceeded only 400 meters before stumbling into a Japanese screen. This time it was the cavalrymen who gave up the fight first and made their way back to River X and safety. These patrol clashes pointed to the possibility of a Japanese attack. Indeed the Americans were jittery, and there was a report (later proven false) that General Cunningham's command post was under attack. In spite of the indicators, the direction of the main Japanese attack caught the 112th Cavalry by complete surprise.

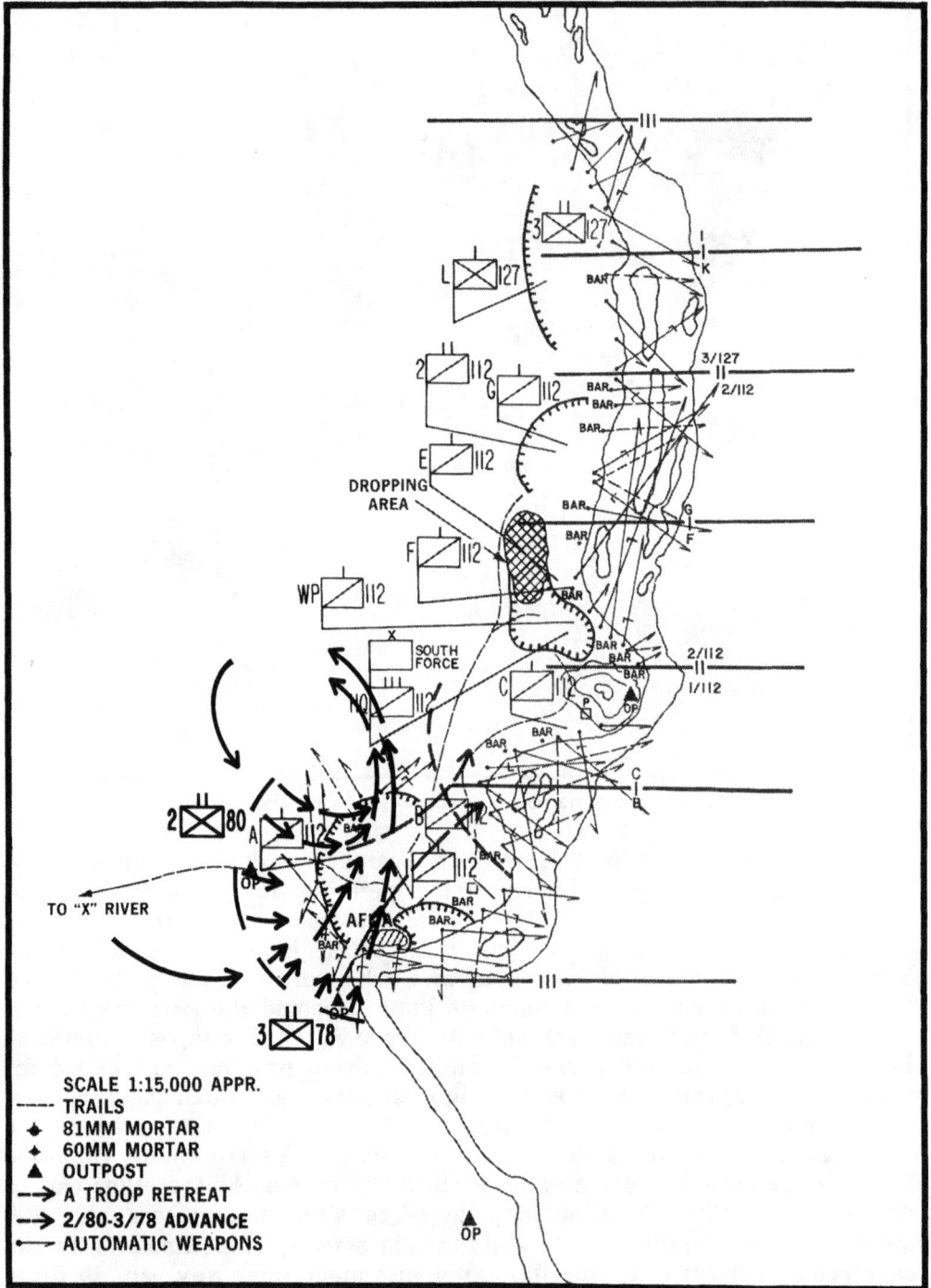

Map 22. Japanese attack against Afua, 18 July 1944

Cpl. Charles C. Brabham was settling into his nighttime defensive position, under a log on the Driniumor bank facing south. It was just before dusk, and having secured the perimeter and strung tin cans on the barbed wire for a crude early warning system, several men were bathing in the river. Suddenly a machine gun roared, and Japanese soldiers in skirmish line formation emerged from the jungle, walking and firing into Troop A's perimeter from the south and west (see map 22). The 112th Cavalry was being attacked from the rear in strength. Pfc. Walter Stocks, a rifleman, was sheltered in a bomb crater that served as an outpost. He recalled, "One shot was fired and everything broke loose. Japanese fighting patrols, ten here, ten there, spreading out to flank. I called for artillery." His machine gunner dropped down into the crater, stunned by a Japanese bullet that creased his skull. The few other Americans in the crater fought back, and Stocks himself ducked into the crater with the wounded gunner, but still traversed the machine gun back and forth with one hand, spraying bullets at the menacing Japanese foot soldiers. A bullet hit Stocks in the hand. When a white phosphorus grenade exploded, the men in the outpost used the diversion to clear out with their wounded back to the main force.[66]

All the men in 1st Squadron knew was that machine guns and mortars were blasting away behind them. Troop A took the brunt of the assault conducted by the Japanese 3d Battalion, 78th Infantry, and 2d Battalion, 80th Infantry. Despite heavy losses attacking across the Driniumor on 10—11 July and despite being out of supply and usually out of communication with other Japanese formations for the next week, the Japanese fought fanatically. The infantrymen were undernourished and exposed to torrential rain, mosquitoes, and insects. These particular troops had not eaten since the previous day and had been reduced to living on grass or tree bark.[67] They were weary, and their uniforms were becoming ragged. They had seen and felt the death or mutilation of hundreds of their comrades. But when ordered to attack, they advanced. It seemed the sheer desperation of their condition served to drive their attacks forward.

For two hours the struggle raged. A few men here and there appeared briefly out of the jungle or over the lip of bomb craters to fire several hurried shots at real or imaginary enemies. Intermittent showers and darkness compounded the confusion, but the Japanese capitalized on their initial surprise and forced the shaken troopers back about 300 meters to the north. Troop A used communications wire to guide its retreat. Like the ball of yarn that enabled Theseus to escape the Labyrinth, the communications wire became a lifeline that guided the cavalrymen and their sixteen wounded comrades to safety in the featureless black maze. Two cavalrymen had been killed.

With Troop A driven back, Troop B called in its upriver outpost, pulled its southernmost platoon from the Driniumor, and moved it southwest to protect Troop B's south and rear. Meantime, the Japanese moved northeast to their reassembly areas in order to reorganize after the attack. With the cavalrymen retreating northwest and the Japanese regrouping northeast, contact between the combatants was severed. Nonetheless, the 112th Cavalry spent an edgy night, as illustrated by the fate of a courier who was making his way to Troop B around midnight. The officer stumbled into a 112th Cavalry foxhole. Presuming he was Japanese, its occupants instinctively attacked and seriously wounded the lieutenant. In the middle of this confusion, General Cunningham had to sort out Troop A, reinforce it, and plan a dawn counterattack to retake the lost ground.

He used a platoon from Troop E, an antitank platoon of Headquarters Troop, and one rifle platoon from the 3d Battalion, 127th Infantry, to counterattack at 0700 on 19 July and retake Troop A's former sector. The attackers encountered almost no Japanese resistance and regained their previous day's positions. Patrols reported, however, that numerous small parties of Japanese troops were moving nearby in the jungle thicket. General Miyake had again rallied his decimated troops for a daylight attack against the Americans. The opposing forces blundered into each other on the west side of Troop A's positions. The men of the 3d Battalion, 78th Infantry, had set up heavy machine guns in thick vegetation across a creek to the west and provided themselves enfilading fire with machine guns firing from a swampy area to the south. The cavalrymen unwittingly walked into this ambush, suffered losses, and pulled back to await artillery support. The Japanese did not take advantage of the delay to redisposition themselves or to move against the Americans, perhaps because they thought help was on the way from the northwest. Indeed, Japanese small arms fire was coming from that direction, but the elements were, at most, squad size. During the "considerable time" lost in coordinating American artillery fire, a platoon leader in Troop E, 2d Lt. Dale E. Christensen, ordered his men to stay under cover while he crawled forward through the jungle undergrowth to pinpoint the Japanese automatic weapons and to find a possible avenue of attack. Although Japanese small arms fire hit his rifle and knocked it from his hands, Christensen crept on until he found the machine guns. He used hand grenades to destroy one Japanese machine gun and kill its crew, after which he returned to his men. Finally, American artillery began exploding among the Japanese positions, although the long-delayed barrage prevented the Americans from attacking until 1400. At that time, Christensen took his men to the point he had previously reconnoitered for the attack and led their charge against the dazed surviving Japanese.* Those Japanese who still could, fled into the jungle. The cavalrymen killed any Japanese wounded. This was the worst day of fighting so far for the 112th Cavalry. They had lost six men killed and twenty-nine wounded, mostly to Japanese small arms fire. Colonel Miller's personal count of Japanese corpses totaled 139. It had been a grim struggle, because the firm wills of their respective commanders had determined that both sides were to stand and fight, a rare occurrence in the tropical rain forest.

For these and earlier actions, Christensen would be awarded the Medal of Honor.

By late afternoon, Troop A had reestablished its original positions. There was no time to pause for congratulations. Tired and frightened men had to perform the most menial of tasks, such as burning the excrement in Japanese field latrines, which they rightly regarded as a source of possible disease. Litter teams carried out the wounded and the dead. Aside from the enormous physical energy required to carry a litter in the tropical heat and high humidity, the unarmed parties worked in constant peril of imminent deadly attack. The morning of 19 July, for example, four litter bearers of the 107th Collecting Company were combing the bush just north and behind Troop G's lines for American casualties. Suddenly, crashing through the bush, came a sword-waving Japanese officer or senior NCO who fatally slashed one litter bearer. Death or maiming from accidents also increased as the cumulative fatigue dulled the men's senses. Infantrymen were killed in accidents, like the one crushed to death when a C-47 dropped free-fall rations and overshot the drop zone. In the middle of intentional mayhem, such absurd accidents were especially cruel blows.

Combat on 18 and 19 July had almost destroyed the already decimated Miyake Force. Small groups of Japanese troops cut off in the daylight fighting tried to use the cover of darkness and heavy rains to recross the Driniumor to the east. One group of fifteen Japanese stragglers used its last mortar rounds, grenades, and light machine gun ammunition in a surprise attack to break through the north flank of the 3d Battalion, 127th Infantry, from the rear. One Japanese was shot to death in the attempt. The others made it through and left in their wake two dead and five wounded Americans. In the jungle the opponents were so intermingled within each other's formations that mortal enemies could be almost within arm's length of each other, yet remain unaware of the proximity. The conditions were at that moment worsening.

The Americans and Japanese near Afua doggedly regrouped on 20 July. Miyake Force's battered regiments, now reduced to company strength, finally received reinforcements when the 79th Regiment, 700 strong, along with a sixty-man mountain artillery company possessing a single gun, joined forces with General Miyake south of Afua. Additional men and supplies were also on their way. On 19 July, General Adachi, at 18th Army Headquarters, originally had ordered the 66th Infantry to attack near Kawanakajima in order to cover the north flank of the 20th Division. When he learned the actual extent of the 20th Division's losses, he canceled the attack order for the 66th Regiment and instead employed those troops as bearers to haul supplies to General Miyake's desperate troops.[68] Miyake meantime coordinated his attack plans with Lieutenant General Nakai, who had moved 20th Division headquarters forward together with the 79th Infantry. At the same time, General Cunningham and the 112th Cavalry prepared their defenses to stop another Japanese thrust. He switched the battered Troop A from its ostensibly "reserve" position and substituted Troop C on the drawn-up right flank. Troop C occupied a place the Japanese called Tsuru. The entire 79th Infantry would attack Tsuru at 1600 that day.

Forty-five minutes after the scheduled H-Hour, the 79th Infantry's lone mountain gun barked as the first of the eight rounds it would fire smashed into Troop C's perimeter (see map 23). The Japanese had manhandled the gun in pieces through the foliage to within 300 meters of the American defenses. One 112th Cavalry veteran remembered his fear as he listened to the Japanese out in the jungle setting up the gun and hammering aiming stakes into the ground. The Japanese fired at point-blank range, aiming at the distinctive headquarters tent. One shell explosion wiped out all tactical command by wounding the commanding officer, 1st Squadron, the commander, Troop C, and an artillery liaison officer. Even before their mountain gun stopped firing, Japanese infantrymen were closing on Troop C.

Any firefight is initially a confused melee, but this one was especially so. Just before the Japanese attack, an American observation plane circling overhead dropped a message to Troop C that U.S. troops were in front of C's lines. That mistake permitted the Japanese infantrymen to walk into Troop C's perimeter. The cavalrymen were reluctant to fire, not wanting to kill fellow Americans. The pilot's error was excusable, because to compound the chaos, many Japanese soldiers wore American ponchos draped over their shoulders as well as other items of American equipment. The Americans themselves were dirty and grimy after more than three weeks on the line, making it impossible to distinguish friend from foe more than a few yards away. It was literally face-to-face combat. One Troop C NCO said, "Unless you looked them in the face you didn't know whether they were enemy or not." A Japanese infantryman walked right up to this same American sergeant, who shot at him and missed. The Japanese soldier then dived into the high, above-ground roots of a mangrove tree, and an American machine gunner loosed a short burst of fire that killed him.[69]

The 79th Infantry apparently assumed that Afua had already been secured, for the Japanese just walked right into Troop C's defenses without firing. Neither group did anything to alarm the other. Both sides had the impression that they were meeting friends. Once heavy firing broke that spell, the Japanese spread out, fanlike, and encircled Troop C. The Japanese attack struck from the south to force its way between Troops C and B. They had initial success, driving back Troop C, mainly because of American communication difficulties that had caused a forty-five-minute delay in delivery of preregistered artillery fire. Once the artillery began to explode and the cavalrymen recovered from their surprise, the men of the 79th Infantry, who had wedged themselves into the U.S. defenses, found themselves, in turn, surrounded by the Americans. Shortly afterward, the remnants of General Miyake's forces attacked Troop C from the west and again isolated the Americans from their regiment.

Maj. Takada Sajuro, a 20th Division staff officer, was just then trying to contact Miyake's forces, whose headquarters were in deep jungle. Even there, enemy shells were screaming overhead or exploding randomly. Everything was in disarray. Takada searched for the 78th Infantry commander,

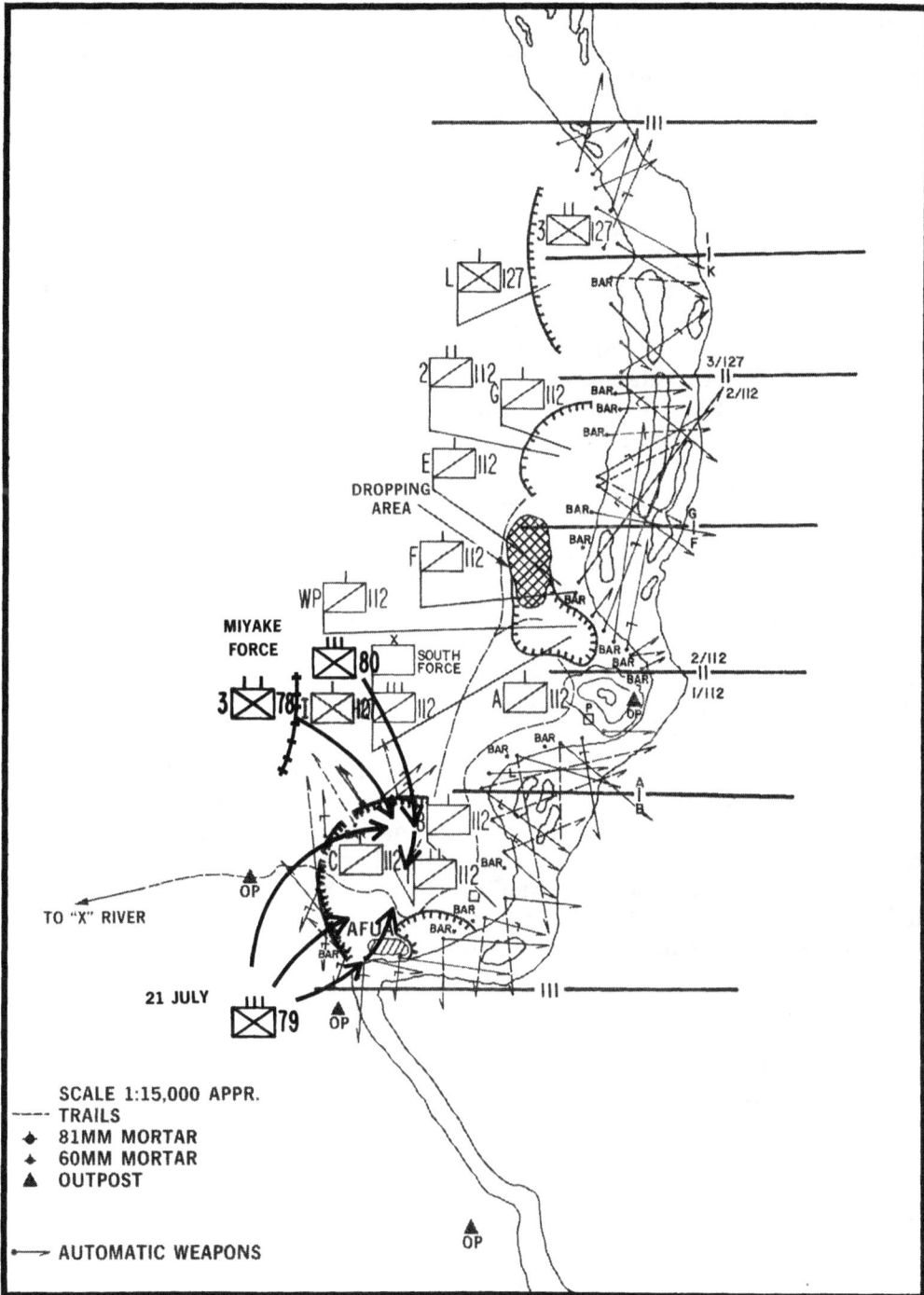

Map 23. Encirclement of Troop C, 21 July 1944

whom he found wounded and sitting cross-legged under a tree, clutching the regimental colors. Takada could hear gunfire reports all around, but because of the jungle veil could not tell its precise direction. His overriding feeling was that everything was messed up. He thought in sorrow of the troops who had to watch helplessly while the enemy flew in transport aircraft to airdrop supplies, while Japanese had only rainwater to drink. His reverie was broken when several wounded Japanese infantrymen stumbled or were carried past him into the regimental headquarters. Takada felt the agony the frontline commanders were going through because they had been ordered to accomplish a mission that was beyond their means.[70] Whatever those officers privately thought, they led their troops with fanatical courage. The American artillery bombardment finally broke up the Japanese attackers, who took refuge in small groups scattered along the fringes of the jungle. The Japanese attack to roll up the 112th's south flank had failed, but it had managed to surround Troop C.

Troop C suffered fifteen casualties, including at least two dead. Early in the fighting, a few of the wounded from the Troop C sector managed to make their way back to the squadron headquarters, where they reported that two platoons of Company I, 127th Infantry, also had been pushed into Troop C's perimeter by Japanese troops attacking from the north. The wounded men also stated that they believed enemy casualties were very high, mainly because of the effectiveness of friendly artillery fire. That observed fire, though, lasted only until about 1900, when Japanese soldiers cut the 112th's communications lines, after which the artillerymen had to resort to blind interdictory fire throughout the night. The Japanese used the cover of darkness to probe Troop C's defenses, mainly by fire with small arms and automatic weapons fire, and an occasional mortar round. Both sides had probably spent themselves, but neither would acknowledge it. The fighting continued spasmodically throughout the night as Japanese infantrymen sneaking close to the cavalrymen's perimeter would shoot at anyone careless enough to show himself in the moonlight.

The troopers of C and infantrymen of Company I resorted to a circle perimeter about 150 meters wide, where about one hundred Americans faced perhaps four or five times that number of Japanese. About 275 meters separated them from their 1st Squadron, but in the isolation of the jungle thicket, it could well have been 275 kilometers. Troop C was cut off and alone. Their Japanese tormentors, however, were also disorganized during their attack and subsequent night fighting. They, too, had to reassemble in intermittent rainshowers and deadly American artillery. So the Japanese laid ambushes on the trails leading to Afua and sent squad-size units crawling forward to test the American defenders' resolve.

At the 112th Cavalry command post, preparations to break the Japanese siege and to rescue Troop C were already underway. Troop B had started to move from Afua the previous night, but the combination of darkness and Japanese infantrymen from the 79th Infantry along the trail barred the Americans' way. Early on the morning of 22 July several American patrols from the 112th and 127th Infantry tried to reestablish contact with Troop C. Each in turn hit a Japanese ambush and fell back, unable to locate precisely Troop C. Gunfire reports to the south added to the uncertainty, for no one knew if it came from Troop C, from American patrols trying to reach C, or from a 112th patrol operating in the area. A spotter aircraft pilot reported only Japanese soldiers at the suspected location, because when the plane flew over, the men on the ground all ran for cover. To attack unprepared was better than to wait for all possible information, which might arrive too late to prevent the destruction of Troop C. So around 1300, Troop E began its attack with about sixty men (see map 24).

Troop E passed through Troop B's sector and then moved southwest into the jungle. Suddenly prolonged bursts of small arms fire hit Troop E from the front and flanks. Without warning, a booby-trapped American bomb exploded in Troop E's midst as the men scurried for safety. When the dust settled after the explosion, one cavalryman was dead, the three others maimed. Still under enemy fire and suffering losses, the troop commander received permission from headquarters to withdraw. The men were badly shaken, and General Cunningham sent them to the vicinity of the dropping ground, a relatively quiet sector just then, to regroup.

Elsewhere a similar story trickled back to headquarters. A wire party of twelve men managed to reach to within 300 meters of suspected Troop C positions, where a Japanese trail block prevented any further advance. Two Americans fell wounded, and both sides escalated the fight. First, about twenty men of Company I went to reinforce the ambushed communications party in hopes of pushing through to Troop C. They deployed a firing line, attacked the Japanese, pushed them back perhaps one hundred meters, but then encountered Japanese reinforcements. Thinking an imminent break-through to Troop C was possible if just a bit more pressure were applied, General Cunningham sent a captain and three enlisted troops from Head-quarters Troop and a lieutenant with twenty men from the mortar platoon to lend support. These cavalrymen, however, stumbled into a Japanese am-bush before reaching the advance party. Japanese automatic weapons operators and riflemen shot down both American officers in the first seconds of the fight. That was enough for the rest of the patrol, which returned to headquarters carrying their wounded officers with them. They claimed to have killed four Japanese in the short, bitter firefight. Lacking reinforcements, fighting against determined Japanese resistance, and with night approaching, the advance wire party and Company I men also pulled back to protect the rear of General Cunningham's command post for the night. It had been a frustrating day for the Americans.

It was even more so within the small Troop C perimeter, because the cavalrymen could do little to help themselves. Japanese snipers had climbed nearby trees and fired down at anything that moved. Anyone standing up was a potential target, and the tension was enormous. Any movement was

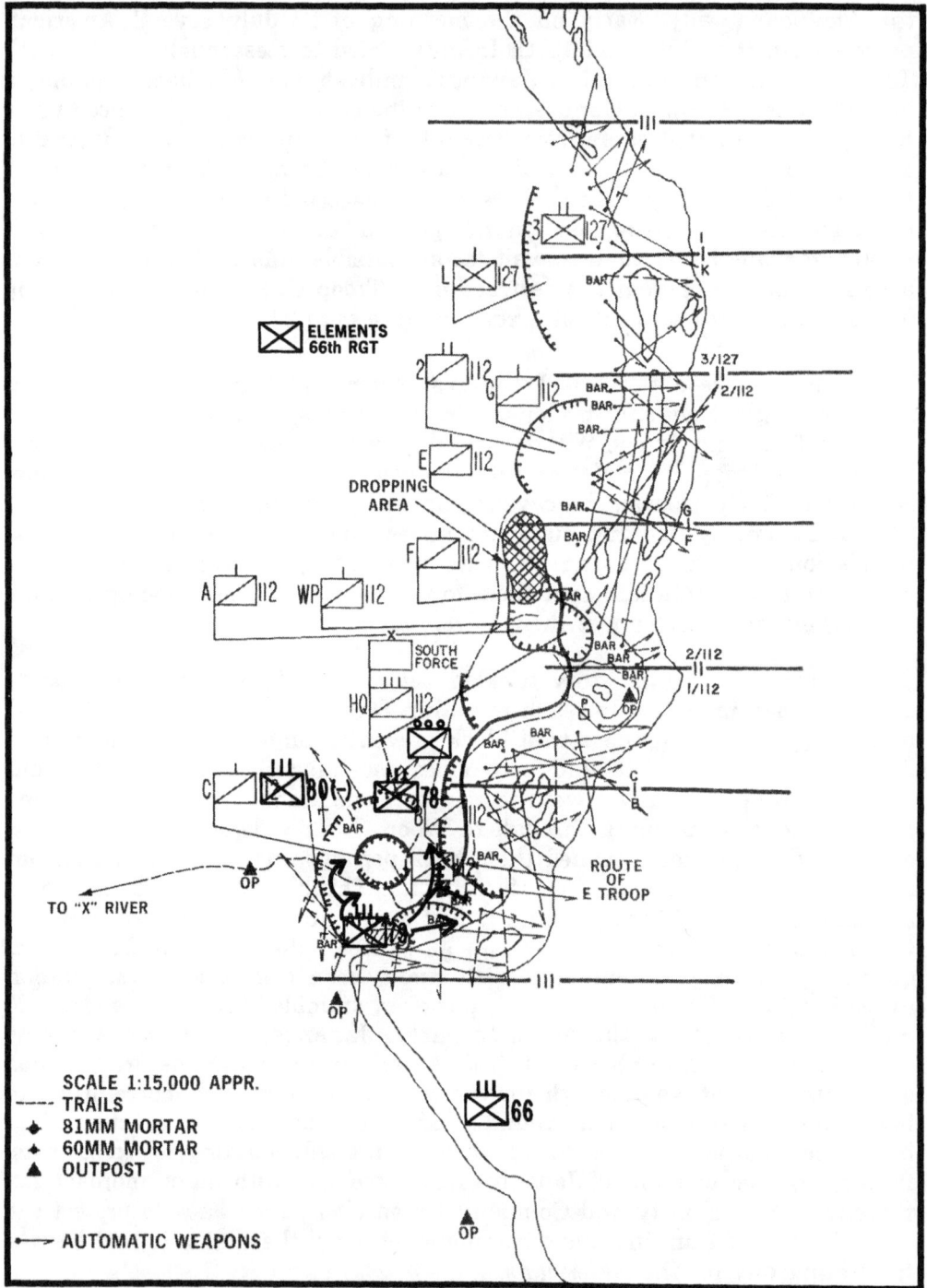

SCALE 1:15,000 APPR.
----- TRAILS
◆ 81MM MORTAR
♣ 60MM MORTAR
▲ OUTPOST

•——→ AUTOMATIC WEAPONS

Map 24. Attempted relief of Troop C, 23 July 1944

dangerous because Japanese infantrymen less than fifty meters away could fire into the tightly packed perimeter. Furthermore, a slough filled with old logs and other debris from previous flash floods ran into the perimeter. This slough provided the Japanese excellent cover to crawl closer and closer to Troop C's lines. All the cavalrymen could do was fight back, tend their wounded, and, under cover of darkness, bury their five dead. According to veterans of that fight, they really did not expect any relief. They understood that the regiment might be simultaneously fighting for its life and that their situation, though desperate, was not unique. Beyond that, they could depend on one another. "You knew the guy that had been back there. You trusted him. You knew if you needed him he was there." That confidence, buoyed by the fight for self-preservation, and an infantryman's fatalism, expressed as "You lived from day to day and accepted it as a way of life," gave them the will to resist and endure. Similar emotions probably provided the same impetus to Japanese soldiers. So Troop C fought on alone against the Japanese, completely out of contact with other American units, yet only a few hundred meters away.[71]

Following the failure of the first day's efforts to rescue Troop C, the commanding officer of the 127th Infantry and assistant operations officer (G-3), 32d Division, arrived at the 112th's command post at 1800 for a council of war with General Cunningham. Their original plan called for the 127th Infantry to rescue Troop C and to relieve the 112th Cavalry. The 112th would then establish positions along the Afua-Palauru track, halfway between the Driniumor and River X, to cover the area south to the Torricelli Range and to act as a general reserve for the covering force. These orders were never executed, for between the time the orders were written and the time they were passed, the battlefield situation had changed. It seemed clear that the major Japanese attack was directed against the heart of the 112th's defense around Afua. The 112th could not be relieved unless General Hall chose to abandon his entire south flank.

Since there had been no contact with Troop C for the past two days, no one was certain that it still existed. Even if the men were alive, no one knew exactly where they were. On the morning of 23 July, a pilot erroneously reported "a large group of Americans" 700 meters southwest of Afua. All that the combat patrols found was a Japanese machine gun nest, which they destroyed. Shortly after noon, the same pilot made amends by discovering Troop C's location. He was sure this time because some of the men were without shirts and he could easily recognize their white skin in the clearing. The Americans also detonated a white phosphorus grenade and waved a white flag to signal the airmen that they were still alive. Now that they had been located, they had to be rescued.

The rescue attack started at 1600. The two-pronged American attack had Troops A and B, with a platoon of Troop E in support, attacking to the east, while the 2d Battalion, 127th Infantry, attacked from the west (see map 25). About one hour later the cavalrymen had reached about 185 meters from Troop C, but were meeting increasing Japanese resistance.

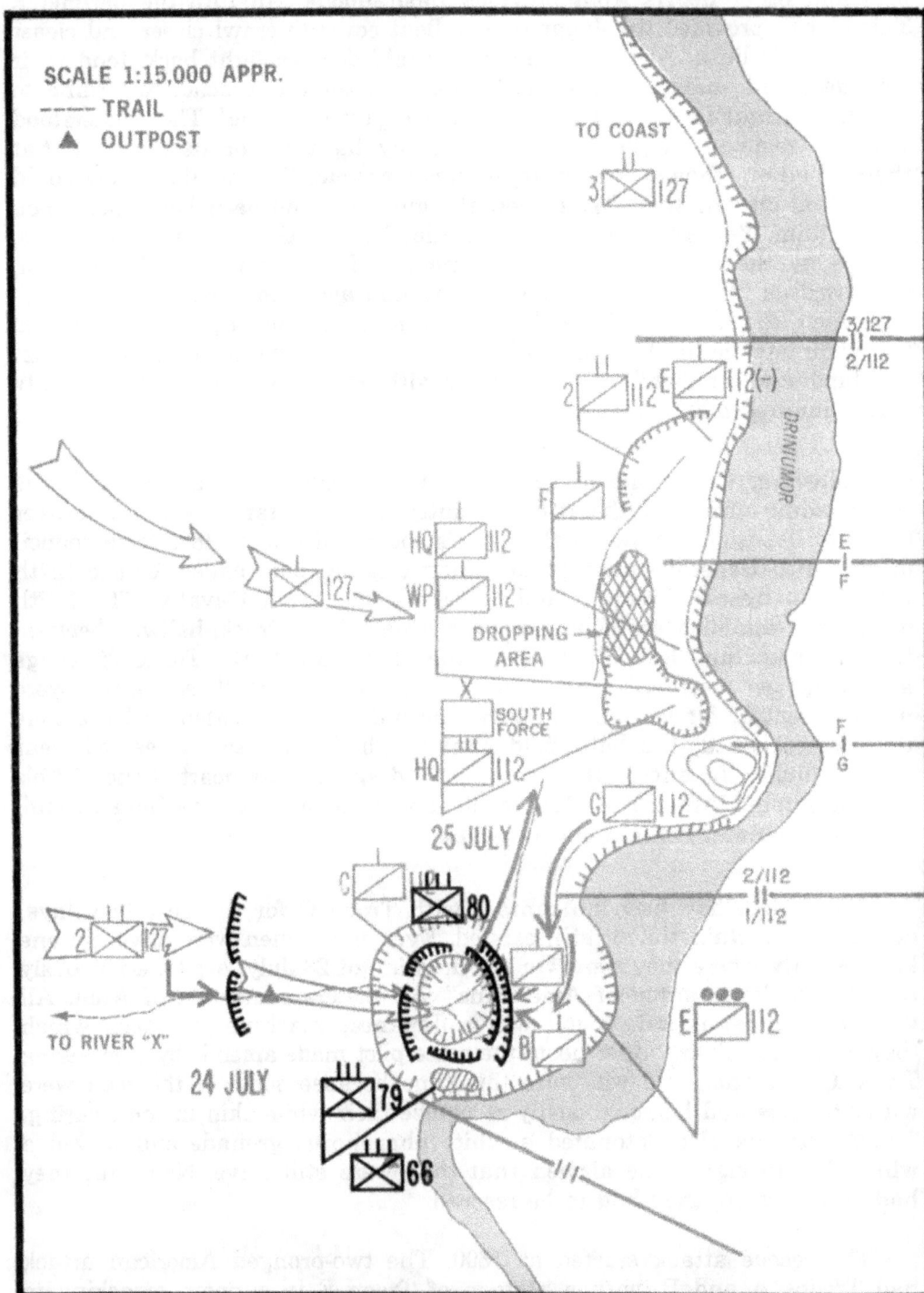

Map 25. Relief of Troop C, 24—25 July 1944

The two advance American platoons deployed and built a firing line. Orders were for Lieutenant Boyce and his platoon to attack the Japanese left flank. They attacked, but could gain only a few meters before heavy Japanese small arms and mortar fire forced the men to crawl to cover. Boyce saw a slough that seemed to offer an avenue of approach against the enemy position. He led his squad into it in column formation. Japanese soldiers defending the shallow depression heaved several hand grenades from above onto the advancing Americans. One grenade landed between the lieutenant and his men. Boyce threw himself on the grenade and smothered the blast with his own body.* That heroic action ended the 112th's attack for the day. A corporal threw a smoke grenade to mark the area for 60-mm mortar fire to cover their withdrawal. They had lost, besides Boyce, one NCO killed and six wounded. The 2d Battalion's attack also had pushed westward, and they were fighting for control of a ridge just west of and overlooking Troop C's positions. As both American units were advancing toward each other, the 112th troops were ordered to withdraw to Afua to preclude the distinct possibility of mistakenly firing on each other. The day's fighting had partially lifted the siege by rooting out Japanese of the 79th Infantry from their roadblocks, thus allowing 2d Battalion to reach Troop C's perimeter just before darkness.

Although the Japanese trail blocks had been broken, small bands of Japanese soldiers continued to fight near Troop C's positions. Even with the added strength of the 2d Battalion, the Japanese refused to release their grip on Troop C. That afternoon, for instance, Troop C tried to break out, carrying its litter cases, but Japanese small arms fire drove the men back. Nevertheless, the cumulative effects of a prolonged battle of attrition were grinding down the Japanese defenders, and Troop C would be able to reach the 112th Headquarters command post by 1000 on 25 July. Instead of the expected mopping up exercise, bitter fighting characterized the day. Cavalrymen fought brief skirmishes with Japanese patrols, probably the screens for 20th Division Headquarters, then moving south of Afua. The day's fighting left commanders on both sides dissatisfied.

Major General Gill, Persecution Covering Force commander, expressed to General Cunningham his "inability to understand slowness in the clearing situation."[72] Gill believed that the 112th was fighting only the Japanese 78th Infantry, but General Cunningham insisted that at least two Japanese regiments, the 78th and 80th, were pressing his troops. Both men were wrong, but they could not know it. The entire 20th Division had arrayed itself against Afua, and according to Japanese sources, by midnight of 25 July at least 2,000 Japanese were to the right (south) and rear (west) of South Force.[73]

General Adachi at Headquarters, 41st Division, learned that the Americans were continuing to strengthen their Driniumor defenses, that the 20th Division's attack against Afua apparently had not gone well, and that the

---

*His actions earned Lieutenant Boyce a posthumously awarded Medal of Honor.

41st Division was preparing its assault near Kawanakajima for 27 July.[74] Morale, he found, was excellent in the 41st Division—junior officers were encouraging each other as they were briefed on the plan of attack. Then the division commander, Lt. Gen. Mano Goro, summoned the small unit leaders to assemble before him. He abruptly announced to his collected officers that the 27 July attack had been canceled and that the division instead would move immediately to Afua. Nothing more was said as the general walked out. After ten days of planning for the 27 July operation, the subalterns wondered aloud why the attack suddenly had been canceled. A persistent speculation was that the 20th Division had lost the "guts" to cross the Driniumor and that the 41st Division was being sent to Afua to do its dirty work.[75] The officers of the 41st Division dismissed the enemy at Afua as decidedly inferior to the Americans they had been fighting near Kawanakajima and so convinced themselves that a frontal attack, brutally delivered, would smash the U.S. units near Afua once and for all. Such contempt for, and underestimation of, their enemies at Afua ultimately would destroy the 41st Division.

Despite the emotional outbursts by 41st Division officers, General Adachi had ordered General Mano to cancel the attack for several reasons. First, the 20th Division was nearly worn out from continual jungle combat, and Adachi realized the Japanese could not turn the Americans' flank without reinforcements. Second, even the strongest Japanese unit, the 237th Infantry, 41st Division, was unable to crack the strong American defenses near Kawanakajima. The solution was to combine the 41st and 20th divisions for a concerted attack on Afua. This concentration of Japanese forces would thereby improve chances of defeating the Americans in detail. Once again Japanese troops swung south towards Afua, though this time they approached on the Driniumor's east bank.

For the cavalrymen around Afua, 25 July just brought more heavy showers. The rain had begun about dusk the previous evening and had poured uninterrupted throughout the night. Soaked and shivering, the men huddled in their holes until the first gray light. They ate in the pouring rain. Patrols departed, but soon reported back that high water in previously near-dry streams made crossing impossible. About mid-morning the storm passed, and the sun appeared as if to greet the men of Troop C, who were just then making their way into the regimental command post area. There was little time for congratulations, because the fighting in the steamy jungle mist near Afua continued on and off throughout the day.

General Cunningham ordered his troopers to push south and west to dislodge Japanese infantrymen who he assumed were holding the high ground southwest of Afua. General Adachi ordered his infantrymen to attack north and west to wrest Afua from the Americans and to seize Hill 56. Thus the 112th Cavalry and the 79th Infantry both believed that they were attacking the other's defensive positions. In fact, they were attacking the same ridgeline. The close vegetation, deep jungle, and broken terrain limited visibility, so neither side knew the other's precise location until someone blundered into an opposing unit. A typical example of a firefight characteristic of the next three days might be as follows:

A Japanese advance patrol, usually four or five riflemen and a light machine gun team, picked its way single file through the undergrowth. When they encountered an American patrol, gunfire might be exchanged, but more likely both patrols would scatter into the thick, tangled vegetation and redeploy in its cover. The Japanese riflemen would disperse to cover the flanks of their machine gunner. The Americans would bring forward automatic weapons to build up their firing line as they called for artillery or tried to outflank the Japanese. If the American artillery fire and movement were successful, the Japanese would flee, and the cavalrymen would move cautiously to finish off wounded Japanese. If the Japanese infantry proved too strong to expel, the Americans would withdraw, carrying their wounded and dragging their dead. As often as not, on first sight of each other, both sides would flee into the safety of the jungle.

Occasionally a single determined soldier could hold up ten or even one hundred men, as was the case during the 112th's 25 July drive against a nameless ridge. There a lone Japanese machine gunner blocked the advance of the center of the 112th's line. The cavalrymen had to deploy and work around the solitary gunner, thus precluding the use of friendly artillery to blast the hill.[76] It was hard, slow, nerve-wracking combat, not at all glamorous, but exceedingly deadly, as fire was often exchanged at ranges of five meters or less. Robert Ross Smith described the nature of the fighting:

> Each side complained that the other held isolated strong points, none of which appeared to be key positions. Both sides employed inaccurate maps, and both had a great deal of difficulty obtaining effective reconnaissance. In the jungled, broken terrain near Afua, operations frequently took a vague form, a sort of shadow boxing in which physical contact of the opposing sides was oft times accidental.[77]

If such horrible circumstances may be described as "routine," then 25 July was routine for the cavalrymen until 1800, when two American 155-mm rounds exploded in Troops A and B's command post area. Excited, hurried calls from the forward observer stopped the artillery shooting, but five more Americans lay wounded, victims of an accident. Likewise, a few hours earlier another unlucky cavalryman thrashing around in the bush was mistakenly shot by his own men. As an aid man tended to his gunshot wounds, a Japanese soldier appeared from the bush to hurl a hand grenade at the medic. The grenade did not detonate, and the enraged aid man turned on the Japanese and killed him. Both American and Japanese soldiers were, in a sense, the victims of bad luck.

On 26 July a light rain and overcast sky added to the problem of identifying fleeting shadows in the jungle. The Japanese took advantage of the morning mist and fog to mask the location of a battalion artillery piece, which fired several rounds that exploded near General Cunningham's command post. The fragmented small unit fighting flickered on and off in the rain near Afua. Most of the 112th's day was spent adjusting its defensive perimeter. The 1st Battalion, 127th Infantry, took positions west of the supply drop zone to cover the rear of the 112th's defenses. The battalion's left flank connected with the cavalrymen's mortar platoon, which, in turn, tied into Troop F on the Driniumor. The 2d Battalion, 127th Infantry, established a line on high ground, tying into Troop E on the left, but exposed on the right. The perimeter resembled a large semicircle facing south and west.

Meanwhile, small units maneuvered and countermaneuvered in search of each other. On 27 July, for example, Troop A and the 2d Battalion, 127th Infantry, attacked a suspected Japanese command post. American artillery cratered the area, so marching through the rain-filled pockmarks left everyone mud-soaked. The men met only scattered sniper fire. They reached the alleged location of the command post, found nothing, and continued to push another several hundred meters southwest, again discovering no enemy soldiers. No one knew whether their "attack" had succeeded or not. All the Americans could do was return to their original positions, thankful no determined Japanese had lurked in the jungle along their route. Farther north, however, there was renewed Japanese activity.

That morning U.S. patrols observed an estimated two companies of Japanese digging in astride the trail from the drop zone to Afua, in effect cutting the resupply link to the cavalrymen near Afua. A hastily organized attack by a platoon of Troop E and a platoon from Company A, 127th Infantry, supported by the cavalrymen's mortar platoon, drove off the Japanese. The mortar crews fired heavy concentrations in support of the foot soldiers. Most of the thirty-five Japanese killed that day fell to mortar fire. Five Americans were killed and six were wounded in the afternoon-long engagement.

The Japanese retreated about 135 meters, which sufficed to keep the vital drop zone-Afua artery open. Cavalrymen searched through the pockets and clothing of the abandoned Japanese corpses and discovered documents and personal identification associating the dead with the 66th Infantry, the first appearance at Afua to date of that unit.*

The fighting then slackened off in the 112th Cavalry's sector. Allied intelligence interpreted the scattered contacts as evidence that 18th Army's excessive casualties and lack of resupply spelled the end of its offensive. Consequently, U.S. analysts reasoned that the Japanese probably had begun to withdraw from the Afua area.[78] Generals Adachi and Hall, however, were

---

*The presence of 66th Regiment elements in this area was probably due to the necessity of using combat troops to serve as bearers to manhandle supplies to Miyake Force. The maneuver elements of the 66th Regiment were operating southwest of this location. According to a Japanese POW captured on 28 July, about fifty infantrymen from the 66th Regiment had been converted to ration bearers.

simultaneously preparing operational plans for what they believed would be the decisive battle of the campaign. Neither general's scheme would come to fruition.

General Hall at XI Corps Headquarters on 29 July decided to counterattack 18th Army. Two days later, three U.S. infantry battalions would attack on line from the coast to about 2,300 meters inland. At Niumen Creek, about 2,700 meters to the east, the battalions would turn south to envelop the Japanese still fighting around Afua.[79] Hall's preoccupation with his major counterattack probably resulted in less pressure on General Gill, Persecution Covering Force commander, to "mop up" Japanese resistance south of Afua. Gill, in turn, reluctantly agreed to General Cunningham's requests to reduce offensive operations in order to shorten his line to the north.

Cunningham spent 28 through 31 July redeploying his forces, strengthening his new defensive perimeter, and sending out reconnaissance patrols to provide information on the suddenly elusive Japanese. The gradual, if unavoidable, erosion of the combat units' fighting strength from battle casualties, accidents, and disease necessitated the redeployment. From 13 to 31 July, the 112th Cavalry had suffered 260 battle casualties, 17 percent of its understrength total. All told, South Force (2d and 3d battalions, 127th Infantry Regiment, and the 112th Cavalry Regiment) had lost 106 killed, 386 wounded, 18 missing, and 426 evacuated because of disease or illness.[80] The Americans estimated that they had killed approximately 700 Japanese during the same period. In other words, in spite of the Americans' overwhelming materiel and fire-power superiority, battlefield casualties were not that dissimilar. The nature of the terrain precluded the Americans from bringing their massive firepower to bear effectively. Instead, small numbers of infantrymen on both sides engaged each other in close combat of attrition, which inevitably resulted in high losses among the infantry.

The men redeployed in a light rain on 29 July, and some, like Troop C, moved just after dark. Redeployment was hard work for men whose physical strength had been worn down by three weeks of continual combat, and they staggered under the weight of their packs and sloshed through the mud to their new positions. Once there, they had to erect shelters, dig latrines, and clear fields of fire—in short, they had to replicate the defensive hamlet they had built just a few days before. The dispositions on 31 July resembled those shown on map 26. General Cunningham had stayed on the defensive and used the respite granted him by higher headquarters and the Japanese to strengthen the 112th's position along the river. His men reorganized and resupplied, Cunningham was now ready to attack the Japanese. His counter-offensive would open 1 August.

Despite no prospect of resupply for 18th Army, its officers and men were confident about their upcoming attack on the American perimeter at Afua. If American reinforcements isolated the Japanese attackers, there would be no alternative for 18th Army but to expend all its force in repeated

114

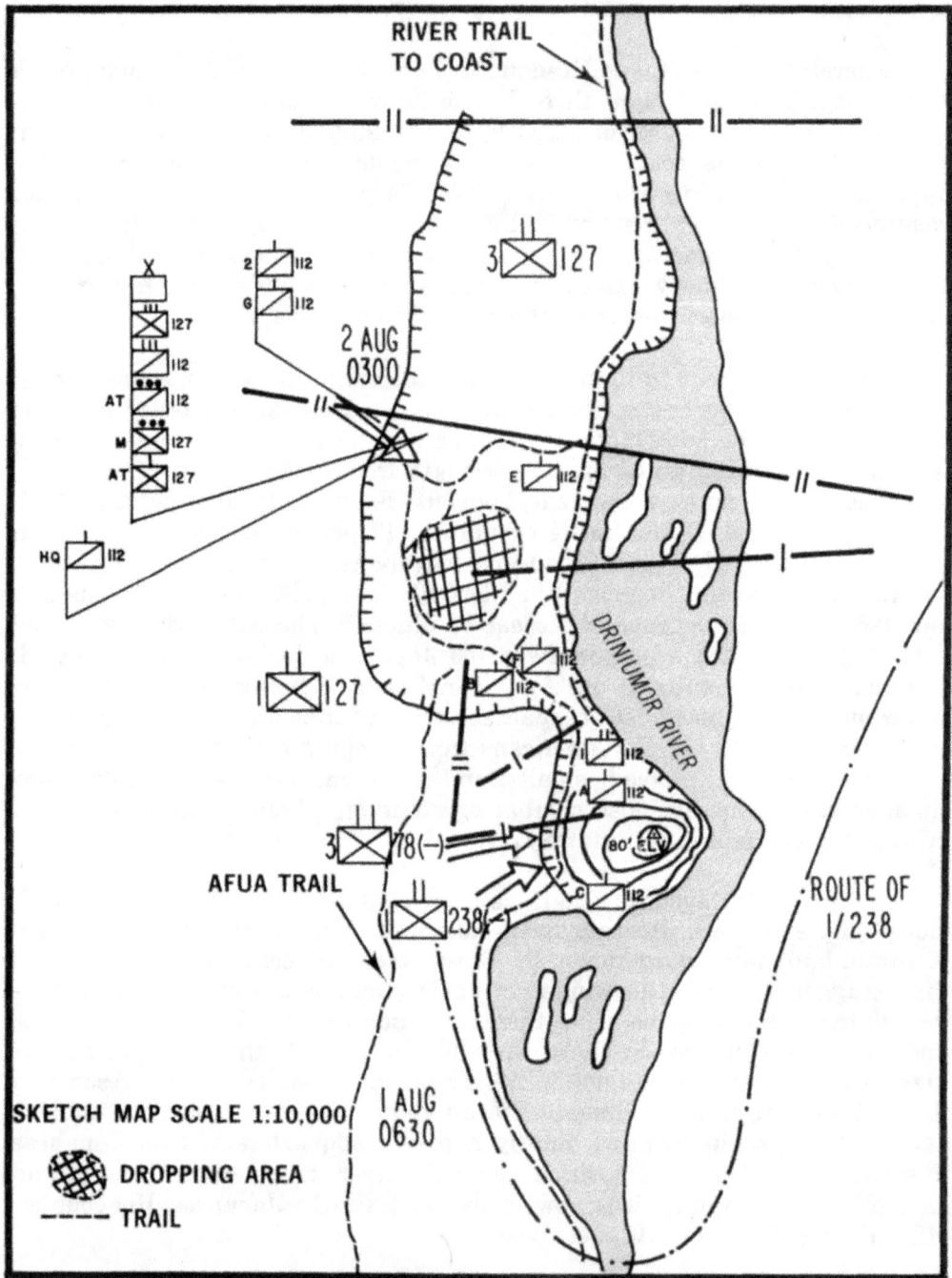

Map 26. Situation, 112th Cavalry and 127th Infantry, 31 July 1944

attacks to relieve them. According to the chief of staff, Lieutenant General Yoshihara, the forthcoming operation would be "literally a fight to the death."[81] Japanese battle casualties and the chaotic Japanese logistics network made more than one major attack impossible. The terrain and insufficient communications made the likelihood of a coordinated, concentrated assault remote. Japanese operational plans called for the offensive to commence at dusk on 30 July. They envisioned the 20th Division overrunning American positions at Afua and Hill 80, with the 41st Division seizing positions on the Driniumor north of Afua. The 112th's withdrawal from its southernmost position, the so-called Tsuru, caused Adachi to alter his plan, essentially moving the objectives of the two divisions farther north, directly into the teeth of the 112th's newly established defensive positions. Adachi's 29 July order clearly revealed his belief that this was 18th Army's final opportunity to snatch victory from the Americans. For the first time in the New Guinea campaigns, 18th Army instructed artillerymen "not to be frugal with ammunition." Everything would be wagered on this battle.[82]

Adachi detailed a rear guard between Kawanakajima and Yakamul to prevent any American attacks through that area. This rearguard defense consisted of men from the 41st Division and "borrowed" combat service support troops from the 4th Field Transport Headquarters, plus one mountain gun and one 70-mm gun to aid in antitank defense. This rear guard also constituted the force that would warn 18th Army of any major American counteroffensive or amphibious landing behind Japanese lines. The remainder of the 41st Division deployed south. By 27 July the troops were still several kilometers from their attack position, so 18th Army had to postpone the date of its projected attack until 1 August. Moreover, the whereabouts of the 239th Infantry were unknown, Japanese scouts being unable to find it. The 238th Infantry finally arrived in its assembly areas the morning of 30 July; the 41st Artillery Regiment and 8th Independent Engineer Regiment, that afternoon; and the 1st Battalion, 238th Infantry, linked up with the 79th Infantry that evening. The next morning the 41st Division Headquarters joined the 239th Infantry. The Japanese artillery deployed on a ridgeline overlooking the Driniumor's east bank about halfway between Afua and Hill 80 in order to support the attacks on those American positions (see map 27).[83]

In contrast to the 112th's relatively smooth redisposition, the 41st Division had to conduct its redeployment under constant Allied bombardment and while dealing with jungle obstacles. Australian and American warplanes dropped tons of bombs along suspected Japanese trails, and Allied warships shelled suspected "Japanese troop concentrations." Japanese supply troops in transportation units labored under the same danger, but over much longer distances. Rain made the trails over which the supply troops carried their heavy burdens slick and muddy. A path that one day provided easy access to frontline units could turn overnight into a quagmire or even disappear into the morass of mud, jungle, and bomb craters. Illness increased dramatically as the Japanese struggled to bring vital provisions forward. The

116

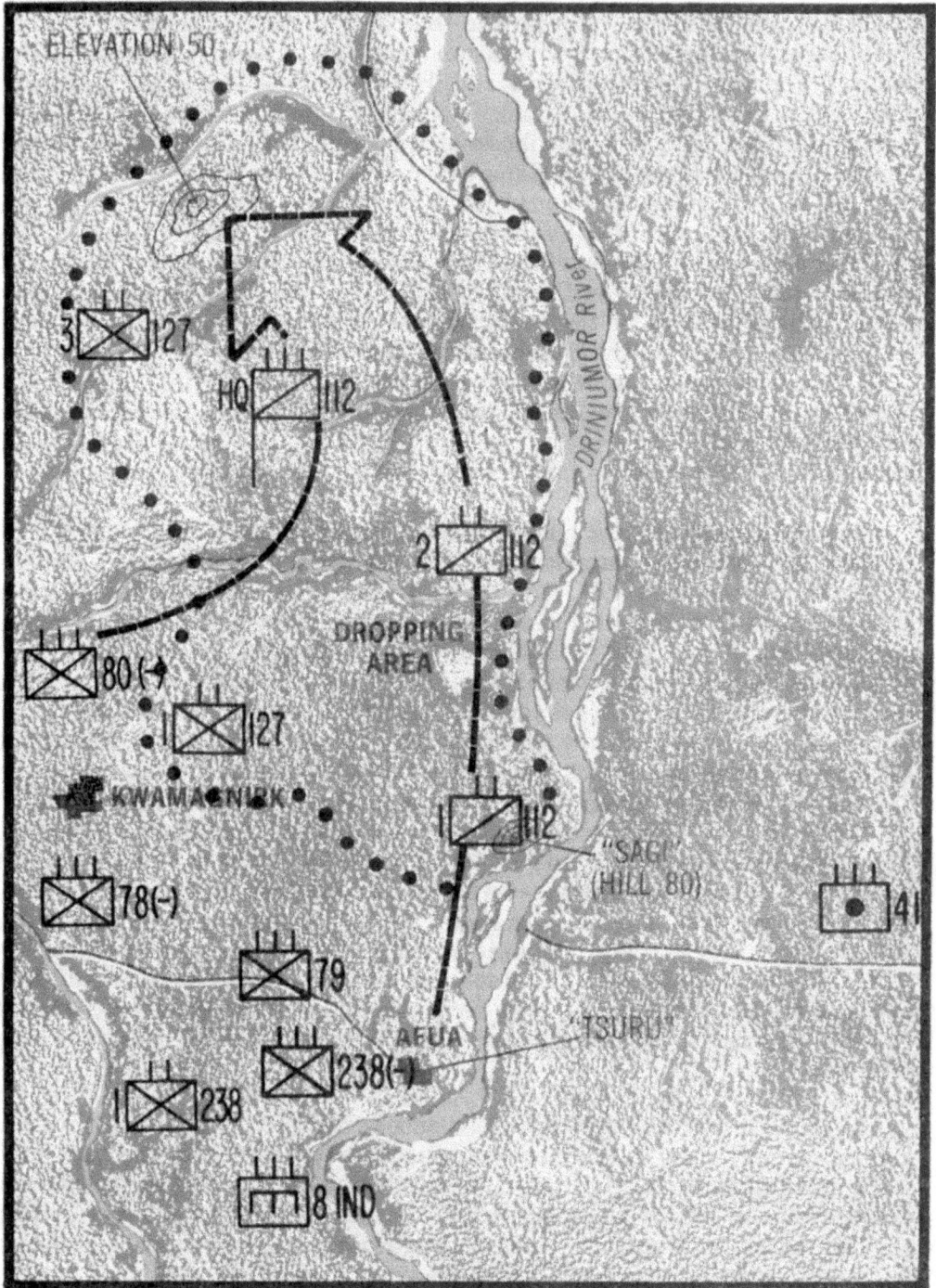

Map 27. Japanese deployment and proposed plan of attack

tribulations of the rear service mattered little to the frontline Japanese fighters, who bitterly complained, "Our supply services kill more of us than enemy bullets."[84] In the face of such hardships, the Japanese had managed to concentrate the remnants of two infantry divisions and an understrength infantry regiment (perhaps 4,000 combat troops total) east, south, and southwest of Afua.

The 112th Cavalry and 127th Infantry focused their attention on the southern flank, where they expected any Japanese attack to originate. Patrols searched west, south, and southwest for signs of Japanese activity. They found stragglers, whom they killed, and well-armed, fully uniformed Japanese infantry, whom they avoided. Small groups of three or four Japanese stragglers appeared west of the cavalrymen's defenses, either scavenging in American garbage for food or discarded clothing or wandering almost in a daze through the jungle. Such preoccupied men were easier and safer to kill than to attempt to capture as prisoners. A patrol working in the rear of 1st Squadron had indeed tried to take a Japanese prisoner, but the would-be POW instead activated a hand grenade, pressed it to his chest, and killed himself. Stories of such fanaticism made the rounds of the 112th quickly and confirmed stereotypes of Japanese and the risks involved in taking prisoners.

Patrols to the south did not run into ragged stragglers. They caught glimpses of well-equipped Japanese combat troops. A heavy rain on 29 July restricted visibility, but in their potentially lethal game of hide-and-seek, patrols continued to report enemy sightings. The next day, American patrols operating near Afua, vacated the previous day by 112th, reported Japanese soldiers already occupying foxholes in the shell-marked village. Other patrols found the partially decomposed remains of Japanese corpses or the mutilated victims of artillery fire, occasionally as many as ten dead at one location. It was grisly, ghoulish work to pry weapons or personal items from these stinking corpses that fell apart when touched. It had to be done, however, because higher headquarters demanded information that might identify the Japanese units arrayed against South Force.

An order for such information resulted in a Troop A combat patrol being sent east across the Driniumor to search for Japanese. Their faces chapped and weathered by the sun, their uniforms ragged and caked with dirt, sweat, and grease, the men were absorbed by the lush jungle growth. They proceeded in column formation at dispersed interval, so each man could just see the back of the man in front of him. As the Americans tramped southeast on a native trail, two Japanese soldiers fell into the rear of the column and apparently marched along with the patrol for some time, both sides unaware of the presence of their enemies. Perhaps it was indicative of the effect of the tropical rain forest on the opponents. Boots falling apart from continual immersings in water and pounding on the rugged terrain, uniforms tattered and stained black with sweat, exposed skin burned, darkened, and soiled, all combined to make Japanese and American combat troops indistinguishable in outward appearance. This strange procession abruptly ended when a cavalryman finally noticed the Japanese behind him. He shouted a warning and in response one Japanese threw a grenade at the Americans, and both then escaped unharmed into the jungle. The cavalrymen, also unharmed, continued their long patrol.

Amidst this extensive patrolling, a major action occurred on 29 July, when the 2d Battalion, 127th Infantry, deployed to reoccupy its former positions southwest of Afua. It ran directly into the 66th Infantry, which was in the process of attacking northeast against the Americans. Once again the meeting engagement broke down into a series of small, isolated combats, with both sides under the impression that they were attacking the defensive positions of the other. The Americans, as had now become a standard tactic, called for all available artillery support, but as the shells crashed into the area, the light rain and mist made accurate spotting nearly impossible. After shelling a point for several minutes, the artillery would lift, and the infantry point would cautiously move forward. If any Japanese fired on them, the Americans would quickly pull back and restart the artillery bombardment. The Japanese seemed to the Americans to be withdrawing, but the 66th Infantry was maneuvering away from the lethal artillery fire and around the right (west) flank of the 2d Battalion (see map 28).

Maj. Okamoto Takahisa, commander of the 3d Battalion, had the mission to envelop the American positions threatening the 20th Division's flank near Afua from the east and then to attack south. In theory, the attack would carry to the American position known to the Japanese as Sagi, an eighty-foot elevation about 900 meters northwest. As the 3d Battalion advanced, it bumped into the U.S. 2d Battalion, 127th Infantry, which immediately called in massive artillery fire. With artillery exploding all around them, the Japanese suffered several casualties. In the din and smoke, confusion reigned, and Okamoto had to run around urging or kicking his troops to get them to move forward. Okamoto's 3d Battalion was on the extreme right (west) Japanese flank, and he was the only officer who had a map of the area. His company commanders used compasses to guide their path through the foliage. All contact among Japanese units disappeared into the green wall of vegetation they were struggling through. The jungle terrain had fragmented Okamoto's forces, leaving him with no idea how the neighboring company was faring. Instead, small parties of Japanese collided with small numbers of Americans, deployed, and attacked their enemies.[85] Okamoto's men wedged themselves between Companies E and G, isolating these Americans from their battalion, just a few hundred meters away, as the jungle again swallowed entire formations into itself. When General Cunningham, as South Force commander, ordered the 2d Battalion to withdraw at 1800, Company G instead remained on its high ground because of Japanese infantrymen lurking in the vegetation to its rear. Company E also preferred to remain in place because of "the uncertain situation and the danger of being fired on by our own troops."[86] Company E had lost thirty-nine men killed or wounded during the day, including several when a friendly mortar

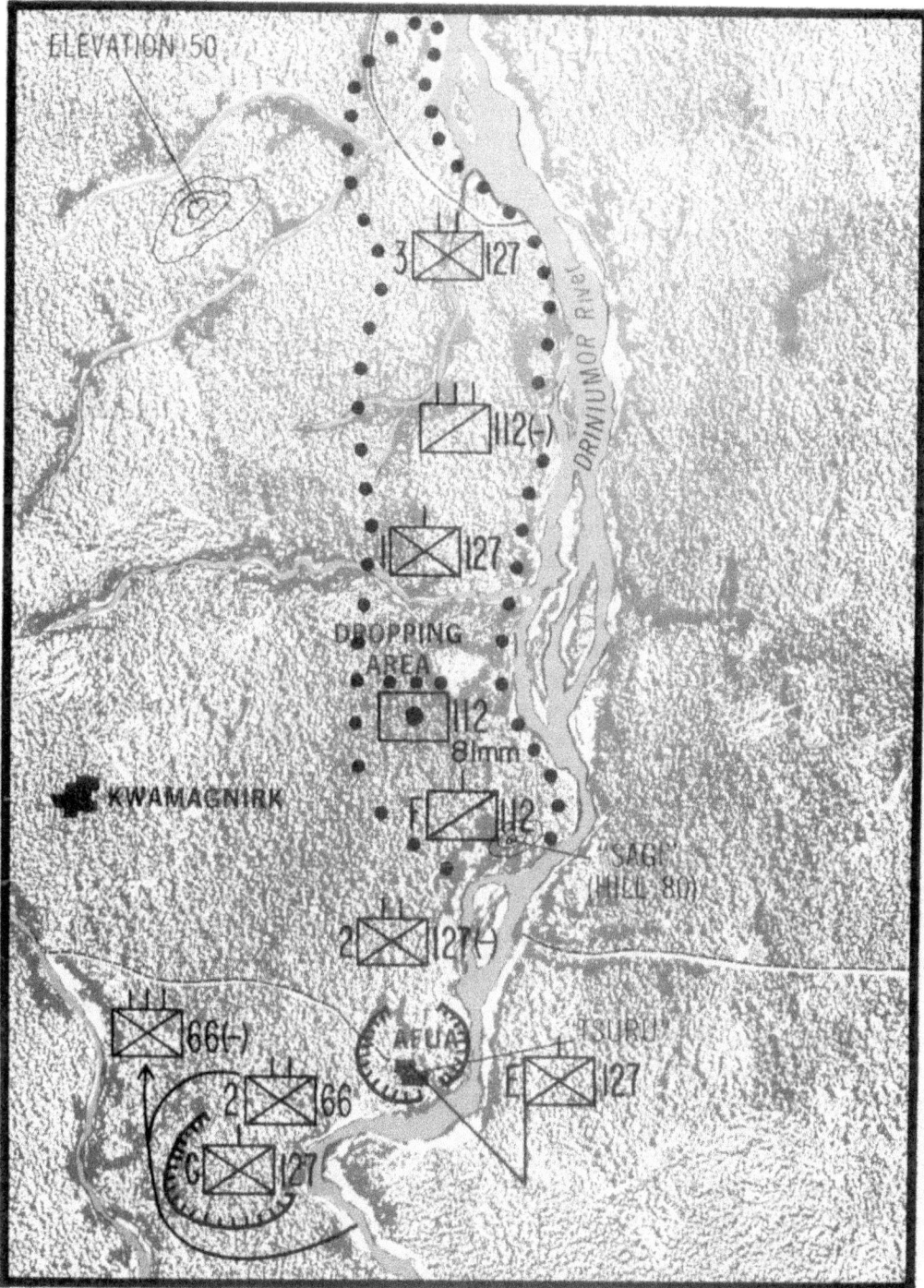

Map 28. 2d Battalion, 127th Infantry, situation, 29 July 1944

round dropped short. The rest of the battalion withdrew north, but was ambushed and attacked by Japanese from the 66th Infantry, who were still advancing east to west. The Americans predictably called on all available artillery support to place a curtain of fire between themselves and the Japanese. The 2d Battalion reported that twenty-six Japanese had been killed by artillery fire.[87] SWPA G-2 assessed the action as characteristic of Japanese inflexibility regardless of losses suffered and indicative of "an apparent lack of control being exercised over enemy operations in the Driniumor sector."[88]

Unbeknownst to the fighting men, the respective commanders had already set in motion another train of events that would climax the Driniumor battles. General Hall's enveloping maneuver, the so-called Ted Force Action, commenced on 31 July, as four American infantry battalions crossed the Driniumor and advanced east. At 1400 the same day, General Cunningham issued a warning order to Troop G and Company K, 127th Infantry, for an attack south and southwest against the Japanese to commence at 0800 the next day. General Adachi, meanwhile, revised his attack plans to conform to the confused, but apparently fluid, battlefield situation. On 29 July the 20th Division reported that it had driven the Americans from Tsuru (Afua) and that they were mopping up that position. Indeed, Cunningham had ordered the withdrawal from Afua that day. The 66th Infantry's fight of 29 July near Afua also influenced Adachi's attack order issued the afternoon of 31 July. According to intelligence, the order began, there was some doubt that the enemy had begun its retreat. Eighteenth Army would continue attacks to annihilate the enemy by advancing northwest to a line from Sagi to north of Elevation 50. In the second phase, the 41st Division would roll up the northern American flank on the Driniumor.*

At Sagi, Lt. Col. Clyde S. Grant, the new commander of 1st Squadron, 112th Cavalry, organized his perimeter in a lazy-S configuration, with Troops B, A, and C deployed north to south and facing west. He also had a machine gun platoon and reinforcements from Troop E. The battle position was just east and around a low hill (Elevation 80) that had many fallen trees scattered around from the continual artillery pounding. The heavy tree trunks and thick vegetation bordering the perimeter made it impossible to clear fire lanes in the area. The men resorted to hammering aiming stakes into the ground to enable them to fire at a particular spot during a defense.[89]

Just before dawn on 1 August, Maj. Imamura Hideo and the 1st Battalion, 238th Infantry, approached Grant's defenses from the southwest after crossing the Driniumor near Afua (see map 29). The battalion was to join forces with the 3d Battalion, 78th Infantry, on its left (west) and seize Sagi. Point men cautiously moved forward, while infantrymen trailed about thirty-five meters behind, with the regimental commander, who led their advance, carrying the regimental colors. Americans in outposts heard the Japanese

*The 41st Division staff officers unanimously disagreed with 18th Army's attack plans but were curtly told, "Even though there are differences of opinion, make the attack."

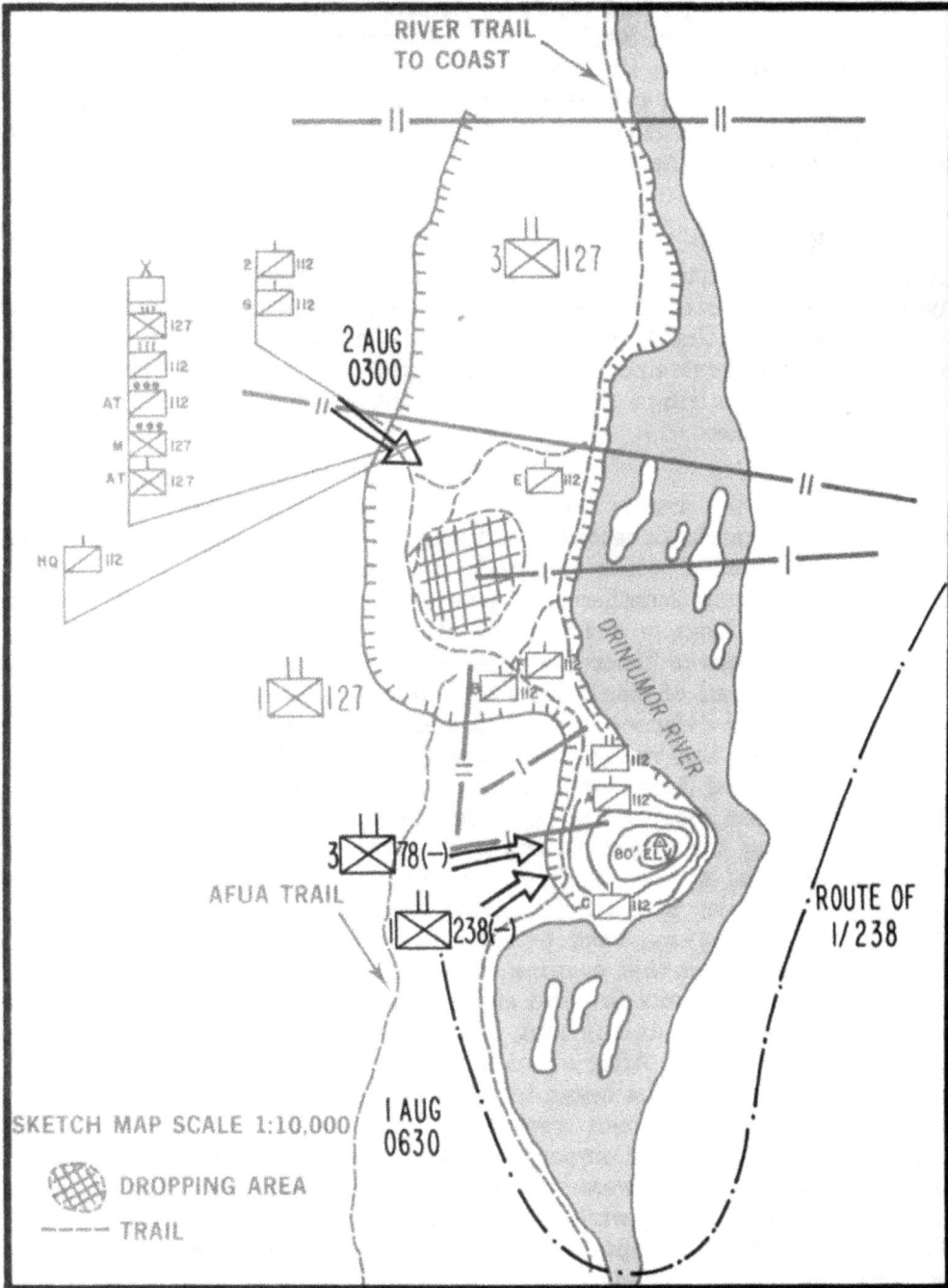

Map 29. Japanese attack, 1 August 1944

approaching from the jungle and withdrew. This movement created the impression among the Japanese point men that all the Americans were withdrawing, and a garbled report to regiment added to the perception that Sagi had already fallen. Regimental headquarters personnel quickly moved forward to capitalize on the American "withdrawal." A few minutes later, an earsplitting roar of gunfire and explosions burst from the direction of the Japanese advance. American artillery shells began exploding all around the Japanese still in the jungle.

Capt. Karai Keiji, commander of 4th Company, 1st Battalion, 238th Infantry, led the attack against Troop C. Karai and his men had been living on parched rice for the past two days, and their greatest ambition was to break into the American positions to steal food and rations. They had been on the move since 0200. Karai urged his weary men forward until they arrived at the fringe of the jungle, about 100 meters outside Troop C's log-strewn perimeter.

All coordination among the Japanese units had dissolved during their night approach march. Consequently, it was left to each company commander to decide individually when to attack the Americans. Once firing began, the Japanese, packed together on a seventy-meter front, rushed like a wave from the jungle. Even in the frenzied attack, few Japanese lived to cover those last 100 meters to Troop C's lines. The infantrymen from 4th Company were hit with a hail of small arms and automatic weapons fire in volleys from well-prepared defenses. Even unaimed American fire into the overcast predawn darkness and rising jungle mists could hardly miss the swarms of two or three hundred Japanese screaming and running at them. Next, artillery and deadly 81-mm mortar fire exploded immediately in front of Troop C's sector, shredding the Japanese ranks. The 1st Battalion commander died as a shell exploded almost on top of him. The bewildered Japanese survivors fled into the jungle, where First Lieutenant Ishiwara, commander of the Machine Gun Company, tried to rally the men, make them dig in, and launch another attack that evening. But there was no adequate cover from artillery, and small arms fire had stripped off much of the vegetation. The Americans poured fire at anything that moved, making it dangerous even to burrow into the dirt. After about an hour of the one-sided fight, concentrated American mortar fire began to saturate Captain Karai's forlorn position. By then about half his men were dead, killed in the artillery maelstrom that had swept over 4th Company. Other Japanese attackers had suffered proportionately, and men were still being killed and wounded. The Japanese had lost perhaps 150 men, while Troop C suffered five killed and six wounded. There was nothing for Captain Karai to do but to escape. In groups of two or three, the beaten Japanese infantrymen melted back into the safety of the deep jungle. That night Lieutenant Ishiwara killed himself to atone for the debacle. Next morning Major Imamura scouted near the alleged Japanese front line, but was unable to locate a single living Japanese soldier. A few stragglers drifted by throughout the day, more often than not with tales of officers and wounded men committing suicide. Only a handful of Japanese soldiers had ever reached Troop C's lines, and they were killed in hand-to-hand combat.[90]

The cavalrymen in Troop C looked out on piles of Japanese corpses and, while still shaken from the violence of combat and the loss of comrades, realized that they had smashed the attackers. Medics and litter bearers moved to Troop C's area to assist with the removal of the wounded and dead. The Japanese attack had made General Cunningham's planned offensive unnecessary. Instead, he ordered Troop G to attack southwest through Troop C's positions. The attackers advanced at 0830 and moved 600 meters against only scattered sniper fire. The Americans killed twenty-seven more Japanese, most of them dazed and confused stragglers trying to flee the carnage. There were no U.S. casualties. Troop A, just north of Troop C, had the distinction of capturing the first Japanese prisoner ever taken by the 112th Cavalry. The prisoner related the destruction of his battalion from the 238th Infantry and revealed that shortly another Japanese battalion would arrive near Afua.

If fortune had smiled on most of the 112th early that day, by afternoon and evening it had deserted them. A Japanese mortar crew firing from the vicinity of the 41st Artillery Regiment dropped about fifteen rounds near the 112th's command post, wounding three men in Troop F. Friendly fire called on to suppress the Japanese gun fell short into Troop E's left flank and wounded three more Americans. Self-inflicted suffering continued that night. About 0300 a small Japanese patrol blundered into Troop G's rear sector on the southwest edge of the dropping zone. In the ensuing melee, Japanese bullets wounded two cavalrymen. Then both sides drew back, regrouped, and the fight erupted again as the Japanese continued their probes. The cavalrymen called for mortar support, but one round of a 60-mm concentration either clipped a tree branch or had a faulty fuse and fell short, killing the 2d Squadron surgeon and two cavalrymen, as well as wounding two more.

But that long night witnessed even more "friendly fire" casualties. Troop F riflemen mistakenly shot five members of their artillery liaison party. The artillerymen had left their foxholes during the fighting to set up a radio, their phone communications having been severed. Their failure to answer the troopers' challenges resulted in two more Americans dead and three wounded by their own comrades. At first light, the Americans discovered one dead Japanese, two abandoned light machine guns, several rifles and helmets, and numerous trails of blood.

About mid-morning on 2 August, a 112th patrol moving towards the Driniumor walked into a Japanese bivouac and had to shoot its way out. Five more men were slightly wounded. In addition to battle casualties, General Cunningham also had to worry about disease, as medical evacuations for illness were doubling every ten days. It appears that the men of the 112th Cavalry had reached the limit of their endurance. But as long as the battle raged, there could be no relief for the fighting men. Postwar reports recognized that men might fake illness or try to reach safer rear areas. Others became fatalistic, failed to take ordinary precautions, and were convinced that they were the only persons the war required to "take it" day and night until they "got theirs."[91] Justified as such thoughts might have been in their role, dwelling exclusively on them led to nervous breakdown. The cumulative fatigue of battle also dulled some of the men's reflexes, deadened their senses, and made what a few days before were normally simple, routine jobs almost unbearably complicated. Mistakes in a line combat outfit invariably swelled the friendly casualty list. Ironically, the men who had been most exposed to death and danger and had lived through it were now regarded as the experienced fighters and thus irreplaceable on the firing line. For them there was no way out.

On the afternoon of 2 August, 18th Army issued orders to continue the attack against South Force. The 20th Division, now reduced to about fifty men in the 80th Infantry and perhaps sixty or so in the 78th Infantry, would combine their forces into a single command and together with the 41st Division strike the rear (west) of the American positions near Hato, then defended by the 1st Battalion, 127th Infantry, and 1st Squadron, 112th Cavalry (see map 30). The Japanese struck initially against the 1st Battalion.

Major Kawahigashi again led his battalion into the attack. His troops were low on ammunition and knew that they could not neutralize the overwhelming American firepower. They devised a plan to avoid it. Masked by dusk, they would simultaneously fire all their grenade dischargers, mortars, and one battalion gun. The surprise and subsequent shock action of a massed infantry assault on a narrow front, the Japanese believed, would temporarily unnerve the American defenders. This paralysis would give the Japanese the time that they needed to cross the killing zone in front of the U.S. lines and to break into the American defenses, where the U.S. artillery could not be used against them.

Men of the 78th Infantry had dragged a 70-mm howitzer through the jungle to within twenty meters of the 1st Battalion's lines. The gun fired point-blank into the American lines to signal the attack, but on the first round, the gun flipped upside down. Japanese attackers, packed together, came running from the jungle screaming. American small arms fire and artillery explosions riddled the dense mob. Despite Japanese jamming of the American artillery communication channels and the absence of any artillery observers, the 120th and 129th Field Artillery battalions pounded the area outside the 112th's perimeter. Cavalrymen called artillery fire to within fifty meters of their lines. Other Japanese troops tried to crawl along the ground toward the American lines to escape the withering fire. Kawahigashi saw that the Americans fired at anything that moved. In the rapidly fading light, Japanese camouflaged with tree limbs and leaves collapsed after several bullets struck them. Darkness settled as flares lit up the sky, revealing the carnage. The attack failed, though not for lack of

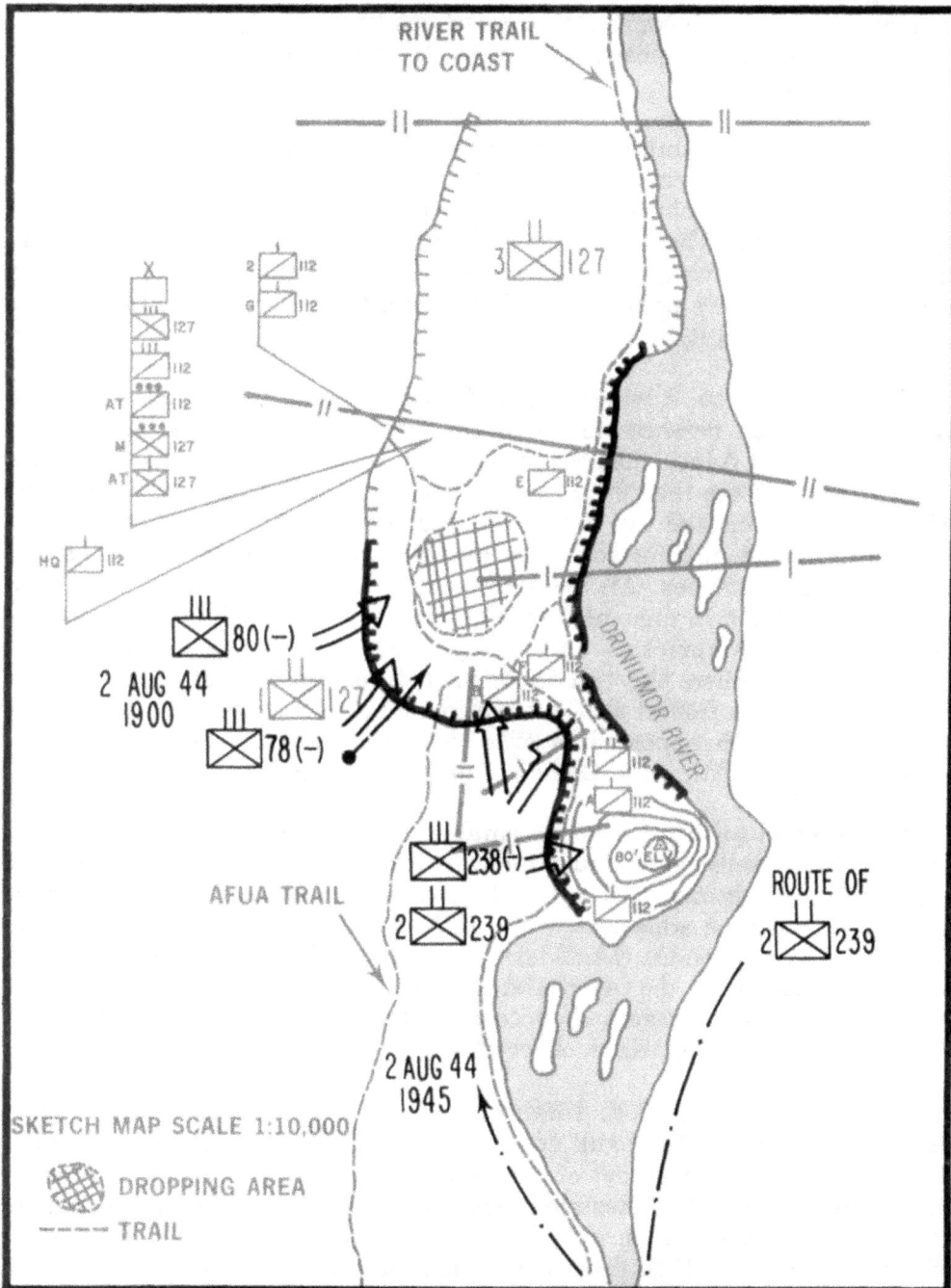

RIVER TRAIL
TO COAST

3 ⊠ 127

2 ⊠ 112

G ⊠ 112

X
⊠ 127
⊠ 112
AT ⊠ 112
M ⊠ 127
AT ⊠ 127

HQ ⊠ 112

E ⊠ 112

⊠ 80(−)

2 AUG 44
1900

⊠ 127

⊠ 78(−)

DRINIUMOR RIVER

⊠ 112

⊠ 112

⊠ 112

⊠ 238(−)

80' ELV

⊠ 112

2 ⊠ 239

AFUA TRAIL

ROUTE OF
2 ⊠ 239

2 AUG 44
1945

SKETCH MAP SCALE 1:10,000

DROPPING AREA

TRAIL

Map 30. Japanese attacks, 2 August 1944

fanatical courage, as all the 78th Infantry's remaining company-grade officers died leading their men in this assault.[92] Wounded Japanese soldiers began to commit suicide with hand grenades, adding to the slaughterhouse in front of the 1st Battalion's positions, where the defenders counted fifty-eight Japanese corpses.

About forty-five minutes after that assault had begun, survivors of the 41st Division hurled themselves at the adjoining 1st Squadron, 112th Cavalry. For the first time in the campaign, the cavalrymen occupied a well-organized defensive perimeter. The Americans could fire their 60-mm mortars effectively and had automatic weapons sited every twenty-five meters or closer. It was a formidable defensive position. The Japanese attackers from the 41st Division had underestimated it.

The 41st Division, it will be recalled, had meticulously planned an attack against American defenses to the north, near Kawanakajima. At the last moment, General Adachi had diverted the division from its scheduled attack in order to reinforce the 20th Division and press home its assaults against Afua. This decision had two important repercussions. First, the 41st Division staff officers had no time to devise an appropriate plan of attack against the American defenses. All their time was consumed moving their men through the jungle to their new assembly areas. Nevertheless, the Japanese dismissed the Americans defending Afua as inferior to those near Kawanakajima, where the 41st Division had been in combat. Against these "inferior troops," a frontal attack conducted on a narrow frontage with forces echeloned in depth appeared to offer the Japanese the best possibility of achieving the breakthrough General Adachi had ordered.

The second problem also originated in the cancellation of the 41st Division's originally scheduled attack. Officers in the 41st Division opposed the decision and complained openly that the 20th Division's lack of courage had caused the Afua stalemate. Word of their dissatisfaction reached General Adachi, who reprimanded the division commander, Lieutenant General Mano. This rebuke infuriated the regimental and battalion commanders, who decided among themselves to regain their commander's honor by overwhelming the American defenses regardless of losses.[93]

The 2d Battalion, 239th Infantry, crossed the Driniumor on 2 August and proceeded along the bank adjacent to the 238th Infantry. Shortly after dark, both units charged out of the jungle against the 1st Squadron's positions. The 41st Artillery Regiment and mortar fire supported the Japanese thrust, but the bunched-up infantrymen simply dissolved under the impact of the concentrated U.S. firepower. Japanese officers regrouped their men under fire and charged forward, determined to prove that the slight against their division had been unjustified. They died in bunches, as heaps of bodies fell in front of the cavalrymen's perimeter. Only darkness saved the Japanese from complete extermination. The 1st Squadron suffered only four men slightly wounded. Nearly 100 Japanese were killed. All night, screams and moans resounded outside the cavalrymen's perimeter. In the early light of 3 August the Americans could see stacks of Japanese corpses marking the axis of attack.

Although the 112th Cavalry enjoyed overwhelming materiel and firepower superiority, the protracted warfare of attrition had ground down the troops, who were now in poor physical shape. Sickness skyrocketed. The Americans detected that they were winning the struggle, but they had no idea how many more of their friends would be killed or wounded in the savage fighting. They were worn out, tired, sick, and understrength. But they could still improve their defensive positions. Registration of mortar and artillery concentrations boomed during the day as the 112th Cavalry surrounded their perimeter with a band of fire, ready on call. Amidst these major preparations, there was no respite from small-scale patrolling, with its usual deadly results.

A Troop G patrol operating east of the Driniumor walked into a Japanese ambush, and its sergeant was killed by machine gun fire. The other Americans quickly ran from the site and then called in mortar fire. Another patrol, later in the day, could find no evidence that the skirmish had ever taken place. A six-man patrol vanished a little more than a football field's length from the 112th's perimeter. The men were on a three-day reconnaissance patrol when they stumbled into a Japanese ambush, probably set by stragglers of Miyake Force still trapped behind the U.S. lines. A patrol from Troop G sent to their rescue was, in turn, apparently ambushed and lost two men killed and six wounded.* Another chilling possibility is that the G troopers reached the ambushed American patrol only to be shot by their comrades. A trooper recalled that he heard someone yell "Watch out!" just before Thompson submachine gun fire raked the men.

On the afternoon of 1 August, the first inkling of the Ted Force envelopment reached General Adachi, when he received reports of enemy landings near Yakamul. That same afternoon, the 237th Infantry arrived in the Afua area. In conjunction with survivors of the 238th and the 239th Infantry, the 237th set out to attack across the Driniumor at 0200 on 3 August. Poor coordination and late arrival of troops caused a postponement. Also on 3 August, General Adachi ordered the Aitape offensive to end at noon 4 August. Attacks then in progress would continue in order to cover the Japanese withdrawal. Shortly thereafter, Adachi heard that about 400 Americans—probably the 3d Battalion, 127th Infantry—had crossed the Driniumor in the vicinity of Kawanakajima and were rapidly advancing east (see map 31). Adachi ordered elements of the 237th Infantry to check this American advance.

*As for the lost patrol, a wounded member was found by the 127th Infantry, and another made his way to the 112th command post. Subsequent patrols found a third wounded cavalryman who had been in the bush three days. He believed his lieutenant and one other enlisted man had been killed. Those bodies were never found.

128

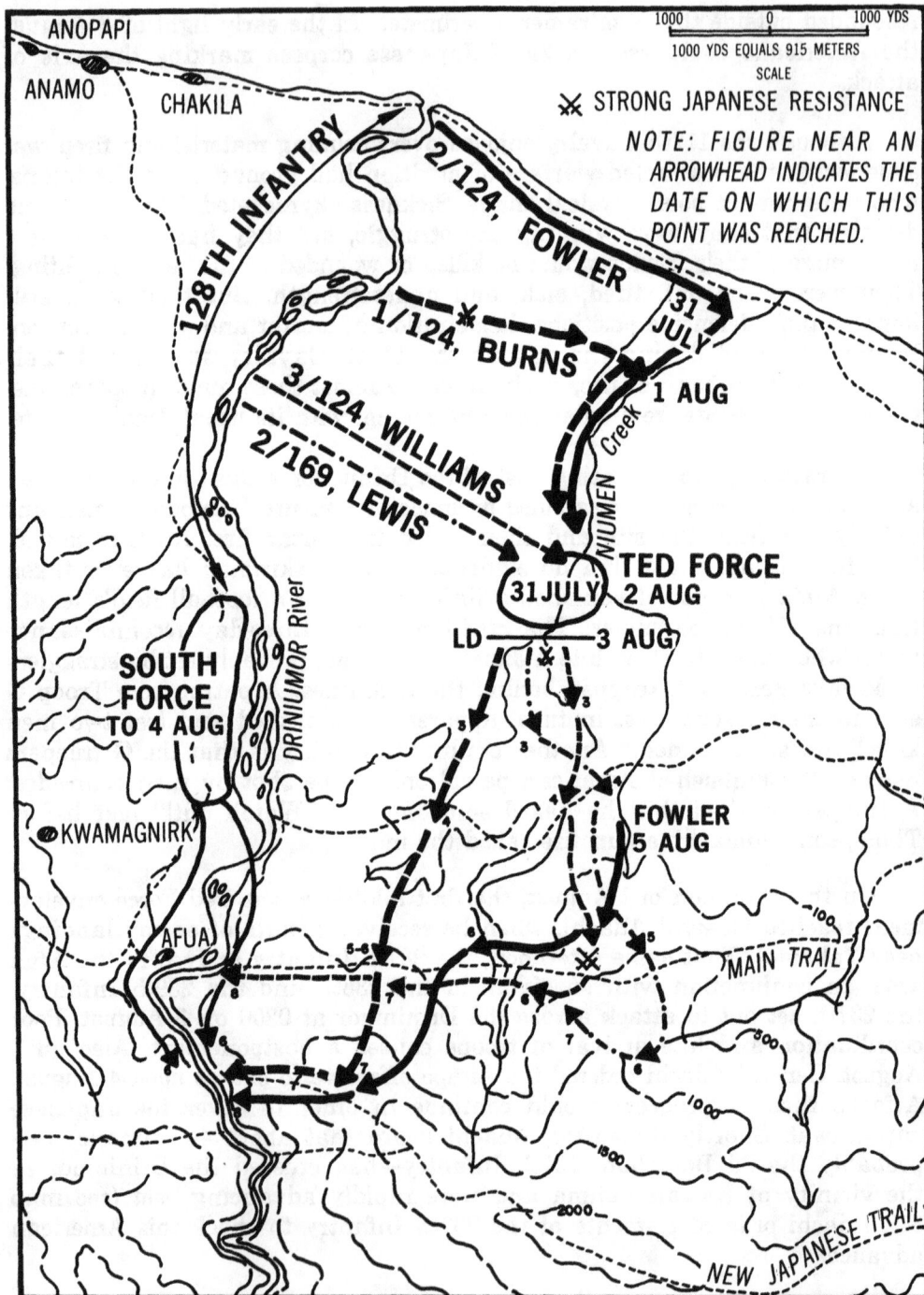

Source: Smith, *Approach*, p. 193

Map 31. Ted Force operations, 31 July—10 August 1944

Elsewhere elements of the 41st Division prepared for what would be their final attack against the 112th Cavalry.[94] Morale was low among the Japanese troops, who had only one day's rations left and were short of medical supplies. Their condition had deteriorated to such an extent that the physically fit soldiers took the clothes and rations from the weaker men.[95] The Japanese had crossed the Driniumor upstream and then swung north to strike the American positions from the jungle and along the west bank of the dry riverbed. Their attack began at 0615 on 4 August.*

Platoon Sgt. Claude Rigsby of Troop B was on the firing line that morning. His troop, part of Lieutenant Colonel Grant's lazy-S line, formed a pocket facing towards the jungle. Rigsby could see very few Japanese because of the thick jungle, and the fleeting figures he could see attacked in open formations. They advanced into the pocket, where U.S. automatic weapons and 60-mm mortars tore them to pieces. Artillery blasted the Japanese remaining in the jungle. The fighting raged as the Japanese tried desperately to break the American lines. A few Japanese actually reached the American outpost line and drove the defenders back. But after two hours, more than 185 Japanese were dead or dying. The squadron commander watched impassively as sixteen wounded Japanese committed suicide in front of his defenses.[96]

As soon as the Japanese attack had begun, General Cunningham alerted Troop E for a counterattack, and at 0900, Troop E deployed to mop up any remaining Japanese and reestablish the cavalrymen's outpost line (see map 32). As they passed through Troop C's lines and walked crouched forward toward the jungle, three Japanese riflemen hiding under the roots of a tree on which an American officer was standing shot and killed Lieutenant Christensen. Enraged cavalrymen killed the Japanese with hand grenades. Six other Japanese died during this sweep, as did another 112th Cavalry lieutenant.

The human carnage along and in the Driniumor was appalling. A member of the 112th's Supply Company arrived at the river around this time and at first glance thought that it was full of logs. Another look registered that Japanese corpses choked the river.[97] If ever during a battle morale soared and exhilaration appeared, it was then, for the cavalrymen seemed to have sensed that the Japanese were finished. So badly were the Japanese beaten that nine surrendered. These prisoners were put to work burying the Japanese dead scattered around the perimeter. While the worst of the 112th's ordeal had passed, the danger permeating the lives of frontline troops had remained.

From 5 through 9 August, 112th Cavalry patrols plunged into the jungles, searching for the Japanese and hoping to cut off the disorganized enemy's retreat. The Japanese, however, withdrew southeasterly, not in the easterly direction General Hall had anticipated. Thus Ted Force, moving south,

*No Japanese record of this attack exists.

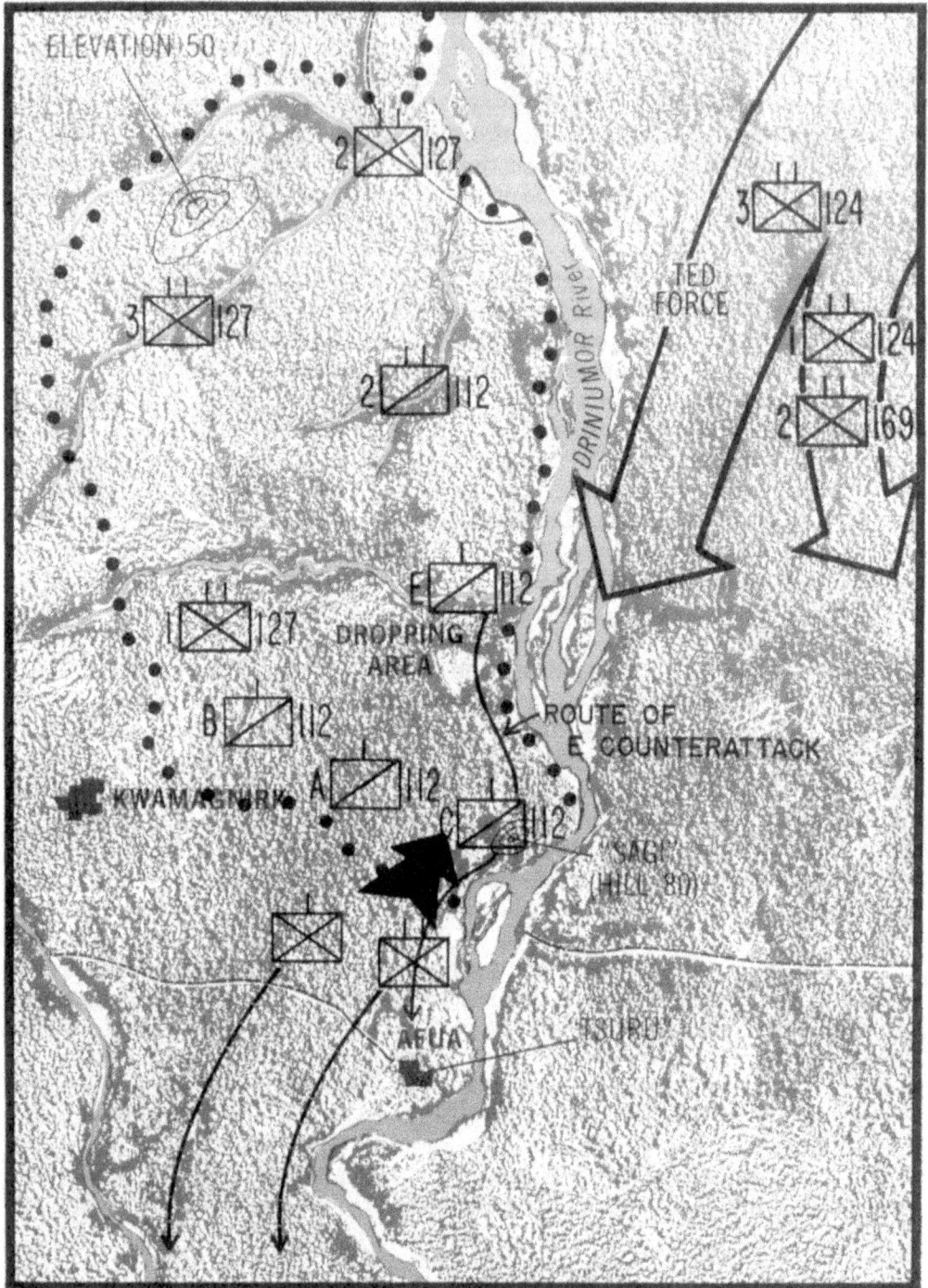

Map 32. Japanese attack and Troop E counterattack, 4 August 1944

encountered some resistance from the 237th Infantry, but most of the Japanese they killed were service support personnel, not infantrymen. Indicative of the caliber of opposition, Ted Force managed to suffer more casualties from friendly artillery fire than from enemy action.

Even the hunt for Japanese stragglers was not always one-sided. Enemy snipers shot and wounded the point man of a patrol on 8 August. He had the unfortunate distinction to be the last 112th Cavalry battle casualty as the campaign was visibly winding down and had degenerated into a chase, albeit a dangerous one, after Japanese stragglers. Cavalrymen shot several stragglers daily and occasionally discovered mass Japanese graves or piles of rotting corpses. On 10 August the 112th received orders to return to Aitape, and the next day they marched north to the mouth of the Driniumor.

U.S. Army Signal Corps

Regimental HQ and squadron commanders, 112th Cavalry, Aitape, 11 August 1944.

Before the cavalrymen reached the beach, where they would board trucks to ride to Aitape, Lieutenant Colonel Grant ordered his 1st Squadron to stop at a stream in order to wash and shave. Then they continued towards the beach. As they emerged from the jungle, the 112th Band began to play and the men fell into march order. After forty-five days on the line, many troopers had jungle ulcers on their hands and feet. Some had blood oozing from their boots. But they marched to their waiting trucks. They had come to the Driniumor in trucks, and they left in trucks. In between, they suffered 317 battle casualties or 21 percent of their authorized strength, probably 26 or 27 percent of their actual pre-Driniumor strength. They claimed to have killed more than 1,600 Japanese, the majority of these during the bloody Japanese attacks of early August and the subsequent straggler hunt. Overall American losses were 440 killed, 2,550 wounded, and 10 missing.[98]

General Adachi's survivors meanwhile made their painful way back towards Wewak. His 20th and 41st divisions had lost more than 8,000 men, including almost all the battalion commanders and company-grade officers. The 41st Division lost 2,519 killed, 237 missing, and 1,740 dead from illness or untreated wounds. The 20th Division's losses are shown below:

Regiment	Pre-Battle Strength	Post-Battle Strength	Losses	Pre-Battle Percentage Lost
78th Infantry	1,300	350	950	73
79th Infantry	700	350	350	50
80th Infantry	1,010	320	690	69
26th Field Artillery	990	450	540	56
Other	2,612	1,570	1,042	40
Total	6,612	3,040	3,572	55

The Japanese lost close to 10,000 men overall. They claimed to have inflicted an estimated 2,000 American casualties, but nearly 3,000 Americans had been killed, wounded, or reported missing. Nor did that end 18th Army's grim saga. Even though General Krueger for "historical purposes" had declared the campaign finished on 25 August 1944, 18th Army fought on against Australian forces until V-J Day in September 1945. During those thirteen months, the Japanese lost another 7,200 killed and 270 prisoners. Australian losses were 451 killed and more than 1,160 wounded. General Adachi formally surrendered 18th Army on 13 September 1945 and shortly afterwards committed suicide at Rabaul, where the Australians had taken him to stand trial for war crimes.

The men of the 112th Cavalry joined the 1st Cavalry Division in the Leyte campaign in November 1944 and later landed at Lingayen Gulf in January 1945. On V-J Day the regiment sailed into Tokyo Bay and the next day began its occupation duty in Japan.

Conclusions

Conclusions

8

The GHQ, SWPA Daily Summary no. 871, dated 9—10 August, summarized the Aitape campaign as an exemplary use of counterenvelopment and exploitation of the Driniumor line to annihilate the 18th Army. It characterized the operation as "possibly unparalleled in the history of military maneuver over this type of terrain." The summary continued that this feat had been accomplished with "negligible loss to our units."[1] Viewed from the theater or army commander's perspective, the statement probably was accurate, but overstated. Maneuver warfare, seen from the headquarters of these higher echelons, did produce a relatively bloodless victory.

MacArthur's bold, multiple invasions at Hollandia and Aitape were classic examples of a maneuver that forced his opponents to fight at places and times not of their choosing. At the so-called "sharp end" the price was paid in lives. Victory communiques aside, the men of the 112th Cavalry knew that they had won their part of the battle along the Driniumor, and they also understood in vivid personal terms that they paid a heavy price for victory. This dichotomous appreciation of the nature of the fighting may originate in the different perceptions of that operation at varying levels—strategic, operational, and tactical—of the Aitape campaign. An analysis of the components that characterized these respective levels may clarify areas of overlap and identify points of divergence in the strategic and tactical conduct of the Aitape operations.

In the strategic and operational contexts, Ultra-derived information about the state of the Japanese 18th Army influenced MacArthur's decision to leap to Hollandia and Aitape. MacArthur's staff also probably used the Ultra picture of weak Japanese defenses to convince the Joint Chiefs of Staff that the element of risk, while always present in a combat operation, had been minimized by the detailed Allied knowledge of the exact Japanese dispositions along the northern New Guinea coastline. In short, Ultra helped to persuade the Joint Chiefs of Staff to approve MacArthur's plan. Ultra also confirmed the success of the Allied deception plan and was instrumental in the destruction of 4th Air Army. These events insured that no substantial Japanese forces would turn the invasion beaches into bloody deathtraps for the Americans.

Despite these successes, SWPA's analysis and interpretation of Ultra, in conjunction with other sources of intelligence (POWs, captured documents, patrol reports) was ultimately flawed. SWPA's preconception of potential Japanese courses of action, its projection of American rationales and intentions on the enemy, and its interpretation that the Japanese intended to attack both the center and flank of the Driniumor covering force affected operational deployments. These dispositions, in turn, facilitated 18th Army's breakthrough on 10—11 July and drastically altered the tactical shape of the Driniumor battle. It is important to distinguish Ultra's operational role from the tactical dimension of battle. At the small unit level (generally division and below), Ultra never was expected to contribute significantly to the actual fighting, because it was usually not timely enough to influence a tactical engagement, and the perishable nature of the lower level unit communications normally rendered them irrelevant within a few hours of transmission. Furthermore, in most cases, protection of the source of Ultra took precedence over temporary tactical advantages. Except in the broadest terms as a yardstick for operational deployments, Ultra was irrelevant to the tactical dispositions. It was, simply put, primarily a strategic and occasionally an operational weapon. During that phase of the Aitape campaign, Ultra was invaluable in guiding General Krueger to set his defenses, to reinforce his troops, and to build a base from which to destroy 18th Army. Ultra was a two-edged sword, and in several instances, Krueger's actions appear driven by Ultra to the exclusion of other relevant tactical, geographical, and sometimes even operational considerations.

The decision to relieve the 163d regimental commander comes to mind as does Krueger's replacement of General Martin following the Japanese breakthrough of 10—11 July. Krueger was impatient with the 163d commander's progress, because he knew that no strong Japanese opposition lurked in the jungles, but this was a luxury the regimental commander was not privileged to enjoy. Martin's relief may have been hastened by Krueger's misunderstanding of the battle based on an intelligence appreciation, not a tactical one. In one sense, Martin became the scapegoat for failing to prevent the Japanese breakthrough. Yet Generals Krueger and Hall had insisted, contrary to Martin's advice, that Martin release his reserves to provide troops for the reconnaissance in force. The decision to develop the battle early backfired. One may surely ask whether, if Krueger had known less about his opponent's circumstances, he would have acted so aggressively, especially when the original mission of Persecution Task Force was to protect—defend—the Aitape perimeter. The accolades Ultra received must be accepted then with significant reservations.

The 25 June intercept provides a case in point. This message, which provided specific tactical-level details of a Japanese attack, was the result of a complex process of decryption, translation, analysis, and dissemination, involving hundreds of people. Without the time-consuming process to place the intercept in context, Ultra was meaningless. It was the recognition of this accomplishment that led Central Bureau to proclaim, "never has a commander gone into battle knowing as much about the enemy as the Allied commander at Aitape on 10—11 July 1944."[2] The assertion conveniently ignores the fact that Central Bureau never intercepted the actual Japanese attack order. Moreover, if the Allied commander knew so much about his enemy, why did he remove his reserves the evening of the Japanese attack? Why did General Willoughby, the very day of 18th Army's offensive, report that the attack probably had been postponed? These questions await definitive answers.

So a brilliant example of maneuver warfare at the operational level degenerated at the tactical level into an unimaginative application of orthodox doctrine—attempted envelopments, large-scale flanking maneuvers, reconnaissance in force—in murderous terrain. The Japanese operations were at least equally conventional, probably more so.

The jungle terrain favored small unit tactics. Both army commanders, however, resorted to conventional doctrine as if it were possible to maneuver large formations intact through the bush. The tactics of the campaign may be seen more as an ad hoc response to particular circumstances than as a logical development of doctrinal thought. A glance at the U.S. Army's Jungle Warfare manuals for 1941 and 1944 reinforces that melancholy observation.[3] Conventional armies applied orthodox, staff school tactics regardless of the terrain. Neither army had a sophisticated doctrine for jungle warfare, so the fighters—that is, the combat soldiers—had to create a doctrine that evolved in the course of the fighting. Within the general principles of offense, defense, reconnaissance, and so forth, the 112th Cavalry did improvise procedures, tactics, and standard operating procedures. The Army Ground Forces Observer Reports were also helpful because they stimulated thought within the regiment about the conclusions cavalrymen had reached from their firsthand experience. Because of its success in the Pacific, the U.S. Army perhaps thought that it had an effective jungle warfare doctrine, but it failed to recognize the smallest cog in that doctrine—the infantryman and his vital role—and instead concentrated on firepower, especially artillery, to engage the enemy.* Instead of adapting American tactics to the environment to achieve victory, American commanders won by adapting the environment to their tactics.

The jungle was not just wooded terrain writ large. It was a totally different physical environment that required almost all a man's energy and determination just to survive its rigors. That these men would turn from existing to fighting is probably more attributable to a primordial urge for survival than sound doctrine and leadership.

---

*That sweeping generalization requires more detailed analysis of the U.S. Army's tactics in its Pacific campaigns. How did combat training change after Buna? After Driniumor? After Biak? After Luzon? After Okinawa? How were those experiences incorporated into the institutional and doctrinal memory of the Army? Those significant questions merit additional study.

138

From the perspective of the combat soldier, it is easy to criticize the staffs at division and corps levels for insensitivity, lack of realism, and outright stupidity. The simple truth is that without the centralized direction the staff provided (as divorced from reality as it unfortunately sometimes became in the confusion of battle), platoons and companies would just mill around purposelessly in the jungle thicket. Without the coercive power of staff orders, it is doubtful that the understandably reluctant combat troops would move forward of their own volition against a dangerous, armed foe. And, at least at Aitape, to a surprising extent, the personalities of the higher commanders who issued the orders impressed themselves on the conduct of the battle.

Both opposing commanders ignored advice from line units—Krueger by his reconnaissance in force and Adachi by his shift of the 41st Division to attack Afua. The mission of Persecution Task Force was to defend Aitape; that of 18th Army, to attack Aitape. General Krueger with his Ultra knowledge changed defense to preemptive attack, apparently, because he perceived Aitape as a sideshow to be concluded as expeditiously as possible in order that he might move on to a more important theater of operations, namely the Philippines. Krueger reacted to changing strategic considerations—particularly the strategic debate between MacArthur and Nimitz concerning future operations against either Formosa or the Philippines—and pressured his subordinate commanders to conclude the campaign promptly. Although his methods may seem overbearing to some, tactics is the handmaiden of strategy. Without a coherent strategy, the best tactics cannot produce overall victory. Yet a sound strategy can capitalize on conventional tactics. MacArthur's imaginative strategy exploited 6th Army's orthodox tactics to the greatest extent possible.

Krueger's reconnaissance in force, conducted to "develop the battle," is entirely out of keeping with his otherwise methodical and plodding generalship, which almost cost him his career in the Philippines.[4] General Cunningham preferred to stand on the defensive and await Japanese onslaughts, always fearful that his vulnerable position was about to be outflanked. General Hall apparently believed tactics could be universally applied, as his textbook envelopment, totally misplaced in the jungles, revealed. Their common opponent, General Adachi, put his faith in the intangibles of battle, and his operational orders and tactical assault formations were uninspired and, as the battle continued, inflexible. To achieve victory, Adachi's tactics had to be exceptional to compensate for 18th Army's shortcomings. His operational plans suggest that his North China perspective did not accommodate itself to the drastically altered conditions of jungle combat. Adachi, like his American counterparts, had been trained to fight one type of war, but told to fight an entirely different one.

These judgments must be understood in the human dimension of leadership. The general officers applied their accumulated military wisdom in accordance with doctrine and experience. They were conventional, not exceptional, battlefield leaders. Officers like Krueger, Hall, Gill, Martin, and Cunningham did nothing spectacular, but they won battles, campaigns, and ultimately the Pacific War with their methodical, almost abstract, style of leadership.[5] They were soldiers who understood the basic principles of warfare and applied them in battle.

At the lowest stratum was the combat soldier, and the tactics that both sides used were more conventional than innovative. It is true that there were successful ambushes, but the usual firefight—if there is such a thing— witnessed American infantrymen pulling back and calling for artillery fire to saturate the suspected Japanese positions. After the bombardment, the Americans cautiously advanced to count the dead.[6] It was methodical and calculated small unit tactics. One must also recognize the important psychological benefits on the morale of combat troops from just hearing the sound of friendly artillery. Perhaps these tactics were appropriate to the nature of the original defensive mission, because everyone vaguely realized that 18th Army had to attack or wither away.

The de facto change of mission and pressure from above to wrap up the campaign demonstrated the limitations of such orthodox tactical concepts. It should be remembered that the presence of many brave men and a few heroic ones who were willing to lead in such conditions made stereotyped tactics work. That the Japanese accommodated the Americans by charging in dense ranks straight into American guns speaks poorly of Japanese tactical innovation. The original Japanese attack on a narrow front did consider the jungle terrain. Adachi's subsequent enveloping maneuver treated the jungle as if it did not exist.

The only time that the Japanese seemed unconventional was after dark, and that was in part because the Americans simply ceased military operations after nightfall, thus surrendering the night to the enemy. Conversely, Japanese infantry doctrine stressed night training and operations. By daylight reconnaissance and trail marking, they marked passages for nighttime movement. The Japanese had been trained to operate at night, and they did. But despite all their emphasis on night training, the Japanese found night fighting extremely difficult to coordinate.

Nonetheless, the Americans never seemed to adapt and take advantage of Japanese errors. The 112th Cavalry's one night march of the campaign, the retreat from the Driniumor, nearly resulted in mob chaos. But was this a deficiency of the infantrymen and cavalrymen along the Driniumor or a basic failure of the U.S. Army to emphasize practical night combat training? After the Papua campaign, the 32d Infantry Division refitted and retrained in Australia. According to their training table, the division stressed night operations. But these lessons were not applied extensively along the Driniumor. It does appear that the 32d Division and the 112th Cavalry closed down at night.

In the jungle combat, the troop and squadron commanders of the 112th Cavalry placed great reliance on the qualities and initiative of junior officers to lead patrols, to lead attacks, to supervise their men, and to scout—all desirable achievements. Yet they recognized that they overburdened these young officers with too many tasks in the oppressive climate.[7] A glance at the casualty figures demonstrates clearly enough that the junior officers of the 112th shared the dangers of combat with their men. In most cases, they led, but the cumulative burden of responsibility, fatigue, and combat used them up at a fast rate.

The casualty returns of the 112th's Driniumor battle provide much area for speculation. Overall, approximately 320 cavalrymen were killed, wounded, or missing,[8] and the Americans claimed to have killed 1,604 Japanese, an exchange ratio of roughly 1:5 in terms of gross casualties. Until 1 August, however, the exchange ratio was about 1:1.5 or 1:2 in the cavalrymen's favor, after which it skyrocketed to 1:8, coincidentally with the Japanese massed frontal attacks against the 112th in early August. Yet, it is difficult to determine with any exactitude a turning point on the Driniumor. Rather, it was a grinding battle of attrition, the ironic ending to a classic example of maneuver warfare. In any case, it was certainly easier to kill men whose formations were disorganized and whose army was breaking apart than to kill them when their organization was intact and functional, despite one side's overpowering materiel superiority. This, of course, harks back to the theories of the nineteenth century French military theorist Ardant DuPicq.

The matter of casualties from friendly fire is unsettling. At least 27, and possibly 35, of the 112th's approximately 320 casualties were victims of friendly fire, or 9 to 10.5 percent. The discouraging feature of these statistics is that they may actually be lower than a commander should expect in jungle combat. A detailed study of U.S. Army casualties on Bougainville-New Georgia and Burma showed that in the first instance, 66 of 393 total casualties "were due to the fire of their own troops. In the former 15.7 percent of the dead and in Burma 16 percent were due to our own fire."[9] This report also stated that carelessness, poor discipline, lack of leadership and judgment, and poor dissemination of information all contributed to the problem. Yet, this same report recognized from empirical data that veteran troops did perform better in combat because they could recognize and react to the stimuli of battle. Perhaps the cumulative effects of a protracted combat situation—not only the actual fighting but also all the other functions required to make combat possible (marching, preparing defenses, organizing attacks, resupplying, eating, personal hygiene, even resting)—drained the body and spirit. The results of such aggregate weariness possibly were the lethal mistakes of friendly fire.[10]

The final casualty account should be understood in the context of the overall campaign. There were slightly more than 55,000 Allied troops, mostly Americans, at Aitape. Among these troops perhaps twelve infantry battalion equivalent size units bore the brunt of the fighting.* Incomplete statistics are naturally suspect, so the following calculations must be regarded as only very rough approximations. By 1943 a U.S. infantry battalion had an authorized strength of 871 officers and men. Ordinarily, the companies in a rifle battalion were under authorized strength, while the headquarters, service, and supporting units were generally overstrength.[11] The 112th Cavalry went to Aitape understrength, with about 85 percent of its complement. The 128th Infantry Regiment had only 77 percent of its assigned officers and 85 percent of its men. The 127th Infantry had 77 percent of its assigned officers, but 92 percent of its men. If these figures can be extrapolated to give a 90 percent authorized strength, a conservatively high figure, a rifle battalion could muster 784 men. Assuming an above authorized strength in headquarters units, one might expect about 175 men in a rifle company (525 per battalion) and another 145 men in a weapons company, or 670 total.** These were the few who actually fought against the Japanese, meaning that perhaps 8,000 of the 55,000 present were engaged in combat, although normally not simultaneously. Again assuming that most casualties occurred in the fighters' ranks (3,010 total battlefield casualties), the result is about a 37 percent casualty rate or above the rule of thumb of 33 percent, which in theory renders a unit unfit for further combat. The figure may seem high, but on the average in fifty-seven U.S. infantry divisions, infantrymen suffered 94.7 percent of division casualties, while they had only 68.5 percent of the authorized strength. Put differently, representing only 14 percent of the U.S. Army overseas, the infantry received 70 percent of the cumulative battle casualties.[12] These figures reinforce the bleak conclusion already enunciated by John Ellis: most fighting in World War II was done by a remarkably small proportion of troops, whose casualties were very high. Nowhere was this more evident than in the six line troops, whose total strength was 665 on 9 August compared with 913 officers and men present on 1 July. On 9 August, Troop A counted only 78 men and 6 officers present for duty; Troop C, 98 and 8, respectively. Not all the absentees were battlefield casualties, because many troops were ill with malaria or related tropical diseases. Altogether the line troops were at 66 percent TO&E strength, whereas on 1 July they had nearly 90 percent of their assigned complement.[13] If this pattern is indeed a trend, planners of future battles must concern themselves with the enormous implications for medical services, replacements, and the ability to fight a sustained land battle in a much more intensive and deadly modern battlefield.[14]

*The units were the 128th Infantry, 127th Infantry, 124th Infantry, and 112th Cavalry. The 163d Regimental Combat Team departed early, the 169th Infantry arrived late.

**On 27 June 1944 of the authorized strength of 35 officers and 836 men, 28 officers and 678 men of the 2d Battalion, 128th Infantry, were present for duty. For the same period, Company E had 6 officers and 156 men of the authorized 6 officers and 187 men. On 10 July, however, Company E reported 6 officers and 183 men present for duty. The following week the figure was 5 officers and 165 men.

This study began with a discussion of the strategic-operational and tactical dichotomy. To return to that originally posed concept, while the levels of warfare are de facto interrelated, the relationship is exceedingly complex. The symbols for corps and divisions moved forward or backward across a map with amazing ease and clarity. Yet, in-depth study of battle reveals that the individuals who form those masses rarely achieve any goal without enormous effort and sacrifice. Small unit combat operations, like the covering force action along the Driniumor, provide the factual details that aid in the identification of the complicated and ofttimes fragile bonds between and among various echelons of combat organizations.

Notes

Abbreviations Used in Notes

Brief History   — U.S. Army, Far East Command, General Staff, Military Intelligence Section, *A Brief History of the G-2 Section, GHQ SWPA and Affiliated Units* (Tokyo, 1948).

"Daily Intelligence Summary"   — U.S. Army, Southwest Pacific Area, General Staff, Military Intelligence Section, "Daily Intelligence Summary and G-2 Estimate of the Enemy Situation."

"Historical Report"   — U.S. Army, 112th Cavalry Regiment, "Historical Report, Aitape, New Guinea, 112th Cavalry Regiment, 21 June 1944 to 25 August 1944."

JM 39   — U.S. Army Forces Far East, Military History Section, Japanese Monograph no. 39: *Southwest Area Operations Record, 18th Army Operations (March 1944 through August 1944).*

Japanese Night Combat   — U.S. Army Forces Far East, Military History Section, *Japanese Night Combat*, pt. 3, *Supplement: Night Combat Examples.*

"MSJAS"   — U.S. War Department, Office of the Assistant Chief of Staff, G-2 Special Branch, Military Intelligence Division, "Magic Summary Japanese Army Supplement."

MTRS   — Boeicho Boei kenshujo senshishitsu [Japan Self Defense Forces, National Defense College, Military History Department], ed. *Minami Taiheiyo Rikugun sakusen 5 Aitape-Puriaka-Rabauru* [Imperial Army operations in the South Pacific, vol. 5, Aitape Empress Augusta Bay-Rabaul] (Tokyo: Asagumo shinbunsha, 1975).

PTF, "G-3 Journal"   — U.S. Army, 32d Infantry Division, Persecution Task Force, "G-3 Reports, G-3 Journal and File, 32d Infantry Division, Aitape Campaign."

The following SRH series documents used in this paper are in "Index of NSA/CSS Cryptologic Documents offered to and accepted by The National Archives of the United States," Record Group 457, National Archives, Washington, DC:

SRH-044 — "War Department Regulations Governing the Dissemination and Security Communications Intelligence," 1943—45.

SRH-059 — "Selected Examples of Commendations and Related Correspondence Highlighting the Achievements of U.S. Signal Intelligence during World War II," 10 January 1946.

SRH-107 — "Problems of the SSO System World War II," August 1952.

SRH-127 — "Use and Dissemination of Ultra in the Southwest Pacific Area," 1943—45.

SRH-140 — "History of the 'Language Liaison Group,' Military Intelligence Service, War Department," 22 September 1945.

SRH-169 — "Centralized Control of U.S. Army Signal Intelligence Activities."

Preface

1. James Jones, *WW II* (New York: Grosset & Dunlap, 1975), 97.

2. The exact ratio of support troops to combat troops in SWPA remains unclear. According to John Ellis, *The Sharp End: The Fighting Man in World War II* (New York: Charles Scribner's Sons, 1980), 157, eighteen men were needed in the supply service for each rifleman. Robert W. Coakley and Richard M. Leighton place the ratio of combat to service troops at one to six in *Global Logistics and Strategy, 1943—1945*, U.S. Army in World War II (Washington, DC: Office of the Chief of Military History, U.S. Army, 1968), 496—98.

Part I

1. Louis Morton, *Strategy and Command: The First Two Years*, U.S. Army in World War II (Washington, DC: Office of the Chief of Military History, Department of the Army, 1962), 596—97.

2. This information is derived from Robert Ross Smith, *The Approach to the Philippines*, U.S. Army in World War II (Washington, DC: Office of the Chief of Military History, Department of the Army, 1953), 22; Allied Geographical Section, Southwest Pacific Area, *Terrain Handbook 21: New Guinea-Aitape-Wanimo*, 21 March 1944; U.S. Department of State, Bureau of Public Affairs, *Background Notes: Papua New Guinea*, January 1980.

3. An excellent summation of the Quadrant Conference and its effect on MacArthur's planning may be found in D. Clayton James, *The Years of MacArthur*, vol. 2, *1941—1945* (Boston: Houghton Mifflin Co., 1975), 331—35.

4. Ibid., 335.

5. *Brief History*, 66—69. Two excellent examples of a critical examination of Ultra in SWPA are Desmond J. Ball, "Allied Intelligence Cooperation Involving Australia During World War II," *Australian Outlook: Journal of the Australian Institute of International Affairs* 32 (December 1978):299—309, and D.M. Horner, "Special Intelligence in the South-West Pacific Area in World War II," ibid., 310—27. A negative assessment of Central Bureau may be found in a 10 July 1945 memorandum, ultimately intended for General George C. Marshall, from Maj. Gen. Clayton A. Bissell, Assistant Chief of Staff, G-2. Bissell wrote: "Akin has built a signal intelligence empire in Central Bureau which in my opinion, judged by results in other areas and by other agencies, is not very efficient." SRH-169, 76.

6. See, for example, the laments of MIS Special Security Officers in SWPA in SRH-127, 23, 29—34, 181.

7. Officially defined, "Traffic Analysis Intelligence" is the term for information obtained by or inferences drawn from a study of the volume, direction, patterns, and characteristics of the enemy's signal communication system and traffic but without reading the texts of such traffic. See SRH-044, 6.

8. SRH-140, 5. According to Clay Blair, *Silent Victory: The U.S. Submarine War Against Japan* (Philadelphia: J. B. Lippincott Co., 1975), 606, U.S. Army troops after a landing on the northeastern New Guinea coast in January 1944 discovered a "trunkful of Japanese army codebooks, buried in the sand along the beach." Presumably this discovery occurred during the Saidor operation conducted by the 128th Regimental Combat Team (126th Infantry and 121st Artillery Battalion).

9. *Brief History*, 18.

10. Smith, *Approach*, 6—9. In late February 1944 Allied airmen reported no enemy reaction to their presence over the Admiralties. MacArthur then ordered a reconnaissance in force of the islands. The 2d Squadron, 5th Cavalry Regiment, 1st Cavalry Division, with attached units, about 1,000 men, made the initial landing on only four days' notice. The cavalrymen surprised the more than 4,000 Japanese defenders and in turn were surprised by the large number of enemy troops. Far from abandoning the islands, the Japanese soldiers had been ordered not to fire at Allied aircraft for fear of revealing Japanese defensive positions. U.S. reinforcements landed shortly after the initial invasion and were able to secure the islands. See Walter Krueger, *From Down Under to Nippon: The Story of Sixth Army in World War II* (Washington, DC: Combat Forces Press, 1953), 45—52.

11. Smith, *Approach*, 9.

12. *Brief History*, plate no. 9 and accompanying text.

13. Smith, *Approach*, 12.

14. See *Brief History*, 28, for an excerpt of the Japanese appreciation. The complete text of the Japanese message appears in *MTRS*, 29.

15. See David Kahn, *The Codebreakers: The Story of Secret Writing* (New York: Macmillian, 1968), 578—79. Wesley Frank Craven and James Lea Cate described Allied aerial operations against the Hollandia airfields in *The Army Air Forces in World War II*, vol. 4, *The Pacific: Guadalcanal to Saipan, August 1942 to July 1944* (Chicago: University of Chicago Press, 1950), 583—99. Of the estimated 351 Japanese aircraft at Hollandia, Allied pilots claimed more than 200 destroyed. Ultra sources mention 410 Japanese aircraft, but only 169 in serviceable condition. In any case, 5th Air Force's new tactics, its redeployment and concentration of heavy bombers, and its ability to extend the range of P-38 escorts via wing tanks, resulted in the annihilation of Japanese air power near Hollandia. In addition, based on information gleaned from Ultra, 5th Air Force and U.S. Navy aircraft attacked and sank several Japanese resupply ships trying to reach the beleaguered Japanese forces at Wewak.

16. Supreme Commander for the Allied Powers, *The Reports of General MacArthur: Japanese Operations in the Southwest Pacific Area*, vol. 2, pt. 1 (Washington, DC: U.S. Government Printing Office, 1966), 263.

17. *MTRS*, 458.

18. It is interesting to speculate on the role of Ultra in MacArthur's decision to leap to Hollandia. His Reno III Plan called for an invasion near Hansa Bay, exactly the area the Japanese expected a landing. Perhaps the increased Ultra revelations of early 1944 convinced MacArthur to take the risks involved in the Hollandia operation because he knew the area would be only lightly defended.

19. Kengoro Tanaka, *Operations of the Imperial Japanese Armed Forces in the Papua New Guinea Theater During World War II* (Tokyo: Japan-Papua New Guinea Goodwill Society, 1980), 83—84. Tanaka was a staff officer assigned to 18th Army.

20. James, *Years*, 447; Krueger, *Down Under*, 62—63.

21. *Reports of MacArthur*, 266.

22. Karl C. Dod, *The Corps of Engineers: The War Against Japan*, U.S. Army in World War II (Washington, DC: Office of the Chief of Military History, U.S. Army, 1966), 532—33.

23. U.S. Army, 6th Army, Assistant Chief of Staff, G-3, "Comments on the Aitape Landing," in 6th Army's *Combat Notes*, no. 3, 15 September 1944, 8 (hereafter cited as "Comments Aitape Landing").

24. The 49th Ordnance Medium Maintenance Company, an eleven-man detachment of the 629th Ordnance Ammunition Company, a four-man antiaircraft repair team from the 253d Company, and about one-third of the 41st Infantry Division's Light Maintenance Company provided ordnance support. See Lida Mayo, *The Ordnance Department: On Beachhead and Battlefront*, U.S. Army in World War II (Washington, DC: Office of the Chief of Military History, U.S. Army, 1968), 375—76.

25. "Comments Aitape Landing," 10.

26. U.S. Army, 6th Army, "Training Memorandum Number 6, Headquarters 6th Army," 6 September 1943, and U.S. Army, 6th Army, "Training Memorandum Number 7, Training Program-Rehabilitation of Units," 7 September 1943. I am indebted to Professor Jay Luvaas for pointing out these changes in training schedules for SWPA units.

27. For details see Smith, *Approach*, 116—20.

28. *MTRS*, 105.

29. The 1st Battalion, 126th Infantry Regiment, lost 18 killed, 75 wounded, and 8 missing in action. Japanese losses in the 1st Battalion, 78th Infantry Regiment, and two companies of the 80th Infantry Regiment were about 100 killed or wounded. Smith, *Approach*, 123; *MTRS*, 75.

30. U.S. War Department, FM 100—5, *Field Service Regulations*, 15 June 1944, para. 597.

31. A cursory review of the two pertinent U.S. Army Jungle Warfare manuals, U.S. War Department, FM 31—20, *Basic Field Manual: Jungle Warfare*, 9 December 1941, and U.S. War Department, FM 72—20, *Jungle Warfare*, 27 October 1944, reveals the 1944 version superior in its section on march and bivouac and more elaborate in its discussion of attack and defense in jungle terrain. The 1941 version spent as many pages on personal hygiene, disease, and jungle living (15) as it did on tactics. The later edition did devote more space to tactics (37 pages) but still spent fifteen pages on hygiene, disease, and living conditions. Of special significance for the covering force on the Driniumor is the fact that the 1944 edition's chapters on Retrograde Movement and Delaying Action (96—98) are verbatim from the earlier manual (45—46). Similarly, the section on night attack in the 1944 version (83—84) is verbatim from pages 47—48 of the 1941 manual.

32. U.S. War Department, FM 7—20, *Rifle Battalion*, 1942, paras. 192, 216, 219.

33. Smith, *Approach*, 126.

34. U.S. Army, Southwest Pacific Area, "Monthly Summary of Operations," May 1944, 10.

35. *MTRS*, 52.

36. Ibid., 76—80.

37. Ibid., 83. The 32d Division lost one regiment to U.S. submarines northwest of Luzon on 26 April during its move from Shanghai to Manila.

38. The officer flew in a heavy bomber which had dropped off supplies at Wewak and returned to Davao with the officer and eight stranded Japanese pilots.

39. Cited in *MTRS*, 97, IGHQ Order No. 1030, 17 June 1944.

40. Yoshihara Kane, "Aitape no shito" [The death struggle at Aitape], *Bessatsu Chisei*, July 1956, 286. Also see JM 39.

41. *MTRS*, 120.

42. Ibid., 139.

43. JM 39, 101.

44. Yoshihara, "Aitape," 286.

45. *MTRS*, 103—4 and app. 5, "A go sakusen kogeki" [Instructions for "A" Operation Offensive], Headquarters, 18th Army, 5 May 1944, 468—74.

46. Krueger, *Down Under*, 71.

47. "Daily Intelligence Summary," nos. 763, 770, 773, 778, 786, 795. Krueger's concern about PTF being bypassed appears in Lt. Col. Millard G. Gray, "The Aitape Operation," *Military Review* 31 (July 1951):51. Gray was the G-3 for Persecution Task Force. I am indebted to Lt. Col. (Ret.) Theodore C. Florey for bringing this article to my attention.

48. A copy of this message may be found in SRH-059, 53. That single message, however, can be misleading. A glance at the various interpretations and translations of a duplicate message gives the layman an inkling of how complex and difficult decryption and translation into English actually were.

49. "MSJAS."

50. "Daily Intelligence Summary," no. 803, 2—3 June 1944.

51. See "MSJAS," no. 80, 7 June 1944; *Brief History*, 23.

52. Krueger, *Down Under*, 71. Statistical information to support the veteran versus green unit performance in battle may be found in U.S. Army Ground Forces, Plans Section, "Study of AGF Battle Casualties," 25 September 1946, 8 (hereafter cited as "Study of AGF Battle Casualties").

53. Smith, *Approach*, 132—33. Krueger's preference for the 112th Cavalry RCT also stemmed from his hope to keep the 31st Division intact for future operations.

54. Ibid., 133. General Gill's remark may be found in William H. Gill, Papers, U.S. Army Military History Institute, Carlisle Barracks, PA.

55. U.S. Army, 32d Infantry Division, Persecution Task Force, "Report After Action 28 June to 25 August 1944, Aitape, New Guinea," 1 (hereafter cited as "Report After Action").

56. Smith, *Approach*, 128.

57. Ibid., 130.

58. The 121st Field Artillery Battalion, the organic 155-mm howitzer support of the 32d Division and Persecution Task Force, had already been sent to the Biak operation.

59. Mayo, *Ordnance Department*, 377.

60. U.S. Army, 32d Infantry Division Artillery, "Summary of Lessons Learned (Defense Perimeter, Aitape Area) 3 May 1944 to 27 June 1944," extract from "Historical Report, 32d Division Artillery, 30 April—27 June 1944."

61. Krueger, *Down Under*, 71.

62. SRH-059, 26. There remains an element of confusion about the provenance of this message. It is cited in SRH-059, but an investigation of the original or "raw" intercepts shows this signal was translated on 18 July 1944 or one week after the Japanese breakthrough. The

"MSJAS" for 27 June 1944, however, refers to this identical message as well as SWPA G-2's analysis and comments. Apparently the copy sent to MIS in Washington was a duplicate or retransmission and thus was decrypted and translated at a later date.

63. SRH-059, 26, 51—52; "Daily Intelligence Summary," no. 821, 21 June 1944; "MSJAS," no. 76, 2 June 1944, no. 99, 27 June 1944; *MTRS*, 104, has the original 5 May 1944 attack directive.

64. Tanaka, *Operations New Guinea*, 203.

65. The scheme of maneuver appeared in the "MSJAS," no. 99, 28 June 1944. What is more remarkable is the fact that after the battle SWPA continued to maintain that a two-pronged attack did occur. See "Daily Intelligence Summary," no. 843, 12—13 July 1944; *Brief History*, 22—25; SRH-059, 26; and "Report After Action," 1—3. Also see Gray, "Aitape."

66. Krueger, *Down Under*, 71. Hall actually took command at 2400, 27 June.

67. Ibid., 71—72; Gill, Papers.

68. PTF, "G-3 Journal," radio from Krueger to G-2, XI Corps, sent 27 June 1017K and received at 1127K the same day.

69. Ibid.

70. "MSJAS," nos. 99 and 100, 27 and 28 June 1944, respectively; PTF, G-3 Journal; "Daily Intelligence Summary," no. 289, 28—29 June 1944.

71. *MTRS*, 144—45.

72. Smith, *Approach*, 144.

73. "Report After Action," 3.

74. Ibid., 2. The wording of Krueger's order provides further evidence of his determination to conclude the Aitape campaign in rapid fashion. According to the order, the mission of the reconnaissance in force was "to locate and develop enemy concentrations and force disclosure of his dispositions and intentions . . . ." Cited in "Report of After Action, Eastern Defense Command," 3, appearing in "Report After Action." According to Gray, "Aitape," 52, experienced jungle soldiers in the division did not agree with the concept of a reconnaissance in force.

75. General Gill believed that Krueger did not think a Japanese attack was imminent, so he refused to reinforce the 32d Division and instead ordered the reconnaissance in force. See Gill, Papers.

76. U.S. Army, 6th Army, Assistant Chief of Staff, G-3, "Action of an Infantry Battalion at Aitape," in 6th Army's *Combat Notes*, no. 3, 15 September 1944, 38, 40 (hereafter cited as "Infantry Battalion Aitape").

77. Gill, Papers; interview with Wendell H. Brewbaker, Milwaukee, WI, September 1982.

78. Smith, *Approach*, 143—45.

79. "MSJAS," no. 113, 11 July 1944.

Part II

1. Interview with Col. Alexander M. Miller III, Dallas, TX, August 1981.

2. U.S. War Department, *War Department Replacement Board, the Pentagon, Washington, D.C.*, tab 41, "112th Cavalry Regiment," 12 June 1947, 7 (hereafter cited as *Replacement Board*). The information about the 112th's unit cohesion is derived from interviews with 112th veterans and correspondence with Col. (Ret.) Philip Hooper, 8 November 1982.

3. "Study AGF Battle Casualties," 3.

4. Ibid.

5. "Historical Report." I am indebted to Claude Rigsby for providing me a copy of this report. Hereafter unless specially identified otherwise, the detailed information on the 112th's operation comes from this "Historical Report."

6. Ellis, *The Sharp End*, 281.

7. Based on Samuel Stouffer, et al., *The American Soldier: Combat and Its Aftermath* (Princeton, NJ: Princeton University Press, 1949), 2:70. The remaining third either could get no food or did not feel like eating.

8. "Historical Report," 16.

9. *MTRS*, 134.

10. "Historical Report," 2.

11. *Replacement Board*, 3.

12. "Historical Report," 2.

13. *Replacement Board*, 7. Also see Smith, *Approach*, 135.

14. U.S. Army Ground Forces, Dissemination Division, G-2 Section, "Report on Equipment for Jungle Combat Troops," 8 August 1944, 1.

15. Interview with Ray A. Titus, Dallas, TX, August 1981.

16. Italics in original, PTF, "G-3 Journal." Next to the comment another person had written "Yes." The racial overtone may account for the willingness of combat troops to kill Japanese but not Germans as evidenced in Stouffer, *American Soldier,* 34, where roughly six times as many Americans said that they would "really like to kill" a Japanese soldier as gave a similar response in the case of a German soldier.

17. *MTRS*, 127; Tanaka, *Operations New Guinea*, 209.

18. *MTRS*, 129—30.

19. JM 39, 89—94; Yoshihara, "Aitape," 287.

20. Yoshihara, "Aitape," 287.

21. Ibid., 288.

22. *Japanese Night Combat*, 605—6.

23. *MTRS*, 141.

24. Ibid., 142.

25. *Japanese Night Combat*, 605.

26. Gill, Papers, 9—10. General Gill also stated that he felt neither Krueger nor Hall believed a Japanese attack was imminent. Based on the intelligence reports they received, specifically General Willoughby's 10 July estimate, Gill has a point.

27. Interview with D. M. McMains, Dallas, TX, August 1981.

28. The 3d Battalion's expectation as cited in Smith, *Approach*, 145; the 112th's as noted in U.S. Army, 112th Cavalry Regimental Combat Team, "Headquarters, 112th Cavalry RCT S-2-3 Journal, 26 June 1944 to 11 August 1944," entry for 07/1631 (hereafter cited as "112th Cavalry S-2-3 Journal"); the 2d Battalion's from "Infantry Battalion Aitape," 38.

29. "Infantry Battalion Aitape," 40.

30. *MTRS*, 150.

31. *Japanese Night Combat*, 613.

32. Smith, *Approach*, 144; "Daily Intelligence Summary," no. 841, 10—11 July 1944.

33. *Japanese Night Combat*, 608.

34. *MTRS*, 154.

35. Ibid., 155, based on Kawahigashi's recollections. My account of the Driniumor battle is based on *MTRS*, 153—60; Smith, *Approach*, 152—58; "Infantry Battalion Aitape," 38—42; and interviews with Thomas E. Bell, Theodore C. Florey, and Karl K. Wilke, Milwaukee, WI, September 1982.

36. At 0120 General Martin sent a terse signal: "C[ommand]P[ost]CO[mpany]E captured. CO E all out of ammunition and cut off."

37. In fact Company E's center platoon remained in position until about 0400 on 11 July, when the men realized that they were surrounded and fought their way out.

38. Company G's account of the battle and its withdrawal appears in "Infantry Battalion Aitape," 41—47. The Company H men had been manning supporting positions in Company E's sector. Martin's message sent at 0525K, appears in PTF, "G-3 Journal."

39. Interview with Serph Smigiel, Fort Leavenworth, KS, June 1981. On 10 July 1944 Smigiel was head of a platoon of Company B, 198th Signal Battalion, assigned directly to XI Corps. See also General Gill's comments on Hall's appreciation of the battle. Gill, Papers.

40. Ibid.

41. "112th Cavalry S-2-3 Journal."

42. See "Daily Intelligence Summary," no. 842, 11—12 July 1944, and "MSJAS," no. 114, 12 July 1944.

43. See "Historical Report," 30. Boyce and his men most likely ambushed members of a forty-man, all-volunteer, Japanese long-range patrol led by a Captain Saito. This patrol crossed the Driniumor in the Torricelli foothills around 10 July. Its mission was to infiltrate U.S. lines and reconnoiter American defenses and airfields near Aitape. Despite the ambush, survivors accomplished that mission and returned to control of the 20th Division on 23 July with the results of their two-week patrol.

44. Smith, *Approach*, 156—57, has a detailed account of the 112th's withdrawal. Martin's comment is from "112th Cavalry S-2-3 Journal," entry for 11 July, 1100K.

45. Smith, *Approach*, 155—56. Krueger's optimistic assessment probably stemmed from his Ultra-derived awareness of the pitiful condition of Japanese logistics. Martin was not privy to such information.

46. *MTRS*, 163.

47. As cited in Smith, *Approach*, 159. Also see ibid., note 10, 159. General Gill recalled, "Anybody that knows anything much about this kind of fighting is that you don't have very long to determine whether this was an overpowering force or whether you were just too weak to resist. You had to get out of there and get back on a stronger position" (Gill, Papers). As expressed in a 19 July 1545 message from Hall to Krueger, Hall's intention was to relieve Gill only of tactical control of Eastern Sector and assign him command of the covering force. According to General Gill, General Martin was "just about played out" after "three or four nights of fighting." General Hall asked Gill who would take over the covering force if he, Hall, brought Martin in for "a chance to rest." Gill volunteered, and the change of command was accomplished (Gill, Papers). General Martin remained as Commander, Eastern Sector, and Assistant Division Commander, 32d Division. According to Professor Jay Luvaas, General MacArthur became more and more loath to approve the relief of senior officers in SWPA because he believed that it reflected poorly on his ability to select qualified subordinates.

48. "Report After Action," 5.

49. As cited in *MTRS*, 163.

50. Details on "North Force" operations may be found in Smith, *Approach*, 161—64. A Japanese account of operations against "North Force" appears in *MTRS*, 162—68.

51. Interview with J. B. Corbitt, Dallas, TX, August 1981.

52. PTF, "G-3 Journal," 11—15 July 1944. The total 105-mm artillery units of fire on hand dropped to 1.6 by 21 July. A supply ship arrived that day with 48,000 rounds of 105-mm ammunition, which built the units of fire to 2.3 by 30 July. Another supply vessel arrived 30 July and brought an additional 43,000 rounds allowing for 2.9 units of fire even with the continued high expenditure. A 105-mm unit of fire was 200 rounds per gun per day. See U.S. Army, 32d Infantry Division, Persecution Task Force, "Report After Action, PTF, 28 June to 25 August 1944, Aitape, New Guinea," annex no. 8, "Ordnance Report," 2 (hereafter cited as PTF, "Report After Action"); and U.S. Army Forces in the Far East (USAFFE), "Report No. 132 USAFFE Board, SWPA Ordnance Questionnaire Inclosure No. 1," 11 August 1944.

53. PTF, "G-3 Journal," 291050K entry.

54. "Historical Report," 47; "112th Cavalry S-2-3 Journal."

55. *MTRS*, 168—69.

56. Interview with Carlos A. Provencio, Dallas, TX, August 1982.

57. Smith, *Approach*, 165—66, explains Cunningham's anger.

58. According to one postwar U.S. Army study, troops were thoroughly disgusted with K rations and dehydrated foods. Hunger had to be acute for troops to eat them in proper quantities. Refer to "Report on Equipment for Jungle Combat Troops," 2. See also, "Historical Report," 16: "However, for a period, 'K' ration was issued and it is unsatisfactory over a period of more than three days."

59. PTF, "Report After Action," annex 7, "Quartermaster Operations Persecution Task Force, 27 June to 25 August 1944"; interview with Albert Earl Gossett, Dallas, TX, August 1981.

60. *MTRS*, 170—71.

61. "Historical Report," supplemented by interviews with Jasper Fortney, Frank Salas, and O. B. Kent, Dallas, TX, 1981 and 1982.

62. *MTRS*, 171—72. The decrypted parts of the message appeared in the 24 July 1944 "MSJAS." The 79th Infantry had been 18th Army reserve.

63. PTF, "G-3 Journal," 15—19 July 1944.

64. James, *Years*, 521—42, provides an excellent discussion of the intricate decision-making process that in September finally resulted in approval for MacArthur's Philippine invasion.

65. Smith, *Approach*, 170.

66. Interviews with Charles C. Brabham and Walter Stocks, Dallas, TX, 1981.

67. *MTRS*, 179.

68. Ibid., 180.

69. Interviews with Joe H. Stinson, Travis McDermott, and Robert E. Baskett, Dallas, TX, August 1981.

70. *MTRS*, 182—83.

71. Stinson and McDermott interviews.

72. "112th S-2-3 Journal," entry for 24 July 1600.

73. *MTRS*, 199.

74. Tanaka, *Operations New Guinea*, 222.

75. *MTRS*, 182—85.

76. PTF, "G-3 Journal," Cunningham to Gill, Situation Report 251600K.

77. Smith, *Approach*, 182.

78. See, for example, "Daily Intelligence Summary," no. 859, 28—29 July 1944; no. 860, 29—30 July 1944; no. 861, 30—31 July 1944.

79. Details may be found in Smith, *Approach*, 188—200.

80. Ibid., 184.

81. Yoshihara, "Aitape," 290.

82. *MTRS*, 184.

83. Ibid., 194—95.

84. Ibid., 189.

85. Ibid., 194—95.

86. "Report After Action," 11. General Hall's daily situation report to General Krueger mentioned this action and noted that two Japanese companies had forced back a battalion, leaving Company G isolated. Several hours later Krueger signaled Hall that "if confirmed," the incident "appears to warrant an investigation." See PTF, "G-3 Journal," entries for 30 July 1944 1100K and 2137K, respectively.

87. "Report After Action," 11.

88. "Daily Intelligence Summary," no. 861, 30—31 July 1944, 4.

89. Interviews with Clyde E. Grant, Dallas, TX, August 1981 and 1982.

90. *MTRS*, 203—5.

91. "Study AGF Battle Casualties," 4.

92. *MTRS*, 205—6.

93. Ibid., 185, 208.

94. Participants in this final attack included members of the 238th and 239th Infantry regiments, 41st Division, 41st Independent Engineer Battalion, and 66th Infantry Regiment, 51st Division.

95. "Interrogation Report, 2d Lieutenant Nakamura Tomosaburo, 2d Battalion, 239th Infantry," 4 August 1944, in "Historical Report," annex, "Operations and Intelligence Journal and Diary," July 1944.

96. Interview with Claude Rigsby, Dallas, TX, August 1982, and Grant interview.

97. Gossett interview.

98. Krueger, *Down Under*, app. 4, 381, gives total U.S. casualties for the Aitape campaign as 441 killed, 2,551 wounded, and 16 missing.

Conclusions

1. "Daily Intelligence Summary," no. 871, 9—10 August 1944, 3.

2. Cited in SRH-059, 25. The popular historian Ronald Lewin uses the same source for his interpretation of the Aitape battles in his *The American Magic: Codes, Ciphers and the Defeat of Japan* (New York: Farrar Straus Giroux, 1982), 253.

3. See FMs 31—20 and 72—20, Hooper correspondence.

4. References to MacArthur's displeasure with Krueger may be found in Robert L. Eichelberger, *Dear Miss Em: General Eichelberger's War in the Pacific, 1942—1945*, ed. Jay Luvaas (Westport, CT: Greenwood Press, 1972), 176—77, 179, 203, 214, 237.

5. Perhaps the consistency of these officers was their strength. Could any army function smoothly with a dozen George S. Pattons or Douglas MacArthurs, or would their personalities and genius make them unable to work efficiently with the other commanders in their units?

6. While it may be fashionable to dismiss such tactics lightly, they did conserve American lives and make use of the United States' greatest advantage, its undamaged industrial capacity. As Maurice Matloff has lucidly noted, "the Allies had from the beginning accepted the proposition that the single greatest tangible asset the United States brought to the coalition in World War II was the productive capacity of its industry. From the very beginning, American manpower calculations were closely correlated with the needs of war industry." Maurice Matloff, "The 90-Division Gamble," in *Command Decisions*, ed. Kent Roberts Greenfield (Washington, DC: Office of the Chief of Military History, U.S. Army, 1960), 367. It is possible then to argue that American strategy dictated tactics that relied on materiel superiority to crush its enemies.

7. "Historical Report."

8. This figure is based on the 260 casualty figure cited in Smith, *Approach*, 184, which covers the period to 31 July 1944. I have extracted the additional 60 casualties from the 112th's "Historical Report," for the period 1—10 August 1944.

9. "Study of AGF Battle Casualties," 12.

10. Several 112th Cavalry veterans do not recall or believe that they became progressively wearier or their sense and reflexes duller as the campaign ground along. They may have been the strongest and most adaptable and thus did not experience the physical and mental exhaustion that others said they suffered.

11. "Study of AGF Battle Casualties," 6.

12. Ibid., 11.

13. These strength figures are based on U.S. Army, 112th Cavalry Regiment, "Morning Reports" for July and August 1944. Simply subtracting the August figure from that of 1 July is misleading because the 112th received reinforcements, replacements, and casuals during the fighting. What the figures do show is the dramatic erosion of manpower in line combat units.

14. Ellis, *The Sharp End*, 162. Incomplete statistics by branch of service for U.S. Army soldiers killed in action in Vietnam also bear out the grim fact that the infantry suffers most. Approximately 69 percent of all enlisted men killed in Vietnam were infantry, and infantry officers accounted for 44 percent of all officers killed. The difference in percentage killed between infantry officers and men is explained, in part because 25.2 percent of total officers killed were Aviation Branch, which reduces the relative percentage of infantry officer casualties. In absolute terms, however, infantry officers and men suffered equally. Figures based on U.S. Army, The Adjutant General Center, "Casualty Extract: Active Army Killed During Vietnam War," 27 July 1982. The AG Center compiled this special casualty study for the author.

Appendix 1

**Ultra Documents
Related to Driniumor**

WAR DEPARTMEN1

~~TOP SECRET~~

F 19959 C-P

<pre>
        de   6648   21 June 44   2210   21
        Tsu   552   on 9849   47   20 June 44 2030
</pre>

ATE: 4 5634 Tena

NANA   Mokinzan   to --M--

MO Staff Message #270, Parts 3, 4, 5, and 6*.

2. (?In answer to your inquiry?), we are cooperating ~~in~~ military operations with the 2nd HOMEN GUN and, completely united we are staking all on an encounter with the enemy in the vicinity of Aitape about 10 July. At present we are preparing this attack --G--

3. The 20th (check 20) SHIDAN is destroying advanced enemy units in the vicinity of Yakamul. It is (?in action?) at present on the right bank of the Rarapu River. Together with one part of the 41st (check 41) SHIDAN, it is preparing to destroy --G-- advanced enemy units on the left bank of the same river during the first part of July. The amount of troops is about 11000 (check 1, --G--, Check 000) (?Large landing barges?) --G-- Same - 20 (check 20) ships + Trucks --G-- - Same 30 (check 30). -

F 19959 C-P

Page 1

~~TOP SECRET~~

WAR DEPARTMENT

SRF. NO   26887

WAR DEPARTMENT

~~TOP SECRET~~

F 19959 A

de   6645   21 June 44   2158   40

YO   Tsu 330   on 5634. 55   20 June 44 2030

ATE: --E--

Mokinzan   to --M--

MO Staff Message #270 Part 1*

The overall situation of the GUM ((?Part 1?))

1. They are gradually increasing (their forces) with the American 32nd division as a nucleus. The --2G-- BUTAI are along a line on the Rarapu River (about 30. (check 30) kilometers east of Aitape harbor)

Parts 3-6 same number.

Trans 18 July 44   (7117-z)   F-19959 A

~~TOP SECRET~~

WAR DEPARTMENT

JAAF circuit

SRF. NO   26885

158

F 19959 B

7160 de 6660   21 Jun 44 2207   30

YO Tsu 531   On 3867   53   20 Jun 44 2030

KEY 565* Teha

Mokinzan (c) to Manila (c)

NO Staff Message #270, Part 2.*

    Enemy scouting is becoming progressively more persistant in the mountainous district between WEWAK and AITAPE but it has not reached the SEPIK RIVER yet. The enemy has not landed yet at HANSA.

* - Parts I, 3-12 same number.

Trans 1405 18 Sept 44 (9575-1)   F 19959 B

DECLASSIFIED per E.O. 12065
by Director, NSA/Chief, CSS
1 December 1978

SRF. NO   26886

WAR DEPARTMENT

~~TOP SECRET~~

(?5?) - (?The 51st (check 51) SHIDAN?), together with
the navy 27th TOKUBETSU --G-- KIKAIKA BUTAI is defending in
particular (the line) from north of the mouth of the Sepik
River to north of --G-- TSU.

• Part 1 same number.

Trans 18 July 44   (7117-z)   F 19959 C-P
                                                        Page 2

~~TOP SECRET~~

WAR DEPARTMENT

SRF. NO   26888

SRS 99

No. 99

By Auth. A. C. of S., G-2
Date   27 June 1944

Total pages—5

War Department
Office of Assistant
   Chief of Staff, G-2
Special Branch, M. I. D.

"MAGIC" SUMMARY

JAPANESE ARMY SUPPLEMENT

Declassified Per Chapter 3,
DoD Regulation 5200.1R (Nov 73)

C.D.   2 Mar 77

1.   New Guinea--Proposed Attack on Aitape:

SEE MAP PAGE 2

a.   The attack planned against Aitape
(JAS 2 and 7 Jun 44) is scheduled to begin about 10 Jul
and to be made by approximately 20,000 troops, according to an Eighteenth Army (HQ Wewak) message dated 20
Jun. The message, reported by G-2 SWPA, contains indications that the attack is to be coordinated with un-

identified operations of the Second Area Army---possibly in the Sarmi sector to the W.

   b. The message confirms earlier indications that the 20th and 41st Divs are to participate in the attack and enumerates the following additional troops

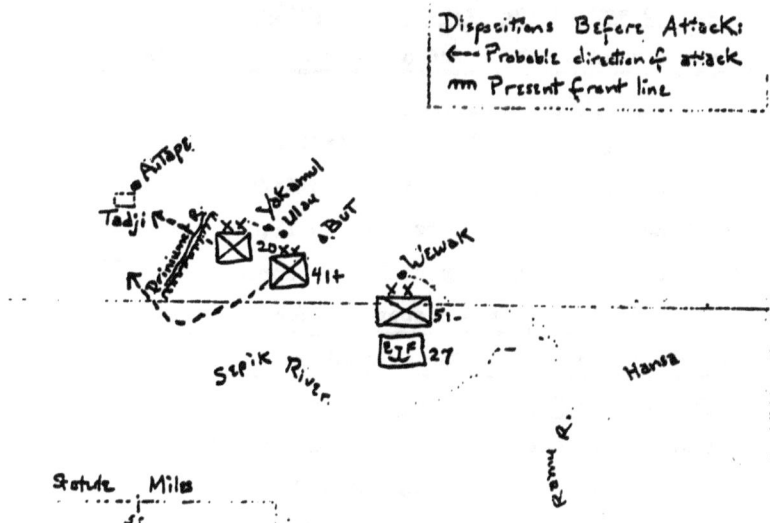

to be attached to the 41st Div: the 66th Inf Regt of the 51st Div, 1 mortar company, and a provisional Army

-2-

162

arty unit composed of Army and Navy AA troops.

c.   The 20th Div is believed to be located
on the right bank of the Driniumor R (about 20 m. E
of Aitape). The 41st Div and the attached troops are
scheduled to be concentrated in the Yakamul--Ulau area
about 5 Jul. The plan calls for the 20th Div to
attack W across the Driniumor R, while the 41st Div
moves around to the S and attacks N and NW toward the
Aitape and Tadji airfields.

d.   With the concentration of these units
for the attack against Aitape, the defense of the
Sepik R--But area is to be left to 11,000 men from
the 51st Div and 27th Special Base Force (Navy). G-2
SWPA comments that the number of troops seems high,
especially in view of the detaching of the 66th Inf
Regt from the 51st Div for the Aitape attack, but
suggests that base personnel is possibly included.

e.   The Eighteenth Army has made a number
of urgent requests for submarine shipment of materials
(principally wire cutters and signal equipment) necessary for the Aitape operations (JAS 2 Jun 44). An
indication that it has been having serious local supply
difficulties as well appears in a 21 Jun message in which

-3-

the Army reported that it had only 60 usable trucks.

2. Biak--Departure of Navy Commander:

On 20 and 23 Jun messages addressed to the
C of S and the CO, respectively, of Base Force 28 (Navy),
which has been on Biak, were routed to Manokwari. This
is the first indication that an evacuation of Navy troops
from Biak may be under way.

3. Allied Submarine Sightings:

A 10 Apr message from Tokyo to major Army
and shipping HQs outside the Empire, summarizing Allied
submarine activity during March, reported 292 submarine
sightings during the month and observed that:

(1) "There appears to be a considerable
number of submarines concentrated in the seas E
of Mindanao and around Saipan and Palau."

(2) "It seems that they are stationing a
[word missing] number of ships in the SW areas,
especially in the seas S of Mindanao and in the
Molucca Sea."

(3) "There are a great many instances of
enemy submarines waiting in areas of the sea in
which our aeroplanes are thinly distributed."

-4-

164

GENERAL HEADQUARTERS

SOUTHWEST PACIFIC AREA

MILITARY INTELLIGENCE SECTION, GENERAL STAFF

SPECIAL INTELLIGENCE BULLETIN

NO.	417	DATE	
	827		27/28 Jun 44

CONTENTS AND SIGNIFICANT ITEMS:

Par. 1 Aitape Area: Plan for attack of 20th Division.   *
Par. 2 Palau: Movement of special type tanks cancelled. *
Par. 3 Estimate of the Situation by 2nd Area Army as of
        17 June.   *
Par. 4 Air Traffic analysed.
Par. 5 Guam: Air reinforcements from Yap.
Par. 6 Philippine Area: Husbanding of Air Strength.   *
Par. 7 Marianas: Air reinforcements probably arriving
        through the Bonins.
Par. 8 Naval Air Group 604 believed ready to join Carrier
        Division 4.   *
Par. 9 Wewak: Air transport of supplies discontinued.   *
Par.10a Balikpapan: Two feet tankers are to proceed to
        Balikpapan.
Par.10b Singapore: Units of Cruiser Division 16, formerly
        on transport run to New Guinea, now at Singapore.   *
Par. 11 Guam: Evacuation of air personnel by submarine.   *
Par. 12a Empire: Bauxite shortage indicated.
Par. 12b Woleai: Torpedo adjustment station completed.
Par. 12c Manokwari: Commander, Base Force 28, now at Manokwari.
Note: Significant items are indicated by an asterisk (*)

I GROUND

* 1. Aitape Area: An operational order of the 20th Division outlines
the following:
            20th Division - Operational Order #24 (24 June)
26 June: 20th Division Headquarters will commence move forward.
28 June: 20th Division Headquarters will arrive at point two kilometers south west of Hill 35 (unlocated).
29 June: a) During the night the 78th Infantry Regiment will cross
the Hanto River (Driniumor ?) at a point approximately 3 kilometers
upstream from the mouth.
b) The 80th Infantry and the Yamashita Battalion will be concentrated
at a point of crossing.
PLAN: a) The 78th Infantry Regiment will attack from south of Hill
56 immediately following the river crossing and gain the Palauru-
Afua track.
b) The 80th Infantry Regiment, supported by the second battalion
79th Infantry Regiment will immediately follow the crossing by the
78th Infantry and will attack toward Paup.

- 1 -

165

c) The Second Battalion, 79th Infantry will then occupy the neighborhood of Paup.

d) The main strength of the Division in the Paup area will assemble in the sector west of Hill 56 and will form a spearhead with a part of the strength for a further push. ('BJ 5825)

COMMENT: The above information is a confirmation of previous intelligence and gives an accurate picture of the enemy's plan and axis of advance for his attack on Aitape. It now appears that this attack will commence with the crossing of the Driniumor River on the night of 29/30 June. This is presumably phase 1 of the operation, and the previous indications of the attack commencing on 10 July were probably meant for the main assault (phase 2) on Aitape. The enemy's proposed plan of attack is shown on enclosure 1. The supply situation in this area, particularly regarding essential combat supplies, is known to be serious, and every effort is being made to get these items in by submarine. Air transport into Wewak, principally of atabrine and batteries probably ceased in May with a staff officer confirming such a stoppage on 12 June. (See par. 9). The enemy has expressed his doubts on his ability to accomplish this mission in time, and consequently it is possible that as in the "TA" operations at Torokina, the actual date of attack may be slightly delayed.

2. Palau: As of 25 June, transport of the remaining special Type "Koo" Tank units, at Palau, was cancelled. (7F, 25 June)

COMMENT: Two special transports with a destroyer escort were scheduled to transport tanks from Palau to Biak late in June. (SIB 376) These tanks are believed to be the 30 new amphibious armoured vehicles described in SIB 375. Apparently basic units were composed of 4, 6, or 10 vehicles, each unit to be divided in sections of 2 each. It is believed that these vehicles were to be used to attack newly formed Allied beachheads from the rear.

* 3. 2nd Area Army Estimate: As of 17 June, the 2nd Area Army believed that there were strong indications that the next Allied landings would be at key points in the Geelvink Bay area. It was also believed not improbable that, in conjunction with the Mariana operations, Allied landings might be imminent in the Palau/Yap and Halmahera/Sorong areas. (MBJ 5824)

II AIR:

4. Air Traffic: A minimum of 72 Army flights were observed, the highest total during the past twelve days. Philippine bases controlled over 50% of the observed Army flights. Naval flights were of no special significance, the relative normal level being maintained. (CB)

COMMENT: Floatplane and reconnaissance activity in the Philippine area continues on a high scale probably indicating heavy shipping in Philippine waters.

5. Air strength at Guam was possibly reinforced by aircraft from Yap on 23 June. (CB)

COMMENT: With the probable arrival of the 705 Naval Air Group in the Philippines from Malaya and Sumatra, the enemy in the Palau area will possibly be partially relieved of supporting the Philippines, hence is enabled to render more substantial support to the Marianas.

6. Indications point towards the continued air reinforcement of the Philippines, Palau, and Celebes via Formosa. (AAF)

COMMENT: During the current month, the enemy has been reinforcing his air strength throughout the Philippine Islands and adjacent areas. Although he

SRS 99

No. 99

By Auth. A. C. of S., G-2
Date   27 June 1944

War Department
Office of Assistant
    Chief of Staff, G-2
Special Branch, M. I. D.

Total pages—5

"MAGIC" SUMMARY
JAPANESE ARMY SUPPLEMENT

1. New Guinea--Proposed Attack on Aitape:

SEE MAP PAGE 2

a. The attack planned against Aitape
(JAS 2 and 7 Jun 44) is scheduled to begin about 10 Jul
and to be made by approximately 20,000 troops, according to an Eighteenth Army (HQ Wewak) message dated 20
Jun. The message, reported by G-2 SWPA, contains indications that the attack is to be coordinated with un-

identified operations of the Second Area Army---possibly in the Sarmi sector to the W.

   b   The message confirms earlier indications that the 20th and 41st Divs are to participate in the attack and enumerates the following additional troops

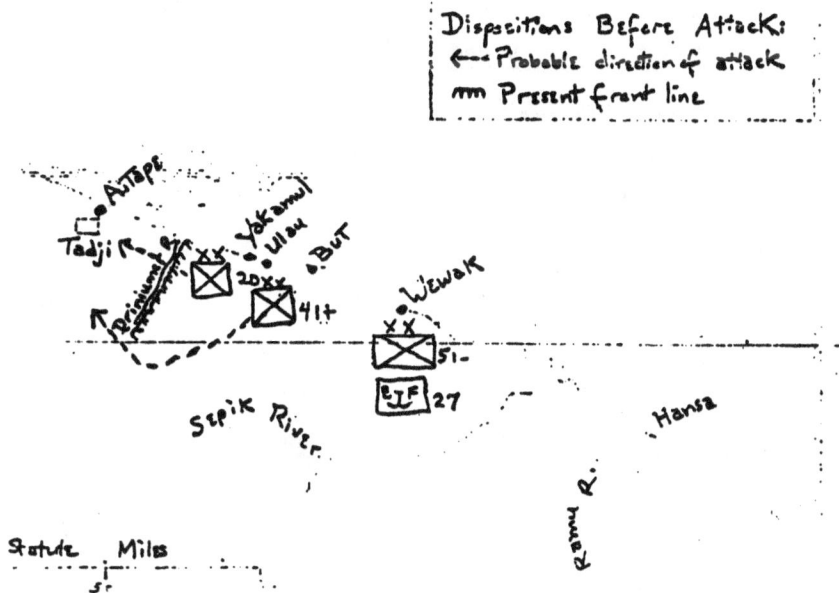

Dispositions Before Attack:
←-- Probable direction of attack
mm Present front line

to be attached to the 41st Div: the 66th Inf Regt of the 51st Div, 1 mortar company, and a provisional Army

--2--

168

arty unit composed of Army and Navy AA troops.

_c_.   The 20th Div is believed to be located
on the right bank of the Driniumor R (about 20 m. E
of Aitape). The 41st Div and the attached troops are
scheduled to be concentrated in the Yakamul--Ulau area
about 5 Jul. The plan calls for the 20th Div to
attack W across the Driniumor R, while the 41st Div
moves around to the S and attacks N and NW toward the
Aitape and Tadji airfields.

_d_.   With the concentration of these units
for the attack against Aitape, the defense of the
Sepik R--But area is to be left to 11,000 men from
the 51st Div and 27th Special Base Force (Navy). G-2
SWPA comments that the number of troops seems high,
especially in view of the detaching of the 66th Inf
Regt from the 51st Div for the Aitape attack, but
suggests that base personnel is possibly included.

_e_.   The Eighteenth Army has made a number
of urgent requests for submarine shipment of materials
(principally wire cutters and signal equipment) necessary for the Aitape operations (JAS 2 Jun 44). An
indication that it has been having serious local supply
difficulties as well appears in a 21 Jun message in which

-3-

the Army reported that it had only 60 usable trucks.

2. <u>Biak--Departure of Navy Commander</u>:

On 20 and 23 Jun messages addressed to the
C of S and the CO, respectively, of Base Force 28 (Navy),
which has been on Biak, were routed to Manokwari. This
is the first indication that an evacuation of Navy troops
from Biak may be under way.

3. <u>Allied Submarine Sightings</u>:

A 10 Apr message from Tokyo to major Army
and shipping HQs outside the Empire, summarizing Allied
submarine activity during March, reported 292 submarine
sightings during the month and observed that:

(1) "There appears to be a considerable
number of submarines concentrated in the seas E
of Mindanao and around Saipan and Palau."

(2) "It seems that they are stationing a
/word missing/ number of ships in the SW areas,
especially in the seas S of Mindanao and in the
Molucca Sea."

(3) "There are a great many instances of
enemy submarines waiting in areas of the sea in
which our aeroplanes are thinly distributed."

-4-

170

SRS 100

No. 100

By Auth.   A. C. of S., G-2
Date   28 June 1944

War Department
Office of Assistant
Chief of Staff, G-2
Special Branch, M. I. D.

Total pages—5

"MAGIC" SUMMARY

JAPANESE ARMY SUPPLEMENT

1. New Guinea—Planned Attack on Aitape:

The following additional information concerning the proposed attack by the 20th and 41st Divs of the Eighteenth Army against Aitape (JAS 2, 7, 27 Jun 44) is now available:

(1) On 24 Jun the 20th Div outlined a preliminary attack, scheduled for 29 Jun, in which the Div was to attempt a crossing of the Driniumor

R (about 20 m. E of Aitape) and secure a foothold
on the trails leading W from the River. The
principal attack is still apparently scheduled
for 10 Jul.

(2) If the main attack is unsuccessful, the
Eighteenth Army troops apparently will attempt to
live off the country in the region between Aitape,
Wewak and the Sepik R and carry on guerrilla warfare.

2. New Guinea--Air Supply of Eighteenth Army:

a. Several messages have indicated that attempts were being made to supply the Eighteenth Army (HQ
Wewak) by air. The last known trip was made on the
night of 12 May by 2 medium bombers from Wasile (Halmahera)
which were to drop supplies by parachute if a landing
was impossible.

b. On 12 Jun air transport to Wewak was ordered
suspended because of the condition of the local airdromes.
That flights might be resumed, however, was indicated
by a 19 Jun message from the Southern Area General Army
stating: "We shall make special arrangements for supply-
ing the Eighteenth Army."

-2-

172

GHQ, SWPA "Daily Summary and G-2 Estimate of the
Enemy Situtation," 1/2 July 1944   Summary 832 - Cont'd

    b. Relative Probabilities:
       1) Defense of Noemfoor: To the present, the only indi-
cated enemy reaction to our landing is desultory artillery or mortar fire.
       2) Activities in the Aitape Area: While observed enemy
activity remains at a minimum, additional information is obtained which
corroborates the imminence of an enemy attack.
       3) Defense of the Maffin Airdrome Area: The enemy con-
tinues to hold terrain that dominates the Maffin strip.
       4) Withdrawal on Biak: Aside from a few isolated pockets
of resistance, the enemy has withdrawn.
       5) Air Defense of Ceram: It is expected that the enemy
will increase his air defense of Ceram bases from which he stages air
strikes against our forward positions.
       6) Naval Activity: A concentration of enemy fleet units
in the Philippine area is noted; also efforts to reinforce his forces in
Amboen is indicated.

V MISCELLANEOUS INFORMATION:

       Attack on Aitape: A prisoner of war from the 3rd Company
of the 237th Infantry (41st Division) gave the following locations of some
of the main components of the 20th Division:
       a) Dispositions:

Unit	Location
Hq 80th Inf (with about 1,000 troops including some from 79th Inf)	On trail 1 mile south of Yakamul
Hq 78th Inf (with about 1,500 troops of 78th and 3rd Co 237th Inf 41st Division)	1500 yards south west of Charov.
Hq 20th Division	On west bank Drindaria River, ½ mile west of Jalup.
U/1 Co 237th Infantry	One mile west of Yakamul with 2 platoons on coastal road.

       b) Plan of Attack: 1st Battalion 237th Infantry plus 79th
and 80th Regiment will attack to the east and parallel to the coast from
assembly point near 80th Headquarters (one mile south of Yakamul). 78th
Infantry to move south (from 1500 yards south west of Charov) and attack
from direction of Afua.
       c) D-day: Between 1 and 10 July.
       d) Supplies: Relayed by hand from Matapau (27 miles east
of Yakamul) west.
       e) Enemy knowledge of our dispositions: Enemy believes
that our main strength is on the west bank of the Driniumor River and that
once breaking through, Aitape will be theirs without further resistance.
Comment: This information from a prisoner of war must be assessed accordingly. In many cases it confirms previous information. The locations
reported as being regimental headquarters are probably regimental areas
and the number of troops might be the strength of these depleted units.
The statement that the enemy believes our main strength is on the west bank
of the Driniumor River probably does not reflect the knowledge of enemy--
rather the prisoner's own opinion--as the enemy's reconnaissance probably has given him a more complete picture of our dispositions than the
statement indicates. The 79th Infantry is indicated by the statement of
the prisoner (though not so stated) as being in the north of the 20th Division headquarters area probably south of Parakovio and near the 80th Infantry, with which it is to launch an attack. The statement that the 78th
Infantry will move south and attack from the direction of Afua, seems to
indicate an attack on the ridge line running north west into Afua (see
Enclosure No. 3), but a study of terrain would rather indicate an attack
due west. The statement that supplies west of Matapau have to be carried
by hand confirms the absence of observed motor vehicle or barge activity
west of Matapau, and probably indicates absence of bridging facilities over
the many rivers between Matapau and Yakamul.

- 5 -

GENERAL HEADQUARTERS
SOUTHWEST PACIFIC AREA
MILITARY INTELLIGENCE SECTION, GENERAL STAFF

G-2 INFORMATION BULLETIN ~~████████████~~

NO: DATE:

W. D. INDEX:.   ATTACK ON AITAPE
    TS-4   3 Jul 44

A compilation of entries which have appeared in Special Intelligence Bulletins during the past six weeks is presented. These entries have been grouped under two main headings, Tactical and Supply. according to their context. For ease in presenting the complete picture, the entries are arranged in chronological order under the two main headings. A reference is appended to each entry in case the reader desires greater detail.

I TACTICAL:

7 May – Orders were issued to the XVIII Army that while withdrawing aggressive tactics would be used against Allied positions. Preparations for the operations against Aitape were to be completed by the end of June. The XVIII Army was also ordered to maintain itself in New Guinea, check the Allies from the present location and delay our plans. but no moves were to be made of a suicidal nature. (SIB 395, par. 1)

10 May – Tokio stated they had not received the XVIII Army plan and asked Second Area Army to advise them concerning it. They also asked for advice concerning the XVIII Army supply situation. (SIB 391, par.2)

14 May – Captured documents conform the belief that an attack by the 20th and 41st Divisions is to be made against Aitape and Hollandia while the 51st Division is to garrison Wewak. (SIB 390, par. 1)

25 May – Present operations of the XVIII Army were considered very effective as a delaying action. (SIB 406, par. 2)

28 May – Southern Area Army expressed regret over the lack of aggressiveness on the part of the XVIII Army and hoped the old spirit would reassert itself in the Aitape operations. (SIB 396, par. 1) In general, the plan for the attack was to attack the airfield and at the same time a guerrilla force was to penetrate; it would create the opportunity for a crushing counter-attack just before the second attack occurred, as in the Torokina operations. In case the withdrawal was too difficult, the Army was to determine whether it was possible to live off the country in the region between Wewak, Aitape and the Sepik River, harassing Allied forces with guerrillas. (SIB 398, par. 1)

31 May – The 20th Division left part of its forces at Yakamul in order to reconnoiter our dispositions. Part of the 41st Division was to move to Yakamul. (SIB 404, par. 2)

8 Jun – On approval of Second Area Army, orders were issued for an attack on Aitape and Hollandia. (SIB 407, par. 4)

11 Jun – The 12th Field Meteorological Unit at Wewak was placed temporarily

under the 51st Division and was instructed to discontinue its
normal mission and engage in defensive duties. (SIB 410, par. 4)
These instructions were later modified, directing that an element
of the 12th Field Unit was to continue its duties because it had
been decided to continue sending meteorological reports from Wewak.
(SIB 413, par. 8)

18 Jun - The XVIII Army was removed from the command of Second Area Army
and placed directly under the Southern Area Army effective on 20
June. (SIB 412, par. 1) Although removed from the command of
Second Area Army, it was to remain under that unit during the
attack on Aitape. (SIB 413, par. 2)

19 Jun - The boundary line between the XVIII Army area and that of the
Second Area Army is to be the 140th Meridian. The XVIII Army will
control all Second Area Army units currently in its area on 20
June. (SIB 413, par. 3)

20 Jun - The XVIII Army's attack plan: Date of attack was believed to be
about 10 July. This operation is scheduled in cooperation with
coming operations of the Second Area Army. The 20th Division is
now located on east bank of the Rarapu (Driniumor?) River, 30 kilometers east of Aitape. The 41st Division is to launch an attack
on the left bank of the Rarapu in the early part of the first ten
days of July. The 41st Division, with the 66th Infantry Regiment
(51st Division), a provisional army artillery unit (with 3 mountain
guns) attached, should be concentrated about 5 July in the Yakamul-
Ulau area. The Army command post leaves on 23 June for an area
south of Yakamul arriving on 30 June. The strength of the above
mentioned forces appears to be about 20,000. 11,000 men of the
51st Division and the 27th Special Naval Base Force are responsible for the defense of Sepik River-But area. (SIB 414, par. 1)

24 Jun - 20th Division Operational Order: Division Headquarters was to
start moving 26th June and arrive south west of Hill 35 (unlocated)
on the 28th. During the night 29/30 June, the 78th Infantry Regiment will cross the Honto River (Driniumor?) 3 kilometers upstream
from the mouth. The 80th Infantry Regiment and the 2nd Battalion,
79th Infantry Regiment, will be concentrated at the point of crossing. The 78th Infantry Regiment will attack toward Paup. The 2nd
Battalion, 79th Infantry will then occupy the neighborhood of Paup.
The main strength of the Division in the Paup area will assemble
in the sector west of Hill 56 and will form a spearhead with a
part of the strength for a further push. (SIB 417, par. 1)

II SUPPLY:

7 May - The XVIII had only half the ammunition required for a major battle
and only enough rations to provide the troops with half rations to
the end of August. After 12 May supply dropping was to take place
at Wewak east airfield from bombers from Wasile. (SIB 395, par. 1)

8 May - Fourth Air Army considered the dropping of supplies at Wewak by
night practicable. (SIB 389, par. 14)

9 May - Orders were issued for two bombers to transport supplies to Wewak.
Air personnel now at Wewak were to proceed to Halmahera in the
bombers on their return trip. (SIB 383, par. 8)
Small or medium type submarines were to make transportation runs
to Wewak. (SIB 372, Navy par. 1)

11 May - Special Base Force 27 (Wewak) was placed under command of the 51st

- 2 -

Appendix 2

Evolution of Persecution Task Force Organization, 22 April 1944—11 August 1944

THE APPROACH TO THE PHILIPPINES

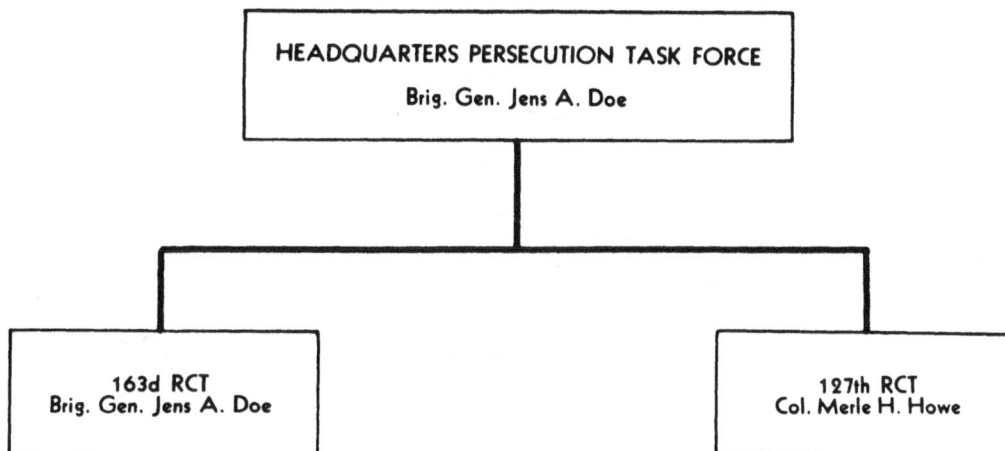

```
        ┌──────────────────────────────────────────┐
        │  HEADQUARTERS PERSECUTION TASK FORCE       │
        │        Brig. Gen. Jens A. Doe              │
        └──────────────────────────────────────────┘
                          │
         ┌────────────────┴────────────────┐
┌──────────────────┐              ┌──────────────────┐
│    163d RCT       │              │    127th RCT      │
│ Brig. Gen. Jens   │              │ Col. Merle H.     │
│    A. Doe         │              │    Howe           │
└──────────────────┘              └──────────────────┘
```

THE PERSECUTION TASK FORCE: 22 APRIL–4 MAY 1944

175

176

THE PERSECUTION TASK FORCE: 4 MAY–28 JUNE 1944

4–19 May

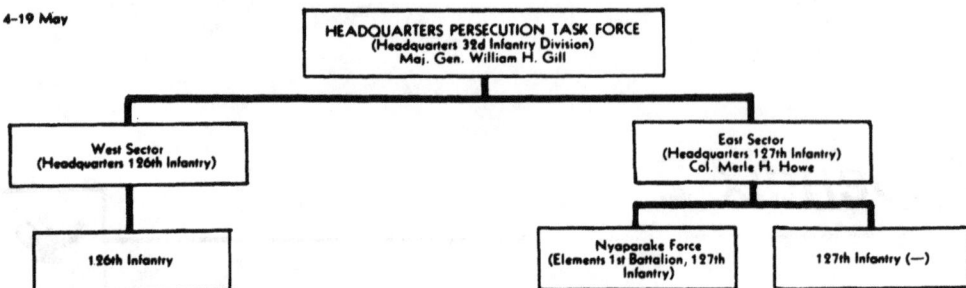

19–29 May

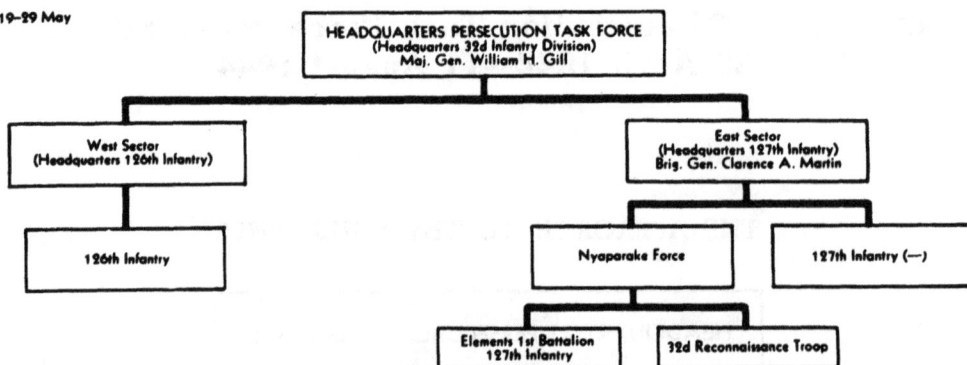

29 May–10 June

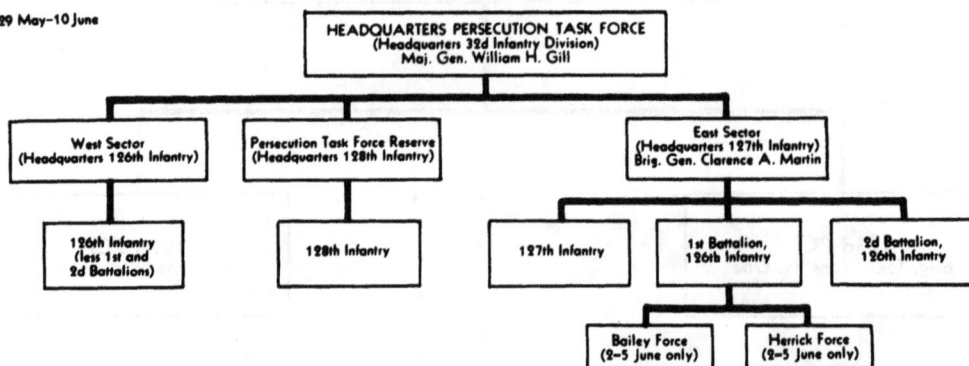

10–28 June

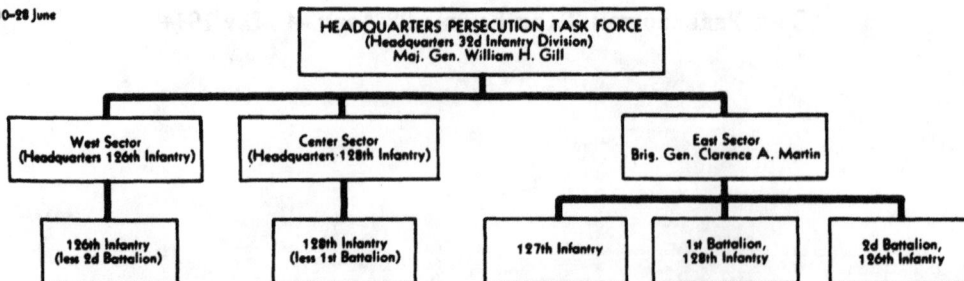

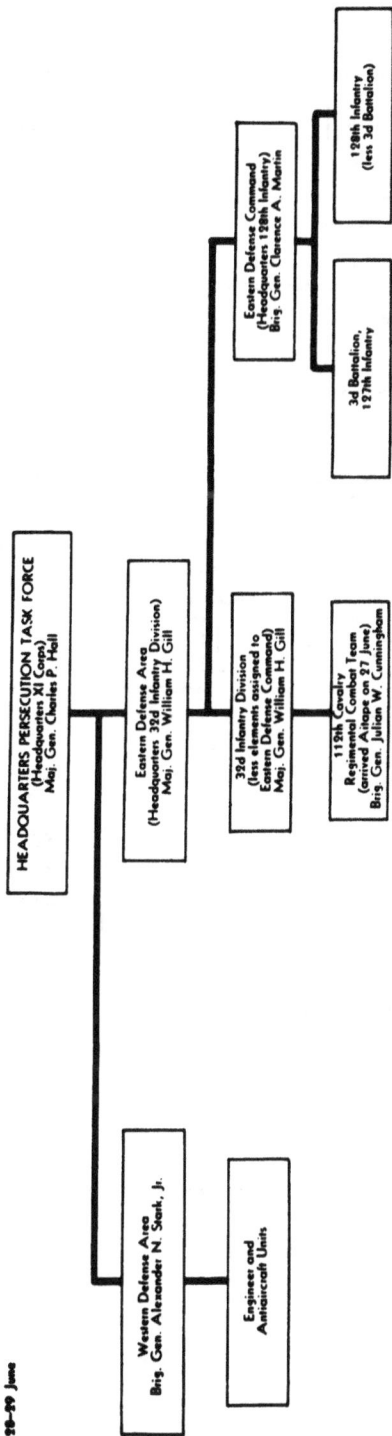

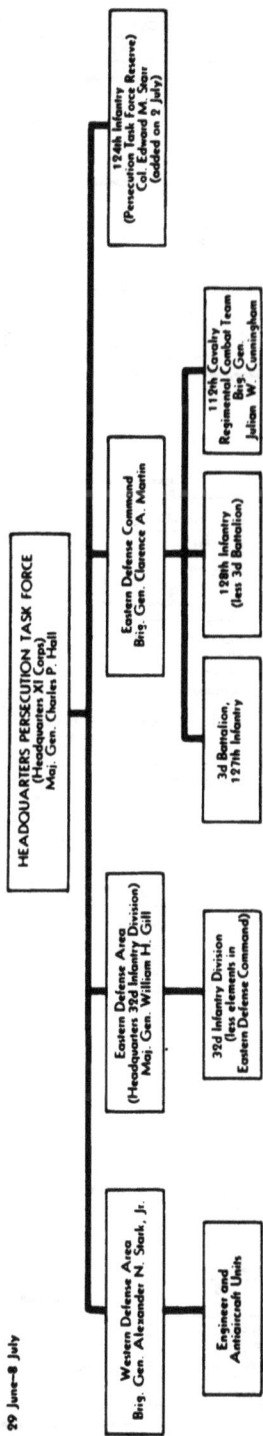

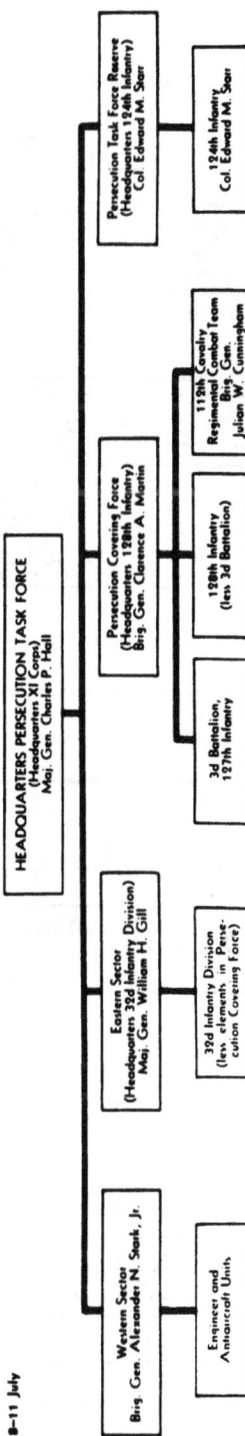

THE PERSECUTION TASK FORCE: 28 JUNE–11 JULY 1944

28–29 June

HEADQUARTERS PERSECUTION TASK FORCE
(Headquarters XI Corps)
Maj. Gen. Charles P. Hall

- Western Defense Area — Brig. Gen. Alexander N. Stark, Jr.
  - Engineer and Antiaircraft Units
- Eastern Defense Area (Headquarters 32d Infantry Division) — Maj. Gen. William H. Gill
  - 32d Infantry Division (less elements assigned to Eastern Defense Command) — Maj. Gen. William H. Gill
  - 112th Cavalry Regimental Combat Team (arrived Aitape on 27 June) — Brig. Gen. Julian W. Cunningham
- Eastern Defense Command (Headquarters 128th Infantry) — Brig. Gen. Clarence A. Martin
  - 3d Battalion, 127th Infantry
  - 128th Infantry (less 3d Battalion)

29 June–8 July

HEADQUARTERS PERSECUTION TASK FORCE
(Headquarters XI Corps)
Maj. Gen. Charles P. Hall

- Western Defense Area — Brig. Gen. Alexander N. Stark, Jr.
  - Engineer and Antiaircraft Units
- Eastern Defense Area (Headquarters 32d Infantry Division) — Maj. Gen. William H. Gill
  - 32d Infantry Division (less elements in Eastern Defense Command)
- Eastern Defense Command — Brig. Gen. Clarence A. Martin
  - 3d Battalion, 127th Infantry
  - 128th Infantry (less 3d Battalion)
  - 112th Cavalry Regimental Combat Team — Brig. Gen. Julian W. Cunningham
- 124th Infantry (Persecution Task Force Reserve) — Col. Edward M. Starr (added on 2 July)

8–11 July

HEADQUARTERS PERSECUTION TASK FORCE
(Headquarters XI Corps)
Maj. Gen. Charles P. Hall

- Western Sector — Brig. Gen. Alexander N. Stark, Jr.
  - Engineer and Antiaircraft Units
- Eastern Sector (Headquarters 32d Infantry Division) — Maj. Gen. William H. Gill
  - 32d Infantry Division (less elements in Persecution Covering Force)
- Persecution Covering Force (Headquarters 128th Infantry) — Brig. Gen. Clarence A. Martin
  - 3d Battalion, 127th Infantry
  - 128th Infantry (less 3d Battalion)
  - 112th Cavalry Regimental Combat Team — Brig. Gen. Julian W. Cunningham
- Persecution Task Force Reserve (Headquarters 124th Infantry) — Col. Edward M. Starr
  - 124th Infantry — Col. Edward M. Starr

THE PERSECUTION TASK FORCE: 11 JULY–21 JULY 1944

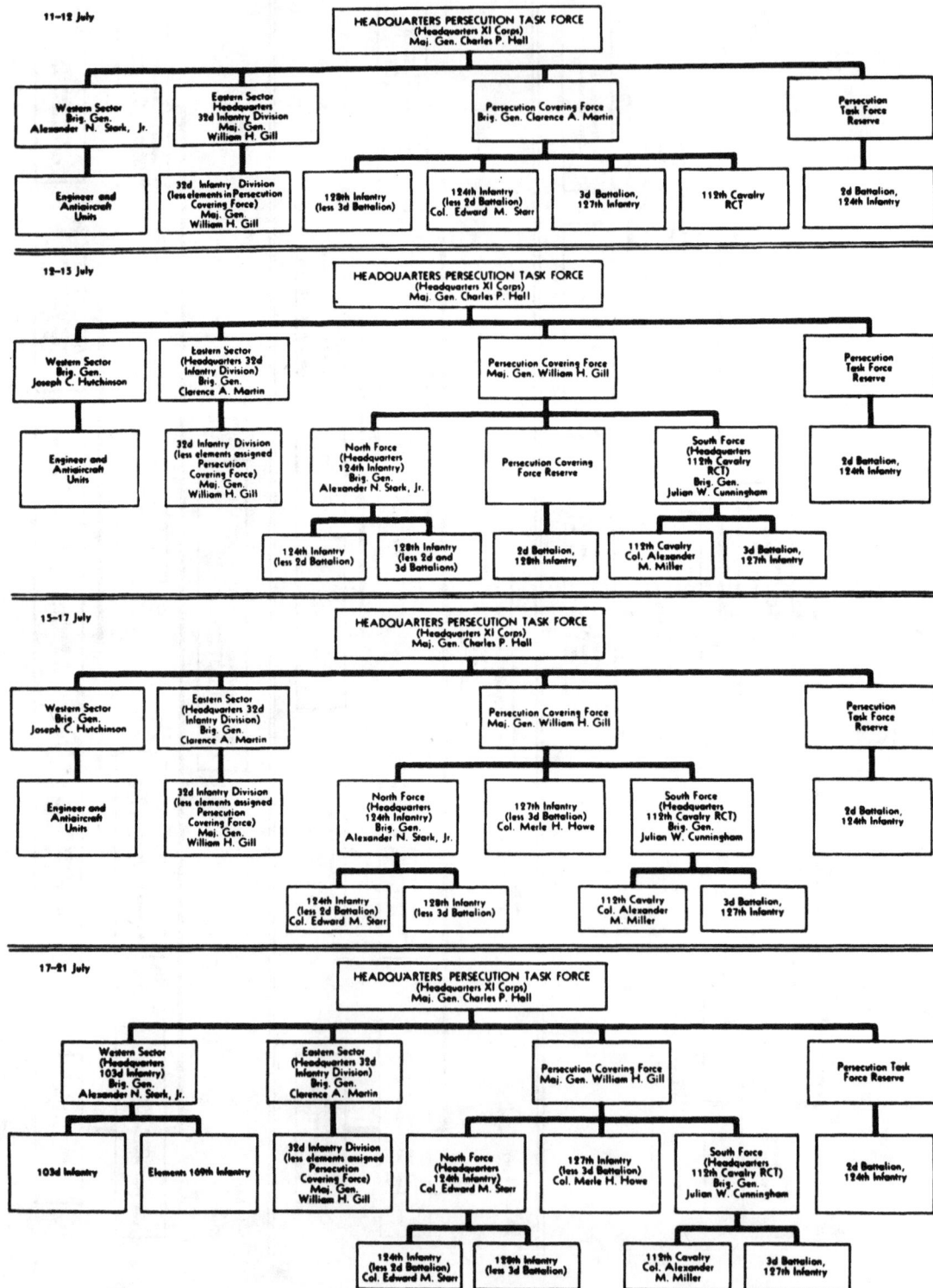

11–12 July

- HEADQUARTERS PERSECUTION TASK FORCE (Headquarters XI Corps) Maj. Gen. Charles P. Hall
  - Western Sector Brig. Gen. Alexander N. Stark, Jr.
    - Engineer and Antiaircraft Units
  - Eastern Sector Headquarters 32d Infantry Division Maj. Gen. William H. Gill
    - 32d Infantry Division (less elements in Persecution Covering Force) Maj. Gen. William H. Gill
  - Persecution Covering Force Brig. Gen. Clarence A. Martin
    - 128th Infantry (less 3d Battalion)
    - 124th Infantry (less 3d Battalion) Col. Edward M. Starr
    - 3d Battalion, 127th Infantry
    - 112th Cavalry RCT
  - Persecution Task Force Reserve
    - 2d Battalion, 124th Infantry

12–15 July

- HEADQUARTERS PERSECUTION TASK FORCE (Headquarters XI Corps) Maj. Gen. Charles P. Hall
  - Western Sector Brig. Gen. Joseph C. Hutchinson
    - Engineer and Antiaircraft Units
  - Eastern Sector (Headquarters 32d Infantry Division) Brig. Gen. Clarence A. Martin
    - 32d Infantry Division (less elements assigned Persecution Covering Force) Maj. Gen. William H. Gill
  - Persecution Covering Force Maj. Gen. William H. Gill
    - North Force (Headquarters 124th Infantry) Brig. Gen. Alexander N. Stark, Jr.
      - 124th Infantry (less 2d Battalion)
      - 128th Infantry (less 2d and 3d Battalions)
    - Persecution Covering Force Reserve
      - 2d Battalion, 128th Infantry
    - South Force (Headquarters 112th Cavalry RCT) Brig. Gen. Julian W. Cunningham
      - 112th Cavalry Col. Alexander M. Miller
      - 3d Battalion, 127th Infantry
  - Persecution Task Force Reserve
    - 2d Battalion, 124th Infantry

15–17 July

- HEADQUARTERS PERSECUTION TASK FORCE (Headquarters XI Corps) Maj. Gen. Charles P. Hall
  - Western Sector Brig. Gen. Joseph C. Hutchinson
    - Engineer and Antiaircraft Units
  - Eastern Sector (Headquarters 32d Infantry Division) Brig. Gen. Clarence A. Martin
    - 32d Infantry Division (less elements assigned Persecution Covering Force) Maj. Gen. William H. Gill
  - Persecution Covering Force Maj. Gen. William H. Gill
    - North Force (Headquarters 124th Infantry) Brig. Gen. Alexander N. Stark, Jr.
      - 124th Infantry (less 2d Battalion) Col. Edward M. Starr
      - 128th Infantry (less 3d Battalion)
    - 127th Infantry (less 3d Battalion) Col. Merle H. Howe
    - South Force (Headquarters 112th Cavalry RCT) Brig. Gen. Julian W. Cunningham
      - 112th Cavalry Col. Alexander M. Miller
      - 3d Battalion, 127th Infantry
  - Persecution Task Force Reserve
    - 2d Battalion, 124th Infantry

17–21 July

- HEADQUARTERS PERSECUTION TASK FORCE (Headquarters XI Corps) Maj. Gen. Charles P. Hall
  - Western Sector (Headquarters 103d Infantry) Brig. Gen. Alexander N. Stark, Jr.
    - 103d Infantry
    - Elements 169th Infantry
  - Eastern Sector (Headquarters 32d Infantry Division) Brig. Gen. Clarence A. Martin
    - 32d Infantry Division (less elements assigned Persecution Covering Force) Maj. Gen. William H. Gill
  - Persecution Covering Force Maj. Gen. William H. Gill
    - North Force (Headquarters 124th Infantry) Col. Edward M. Starr
      - 124th Infantry (less 2d Battalion) Col. Edward M. Starr
      - 128th Infantry (less 3d Battalion)
    - 127th Infantry (less 3d Battalion) Col. Merle H. Howe
    - South Force (Headquarters 112th Cavalry RCT) Brig. Gen. Julian W. Cunningham
      - 112th Cavalry Col. Alexander M. Miller
      - 3d Battalion, 127th Infantry
  - Persecution Task Force Reserve
    - 2d Battalion, 124th Infantry

The Persecution Task Force: 22 July–30 July 1944

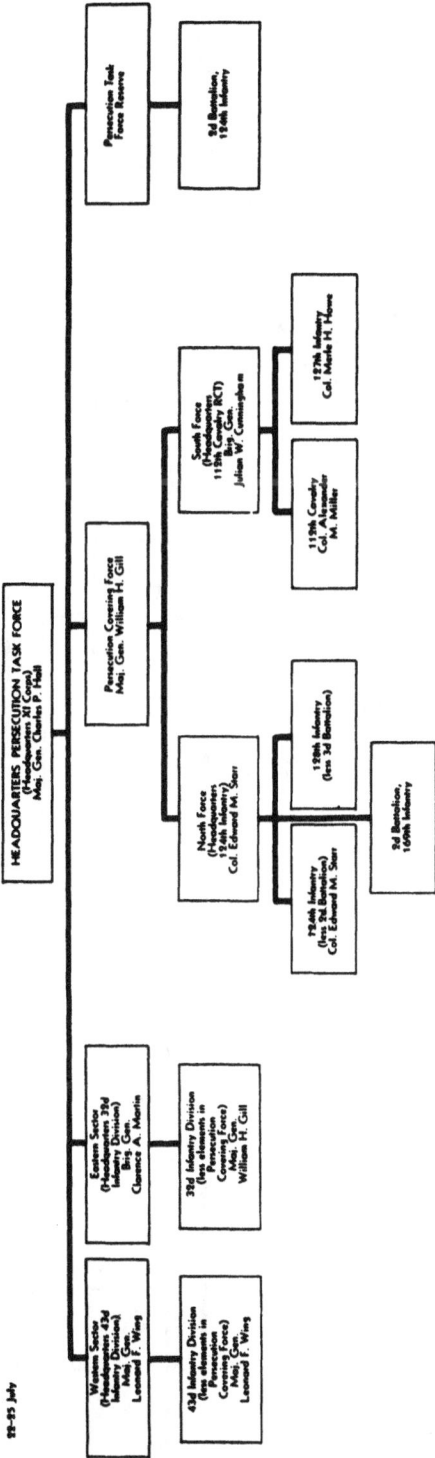

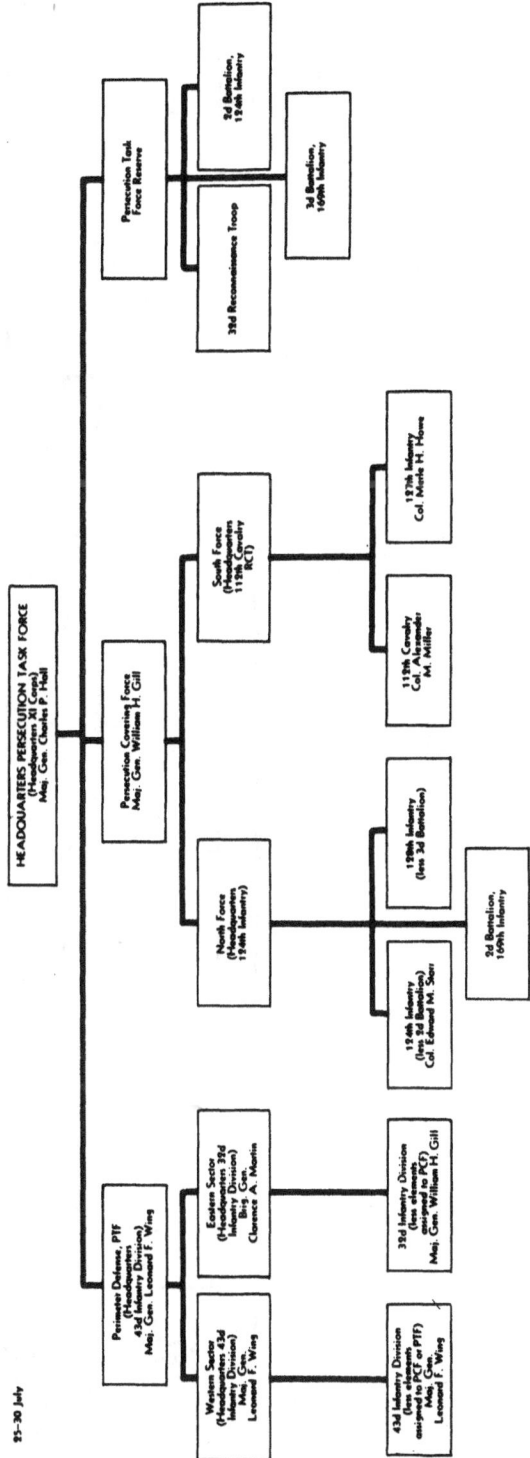

22–25 July

HEADQUARTERS PERSECUTION TASK FORCE
(Headquarters XI Corps)
Maj. Gen. Charles P. Hall

Western Sector
(Headquarters 43d
Infantry Division)
Maj. Gen.
Leonard F. Wing

43d Infantry Division
(less elements in
Persecution
Covering Force)
Maj. Gen.
Leonard F. Wing

Eastern Sector
(Headquarters 39d
Infantry Division)
Brig. Gen.
Clarence A. Martin

39d Infantry Division
(less elements in
Persecution
Covering Force)
Maj. Gen.
William H. Gill

Persecution Covering Force
Maj. Gen. William H. Gill

North Force
(Headquarters
126th Infantry)
Col. Edward M. Starr

126th Infantry
(less 3d Battalion)
Col. Edward M. Starr

127th Infantry
(less 3d Battalion)

3d Battalion,
169th Infantry

South Force
(Headquarters
112th Cavalry RCT)
Maj. Gen.
Julian W. Cunningham

112th Cavalry
Col. Alexander
M. Miller

127th Infantry
Col. Merle H. Howe

Persecution Task
Force Reserve

3d Battalion,
126th Infantry

25–30 July

HEADQUARTERS PERSECUTION TASK FORCE
(Headquarters XI Corps)
Maj. Gen. Charles P. Hall

Perimeter Defense, PTF
(Headquarters 43d
Infantry Division)
Maj. Gen. Leonard F. Wing

Western Sector
(Headquarters 43d
Infantry Division)
Maj. Gen.
Leonard F. Wing

43d Infantry Division
(less elements
assigned to PCF or PTF)
Maj. Gen.
Leonard F. Wing

Eastern Sector
(Headquarters 39d
Infantry Division)
Brig. Gen.
Clarence A. Martin

39d Infantry Division
(less elements
assigned to PCF)
Maj. Gen. William H. Gill

Persecution Covering Force
Maj. Gen. William H. Gill

North Force
(Headquarters
126th Infantry)

126th Infantry
(less 3d Battalion)
Col. Edward M. Starr

126th Infantry
(less 3d Battalion)

3d Battalion,
169th Infantry

South Force
(Headquarters
112th Cavalry
RCT)

112th Cavalry
Col. Alexander
M. Miller

127th Infantry
Col. Merle H. Howe

Persecution Task
Force Reserve

39d Reconnaissance Troop

3d Battalion,
169th Infantry

3d Battalion,
126th Infantry

180

THE PERSECUTION TASK FORCE: 31 JULY–11 AUGUST 1944

31 July–10 August

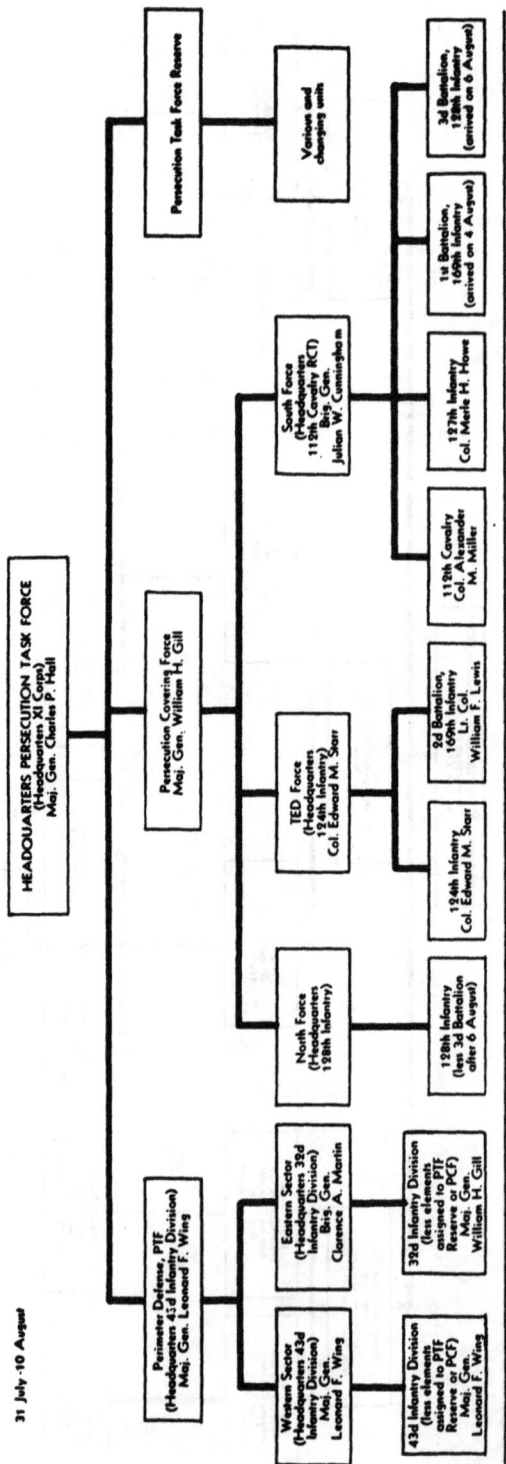

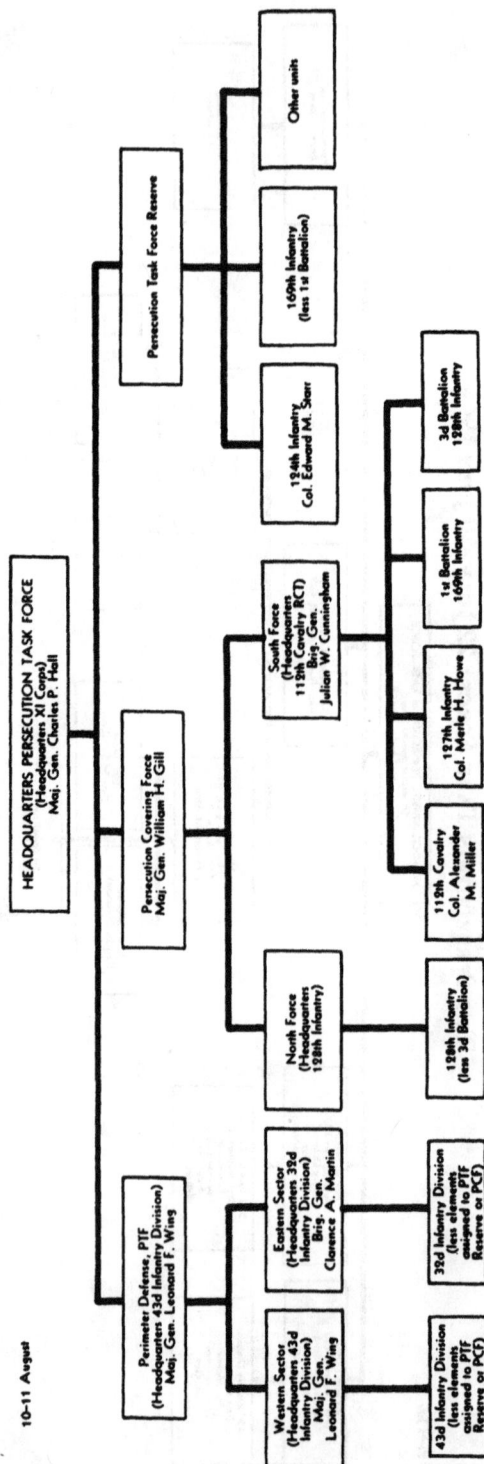

HEADQUARTERS PERSECUTION TASK FORCE (Headquarters XI Corps) Maj. Gen. Charles P. Hall

- Perimeter Defense, PTF (Headquarters 43d Infantry Division) Maj. Gen. Leonard F. Wing
  - Eastern Sector (Headquarters 39d Infantry Division) Brig. Gen. Clarence A. Martin
    - 39d Infantry Division (less elements assigned to PTF Reserve or PCF) Maj. Gen. William H. Gill
  - Western Sector (Headquarters 43d Infantry Division) Maj. Gen. Leonard F. Wing
    - 43d Infantry Division (less elements assigned to PTF Reserve or PCF) Maj. Gen. Leonard F. Wing
- Persecution Covering Force Maj. Gen. William H. Gill
  - North Force (Headquarters 128th Infantry)
    - 128th Infantry (less 3d Battalion after 6 August)
  - TED Force (Headquarters 124th Infantry) Col. Edward M. Starr
    - 124th Infantry Col. Edward M. Starr
    - 2d Battalion, 169th Infantry Lt. Col. William F. Lewis
  - South Force (Headquarters 112th Cavalry RCT) Brig. Gen. Julian W. Cunningham
    - 112th Cavalry Col. Alexander M. Miller
    - 127th Infantry Col. Merle H. Howe
- Persecution Task Force Reserve
  - Various and changing units
  - 1st Battalion, 169th Infantry (arrived on 4 August)
  - 3d Battalion, 128th Infantry (arrived on 6 August)

10–11 August

HEADQUARTERS PERSECUTION TASK FORCE (Headquarters XI Corps) Maj. Gen. Charles P. Hall

- Perimeter Defense, PTF (Headquarters 43d Infantry Division) Maj. Gen. Leonard F. Wing
  - Eastern Sector (Headquarters 39d Infantry Division) Brig. Gen. Clarence A. Martin
    - 39d Infantry Division (less elements assigned to PTF Reserve or PCF)
  - Western Sector (Headquarters 43d Infantry Division) Maj. Gen. Leonard F. Wing
    - 43d Infantry Division (less elements assigned to PTF Reserve or PCF)
- Persecution Covering Force Maj. Gen. William H. Gill
  - North Force (Headquarters 128th Infantry)
    - 128th Infantry (less 3d Battalion)
  - South Force (Headquarters 112th Cavalry RCT) Brig. Gen. Julian W. Cunningham
    - 112th Cavalry Col. Alexander M. Miller
    - 127th Infantry Col. Merle H. Howe
    - 124th Infantry Col. Edward M. Starr
      - 1st Battalion, 169th Infantry
      - 3d Battalion, 128th Infantry
- Persecution Task Force Reserve
  - 169th Infantry (less 1st Battalion)
  - Other units

LEAVENWORTH PAPERS

1. *The Evolution of US Army Tactical Doctrine, 1946—76*, by MAJ Robert A. Doughty.
2. *Nomonhan: Japanese-Soviet Tactical Combat, 1939*, by Dr. Edward J. Drea.
3. *"Not War But Like War": The American Intervention in Lebanon*, by Dr. Roger J. Spiller.
4. *The Dynamics of Doctrine: The Changes in German Tactical Doctrine During the First World War*, by CPT Timothy T. Lupfer.
5. *Fighting the Russians in Winter: Three Case Studies*, by Dr. Allen F. Chew.
6. *Soviet Night Operations in World War II*, by MAJ Claude R. Sasso.
7. *August Storm: The Soviet 1945 Strategic Operation in Manchuria*, by LTC David M. Glantz.
8. *August Storm: Soviet Tactical and Operational Combat in Manchuria, 1945*, by LTC David M. Glantz.

STUDIES IN PROGRESS

U.S. Chemical Warfare Experience in World War I

●

Special Units: Rangers in World War II

●

Counterattack on the Naktong: Light Infantry Operations in Korea, 1950

●

Anglo-French Military Cooperation, March 1939—June 1940

●

Armored Combat in World War II: Arracourt

●

Combat Operations in the Deep Desert: The LRDG

●

Stand Fast: German Defensive Doctrine in World War II

●

Combined Arms Doctrine in the 20th Century

●

Rapid Deployment Logistics, Lebanon, 1958

●

Operations of Large Formations: The Corps

●

Tactics and Doctrine in Imperial Russia

●

Postwar and Prewar Armies: How We Think About War

182

Director
COL William A. Stofft

Curriculum Supervisor
COL Louis D. F. Frasché

John F. Morrison Professor of Military History
Dr. Theodore A. Wilson

CAC Historical Office
Dr. John Partin, *CAC Historian*
Dr. William G. Robertson, *Deputy CAC Historian*

Research Committee
LTC Gary L. Bounds, *Chief*
MAJ(P) Charles E. Heller   MAJ(P) Gary H. Wade
CPT Jonathan M. House   MAJ Scott R. McMichael
Dr. Robert H. Berlin

Teaching Committee
LTC John A. Hixson, *Chief*
LTC Phillip W. Childress   LTC Michael T. Chase
LTC Patrick H. Gorman   LTC Michael E. Hall
CPT(P) Roger Cirillo   Dr. Robert M. Epstein
Dr. Christopher R. Gabel   SFC Robert R. Cordell

Historical Services Committee
Dr. Lawrence A. Yates, *Chief*
Alice M. McCart, *Editor*
Elizabeth R. Snoke, *Librarian*

Staff
SFC Danny G. Carlson   Genevieve Hart
SFC Nelson C. Rogers   Carolyn Conway
Clara Rhoades   Cynthia Teare
Sharon Torres

Leavenworth Papers are published by the Combat Studies Institute, U.S. Army Command and General Staff College, Fort Leavenworth, KS 66027. The views expressed in this publication are those of the author and not necessarily those of the Department of Defense or any element thereof. *Leavenworth Papers* are available from the Superintendent of Documents, U.S. Government Printing Office, Washington, DC 20402.

Leavenworth Papers US ISSN 0195 3451

www.ingramcontent.com/pod-product-compliance
Lightning Source LLC
Chambersburg PA
CBHW080504110426
42742CB00017B/2992

9 781780 392653